A Woman's Guide to

Spiritual Renewal

A Woman's Guide to Spiritual Renewal

Nelly Kaufer and Carol Osmer-Newhouse

Nelly Kauf

HarperSanFrancisco
A Division of HarperCollinsPublishers

Nelly Kaufer and Carol Osmer-Newhouse offer workshops and lectures nationally. For a schedule of upcoming appearances or for information on sponsoring one in your area, please write

    Spiritual Renewal
    P.O. Box 2085
    Portland, OR 97208–2085

Text design by Wendy Calmenson

FIRST EDITION

Library of Congress Cataloging-in-Publication Data
Kaufer, Nelly.
    A woman's guide to spiritual renewal / Nelly Kaufer and Carol
Osmer-Newhouse.—1st ed.
    p. cm.
    ISBN 0–06-250882–2 (pbk. : alk)
    1. Women—Religious.   I. Osmer-Newhouse, Carol.   II. Title.
    BL625.7.K38   1994
    248.8'43—dc20
                                                    93–37438
                                                        CIP

94 95 96 97 98 (RRD)H 10 9 8 7 6 5 4 3 2 1

This edition is printed on acid-free paper that meets the American National Standards Institute Z39.48 Standard.

To our mothers, Ruth Osmer and Adeline Kaufer,
for the gifts of life, love, and spiritual vision

Contents

Acknowledgments

This book could not exist without the womens movement of the early 1970s. The process of self-examination and consciousness-raising in which we participated in those days provided us with a foundation of self-trust and respect for women's experience that never left us. *A Woman's Guide to Spiritual Renewal* is based on that sacred trust.

From Carol:

To all teachers who helped me awaken to myself: Charlotte Cook, Twylah Nitsch, and my root teacher, Ruth Denison, who, by her example, first inspired me to investigate my own spiritual truth and handed me the key to the cessation of my suffering. For this I am eternally grateful. To Annie Hershey for inspiring me to follow my creative spirit.

To the many women whose lives and spiritual struggles have become part of my own: I bow to the Goddess within you all.

From Nelly:

With heartfelt gratitude to the many women whose wisdom, passion, and kindness that have helped me to awaken my own. To the many spiritual friends and advisers who travel beside me, keeping my course safe and steady. To Jacqueline Mandell, for modeling spiritual strength, clarity, and courage. To Ruth Denison for the gift of awareness. To the psychotherapists who guided me toward knowing myself deeply and discovering a self-love that delights and awakens my spirit. To Cheryl Wilton, whose integrity and love inspire my own.

We wish to thank our editorial adviser, Kandace Hawkinson, who supported our vision of women's spiritual renewal and molded our creative journey with her tact and wisdom.

A Woman's Guide to
Spiritual Renewal

Finding Your Path

A Woman's Guide to Spiritual Renewal is an opportunity to participate in an exciting and remarkable experience: the rekindling of your spiritual
self. Even if you feel as though your spirituality was nipped in the bud or never
really cultivated, it is never too late to nourish your spirituality. It will come
back to life in a growthful atmosphere, for your spirituality, like a plant, needs
support and nourishment. Plants need air, sun, water, and nutrients, or they
wither and die. Likewise your spirituality also needs the right conditions to
prosper. In this book you will discover the conditions that energize your spiritual growth. You will make new connections as you embrace your spirit. You
will also have the opportunity to review the past, and heal any spiritual hurts
you may have encountered. You will be able to enter unknown territory and
chart new spiritual directions. This journey of spiritual renewal encourages
self-discovery and teaches self-trust. It is a spiritual journey to the center of
your life.

Of course as individuals we approach a spiritual journey from different
points of view. Some of us may have little or no access to spiritual teachings
and practices. We may be isolated from any form of spiritual community or
organized religion. Others of us may be actively involved in and receiving support from our religion of origin. Others still may have found that our religion of
origin no longer meets our needs and moved on to pursue new spiritual and religious practices. Some of us have an active inner spiritual life; others may
have lost an inner experience of our spirituality. Our commonality lies in a
yearning for greater acknowledgment and participation in a spiritual life.

Although traditional spiritual practices are often based on sound spiritual
principles, their human interpretation can be limiting, especially to women.

As we attempt to discover our own truths, we sometimes discover that traditional spiritual practices and teachings are not compatible with our experience of ourselves and our lives. As women, we can find it a particular struggle to get beyond the difficulties and limitations we have encountered in traditional religions.

Spirituality and Religion

Religion, as we use the word in this book, refers to organized religion, an institution that functions as a container for the teachings. Religion can also provide us with a spiritual identity, for example, Jewish or Christian, Muslim or Buddhist. Many of us have been hurt, confused, or disheartened by some aspects of traditional religion. Religions like Christianity and Judaism are patriarchal, and as women we may suffer more hurt. Some traditional religions are less patriarchal and more inclusive of our experiences and needs as women.

In contrast to the containing and organizing function of religion, spirituality is more open-ended. It is about a process or attitude rather than any specific event. Spirituality refers to a personal inner experience. Therefore it is different for each of us. Spirituality is about everything that is extraordinary, yet at the same time it can be experienced during the most ordinary moments. Listen to the words of women as they speak about their spirituality.

> *"Spirituality is who I am, who I am behind all the masks I wear in daily life, the open, vulnerable part inside me that meets life with both innocence and integrity. It is the moment when I surrender to what is and to who I am at my very core."*
>
> ELLEN, BUSINESSWOMAN, 45

> *"My spirituality is about an essential connection to something more, something beyond what I can see and know, a connection to the essence of life."*
>
> DIANNA, SCHOOLTEACHER, 37

Discovering Your Path Through Experience

We believe that authentic spirituality is experiential, that is, based on experience rather than belief. And finding an authentic spirituality involves learning to trust your experience. Authentic spirituality requires a strong sense of inner connectedness. It is not a conceptualization or an intellectualization. Its basis involves a deeper kind of knowing—a trust in our feelings and our experience. When asked how they were able to trust their spiritual experiences, women repeatedly said they "just knew." They described a process of recognition, remembrance, and connection. Questions like, How do you know that? or Why do you feel that way? were answered with personal anecdotes and stories. When the story was mirrored or shared by other women, it was considered a possible collective truth, but every testimonial stood as a personal truth of its own, regardless of the extent to which it was shared by others.

As women, we have been delegated the tasks of daily life. Many of these tasks are undervalued by the society in which we live. However, the women we spoke with often found spiritual meaning and experience in these tasks: cleaning, cooking, shopping, and child rearing, for example. Perhaps the most ordinary, and at the same time extraordinary, life experience is in the exclusive domain of women: the ability to give birth to human life.

At the same time that we are undervalued or misunderstood, we may also be excluded from the more typically valued experiences occurring within traditional religions. We may be prohibited from touching sacred religious objects or participating in prayer ceremonies. Despite this tendency toward exclusion within many religions, or perhaps because of it, women are rediscovering their spirituality through their direct experience of daily life. We are reclaiming our experiences as valuable, charged with great potential for spiritual growth.

Emotions

Emotions are the energy and atmosphere of our spiritual journey. We make good use of our emotions when we allow ourselves to feel them, while keeping enough perspective to make good choices about how we act upon the feelings. Our emotions then become trusted guides on our spiritual journey. Our feelings often contain a message for us, and we need to learn to accurately interpret the message. Listen to a story from Carol as her emotions guide her forward on her spiritual journey.

A STORY FROM CAROL

One morning driving back from town I passed a giant blue heron lying dead in the road. I picked her up and brought her home. She felt like a gift to me and possibly an omen. As the days passed I sat with her feathers contemplating the meaning of her death, trying to hear any message she might have for me.

I saw her majestic beauty struck down. She was a beautiful and powerful being, yet also quite vulnerable. I saw myself in her, my own strength and my own vulnerability. I realized that she was a waterbird who had strayed too far from the water's edge. I saw that I too had strayed from the waters, my emotional waters, my feelings and intuition. I was out of my element.

The environment where I was living at the time was not supportive of my spiritual journey. As I realized this, I was flooded with a powerful sense of anxiety and then sadness. The full weight of my unhappiness and discontent engulfed me. With the sadness came the understanding that my time in Oregon was limited and that I would soon be moving on. The heron had helped me to reestablish a connection to my feelings and my spiritual self.

Psychological Growth

Spiritual and psychological growth are interconnected. One can open the door to the other. Often healing begins with the personal psychological issues that block us. We may uncover and heal traumas from our childhood. We may dare to experience life directly without the filter of alcohol or drugs to numb us and block our vision. Sometimes psychological healing takes us beyond the personal. We may pause to look at the ways we think and behave and search for new, more fulfilling ways of being. Our spiritual side comes alive. We feel a sense of well-being; we experience a spiritual awakening. At times we do this alone; at other times we welcome the support of a therapist, a close friend, or a group of people.

It is also possible to move from the spiritual to the psychological. Spirituality attempts to end alienation and, through connection, bring compassion and healing to the troubled heart. However, in order to experience true compassion and forgiveness, we may have to confront our unhealthy thoughts and behavior. Often psychology can help us accomplish this, leaving us freer to open to our spirituality. This book will therefore involve you in both.

Voices in This Book

The Authors

This book has grown out of the friendship of Carol and Nelly and our interest in feminist spirituality. It began in 1974, when we first met in rural southern Oregon. Both of us were members of a working partnership of women, a rural collective community and retreat center. Our journey to the country was paralleled by an inner journey. Each step closer to nature led us closer to ourselves. Although we had not yet realized it, we were part of a movement of women journeying to our spiritual selves. Through consciousness-raising groups we began to speak of our unique women's ways, ways that had been silenced until then, ways of meeting together and creating together, and for some of us rediscovering our spirituality together. During our three years living together in the country, we investigated different spiritual practices, sometimes alone, sometimes with others. We shared our discoveries in workshops with women who were on similar journeys of self-discovery. Our years of work and self-exploration created a special bond between us and laid the basis for a professional friendship and collaboration that has endured twenty years and that has given birth to this book.

Although geographically our paths have diverged, in our minds and hearts we have continued to walk side by side, sharing the same spiritual questions and a continuing interest in what we now call feminist spirituality. We have communicated regularly over the years, sharing teaching experiences and providing support and validation for each other's spiritual journey. Carol is a psychotherapist who later opened to her spirituality. She was raised as an Episcopalian. Nelly, although at first drawn to philosophical and spiritual pursuits, eventually incorporated these into a career as a psychotherapist. Her religion of origin is Judaism. Both of us are at present influenced by a strong interest in eastern philosophy and Buddhism, because the practices are based on direct experience. Because of her desire to create a relationship with the feminine divine, Carol also pursues an interest in Goddess religion.

Through personal experience and our work as teachers and therapists, we became acutely aware of the neglect and abuse of women in our culture. Exchanging our stories and discoveries, we came to realize that women's spiritual development had been affected as well. We began to work together again and introduced this idea into our workshops.

We listened carefully as women revealed themselves. With support and encouragement, women spoke of the many ways in which they had felt discouraged on their spiritual path. As we had suspected, growing up in a male-dominated religious world was often a painful and confusing process for women. We were deeply moved by the stories we heard. Despite the lack of support, women had sometimes taken tremendous leaps of faith and followed their spiritual stirrings. Women spoke of feelings of deep joy, peace, and a sense of spiritual connection.

Between 1986 and 1993, we interviewed women, looking for the thread that ran between their childhood spiritual experiences and their spiritual experiences as adult women. Women were happy to tell their stories. These interviews inspired the model for spiritual renewal at the heart of this book.

A STORY FROM NELLY

I remember very clearly when Carol first told me about having gone to a Buddhist meditation retreat led by a woman teacher, Ruth Denison. I knew that something very important had happened to Carol at that retreat. As she spoke of the retreat it almost seemed that her consciousness shifted to a greater calmness and depth.

I had grown to have a great deal of respect for Carol's spiritual journey. She seemed consistently committed to the process of her spirituality, and she shared her insights in a generous yet nonegotistical manner. Most important, I completely trusted her spiritual integrity. And that was a lot to say for me. I seem to be staunchly independent and a bit of a loner spiritually. My mother had strongly advised me not to follow any idea or person or organization blindly. My Jewish heritage bequeathed me a fair amount of fear and reserve, especially of religious zealots who espouse their religion as the best. My feminist awareness left me with a healthy dose of caution regarding male-dominated religions. Yet despite all this I wanted some of what I perceived Carol had found at this Buddhist meditation retreat.

I had always had strong feelings about meditation and Buddhism. I had a love-hate relationship with what I imagined meditation to be. I got angry at the idea of shutting my mind off, perhaps because it seemed like such an impossible task. My self-esteem and Jewish identity rested upon my ability to think critically, to analyze and strategize. What's more, as a woman I had been shut up long enough. I was very attached to my ideas. Yet my mind never quieted down, and I sensed that all the inner chatter was distracting me from really experiencing life. I remember my mother had talked about Eastern religious ideas when I was a child, and I was always fascinated by ideas such as reincarnation. Perhaps Carol had uncovered a safe enough way for me to check out this fascination. Perhaps I too could have some of the calm and insight Carol seemed to have discovered.

My first meditation retreat turned out to be one of the most powerful experiences in my life, both wonderful and difficult at the same time. I confronted the patterns of my mind without the luxury of distraction. I saw how painfully hard I pushed myself. But at one point, I moved beyond the painful focus on my inner struggle and saw a new vision of the world around me. Suddenly, in a flash of insight, life made sense to me. There was a universal pattern or plan to which I was intricately connected. There are no adequate words to explain the experience. I was transformed after that retreat, and my spiritual path became clearer.

A STORY FROM CAROL

I see Nelly sitting on the floor before her altar, such a look of determination on her face. Every morning she sits there staring at her tarot cards, studying the Kabbalah and the Tree of Life. Sun streams through the window, illuminating the devil card, the tarot card she is studying today. I feel the seriousness of her intention, the depths to which she investigates the image. I hope that studying the tarot will help her to make sense of her life, because that is the way it was for me.

I was introduced to the tarot in 1971 by Mary, a client at the adolescent drug treatment center where I was working as a counselor. She offered to do a tarot reading for me. I saw this as an opportunity to establish trust with this teenager and gain insight into her problems. As she laid out the cards, I silently asked a question about the man I was involved with at the time and about the future of our relationship. Discussing the images did prove to be helpful in understanding my client. However, I unexpectedly gained insight into my own dilemma as well. It seemed as though the cards were speaking directly to problems in the relationship. After that experience, I continued to work with the tarot cards. As the months passed I realized that the tarot was a tool that was helping me to understand and validate my childhood inclination toward "trusting a hunch." The cards provided me with a system for checking out my intuitive messages and delving deeper into the situation. The images became a container for my sometimes vague or contradictory intuition. The pictures illuminated life for me; they were windows into the future. When I was feeling something about a situation, I would pick a card and then gaze at the image I had chosen; insight seemed to float to the surface of my mind. As I trusted myself more, I learned to act upon my insights. To this day the tarot remains an important spiritual tool in my life. I still have the original deck I purchased that day after my session with Mary, more than twenty years ago.

In those early days in Oregon, Nelly and I shared our interest in the tarot. Although our religions of origin and spiritual stories were quite different, we came together over our interest in tarot. We learned to consult each other and share the spiritual prescriptions we received from the cards. Nelly trusted me. She helped ground my intuition.

Other Voices in This Book

A Woman's Guide to Spiritual Renewal came out of the life experiences of hundreds of women. These experiences were collected by the authors in interviews and conversations over a seven-year period. As we listened, we heard the pain of women who felt silenced and discounted within traditional religions, who felt out of touch with their spiritual selves. We heard women yearning to connect with their inner self and with the world around them, the quest of one soul reaching out to another. As we listened to the stories, we were inspired to write this book.

In places you will read the actual words of these women as they share their memories and voice their spiritual truths. Many of them have never shared their stories before; their wisdom has previously been unacknowledged. We invite you to use other women's words and experiences to awaken to your own spiritual story.

Your Voice

The process of spiritual renewal is an active one, involving introspection and reflection and an interest in looking inside yourself. You will see that we have created exercises to facilitate this process. Use an exercise like a mirror, to reflect back parts of yourself not clearly seen. There are several types of exercises; choose the ones you are drawn to. You might want to complete all the exercises, or pick and choose among them. You may want to work with the exercises in an order other than suggested. You may find you return to exercises, working through them more than once. In some of the exercises, we suggest that you make a change in your behavior or take action in the world. Although spirituality is rooted in the inner life, it is essential to bring it into our daily interactions, our relationships and our work. This is where our visions and beliefs are tested. This is where they can be supported. The more you bring your spirituality into action, the more empowered you become.

Perhaps you are feeling somewhat out of touch, not fully present to your life, disconnected from your spiritual self. This guidebook can help with any feelings of alienation that may have found their way into your heart. Use it as a guide along the pathway to your spiritual self. As you move through the exercises you will reconnect with fragmented parts of your spirituality. As the director of your journey, you will choose the appropriate spiritual activities to propel you forward. Use the exercises in evaluating your progress. You may sample different approaches like meditation, guided imagery, opportunities for sharing, and ritual creation. They will provide many different doors or points of access through which you may choose to pass, and windows through which you can observe your journey.

As you enter new spiritual territory there will be a need for safety and support. The anecdotes and shared experiences of women in spiritual pursuit will provide a sounding board for your own experiences. We will discuss the possible obstacles and pitfalls of your journey and suggest safeguards. You will find many suggestions of ways to support your progress and maintain your sense of safety along the way.

Writing this book has been an challenge as well as an invaluable healing experience for us. We offer it as a challenge and a gift. We affirm the strength and beauty of women's experiences and wish you well on your journey of spiritual renewal.

Developing a Firm Footing

2

As we begin our healing journey it is helpful to have basic practices we can trust, practices that really work for us, practices to which we can return. Faced with many different spiritual paths and disciplines, many different tools and practices, how are we to know what is best for us and what may be inappropriate or even harmful? At times, we all become confused and overwhelmed when attempting to pursue our spirituality. To make good choices and travel our chosen path with relative speed and grace, we need firm footing.

We want to find a path that supports who we are, a path that fits our special needs and interests. And we want to walk that path with feet solidly on the ground, in contact with the earth, in touch with reality.

Developing firm footing is about taking care of ourselves. It is about getting to know ourselves and finding ways to stay in touch with that knowledge. It is about establishing safe spaces and practices for ourselves. It is about determining the amount of structure and discipline that helps rather than hinders us. And it is about seeking the support we need. It is about building a dependable place to come home to even as we journey.

As you move through this chapter, you will want to develop firm footing for your journey.

Knowing Yourself

"When I get into spiritual pursuits, I get all caught up in the ideas, philosophy, and even charisma of the leaders. I forget myself somehow. It's as though I get swallowed up and carried away by some big wave of spiritual enthusiasm. It

really feels great at the time, but later I sometimes feel empty inside, as though I have lost something of myself somewhere."
STUDENT OF LAND MANAGEMENT, 24

In the course of any journey—even a journey within ourselves—it is easy to lose our bearings. It is easy to lose ourselves. So let's look first at some basic spiritual tools and practices that can help us connect with ourselves and come to know ourselves more deeply.

You will want to take the time at this point to consider each of these tools and practices carefully. You will want to understand how these tools function. And you will want to experiment with their use.

Throughout the course of your spiritual journey, these tools and practices will be of use to you. At various times we suggest the use of one tool or another. At other times, you yourself will feel the need for one of them.

Some of these tools and practices will feel comfortable to you immediately, and some will challenge you. With use, you will determine what works best for *you*.

Grounding

An excellent way to stay safe on the spiritual journey is to stay grounded. Being grounded means being connected to your body and, through your body, being connected to the earth. Grounding is about staying in the present moment as much as possible and knowing that you are present. It is about "showing up" for yourself and others.

Grounding meditations are useful spiritual tools. You can use them to help you relax, to comfort you, to bring you home to yourself. Grounding meditations are especially helpful when you feel confused or disoriented.

Grounding Meditations

Here we offer you three grounding meditations. Each has a particular emphasis. Choose the one that feels most comfortable to you and practice with it so you can use it whenever necessary throughout your journey.

Meditation 1: In the Arms of Mother Earth. This meditation brings us back to the actual experience of being supported by the earth. We rest upon her surface our entire lives but tend to forget what a constant source of comfort and safety she is. She is ultimately our Mother, and she is ultimately our home. Acknowledging this truth in our minds and bodies allows us to receive the love and support she provides.

Slowly take three deep breaths. While continuing to breathe deeply, notice the gentle pull of gravity on your body, holding you down to the earth's surface. Let go and feel yourself being held. Feel the pressure of your body where it meets the earth's surface. Feel the earth beneath you. As you exhale, let go of any unnecessary thoughts or feelings you have gathered. You are home. You are safe. Feel your body from head to toe. Allow yourself to be held by the earth. Feel how you are supported by her. Relax more and more as you are held by her. Open your heart to her in gratitude.

Meditation 2: I Am My Breath. Focusing on the breath is emphasized in many spiritual disciplines. Here it is offered as a practice for getting in touch with the body at the basic level of life force. The breath enters the body, releases life-giving oxygen, picks up carbon dioxide, and as we exhale, returns energy back to the environment. This breathing meditation is designed to bring us back to ourselves and to the basic truth of our existence. It is who we are at a most basic level.

Feel your chest rising and falling. Keep your awareness at your chest area, and follow the movements of your breath, the inhalation and the exhalation. When your mind wanders, bring it gently back. Don't force the breath; just watch it. Let it happen naturally. Realize that we act in cooperation and exchange with all life on our planet by this simple act of breathing. Feel your chest rising and falling again. Open your heart to all beings in gratitude.

Meditation 3: Become a Tree. Nature provides us with many examples of balance and perfection. Learning from the tree, we can come into balance with ourselves and into proper relationship with our world. In this meditation, we practice standing firmly rooted to the earth while reaching for the sky in confidence and strength.

Become a tree that is firmly rooted. Feel your roots reaching deeply into the ground. Trace them with your mind. Feel your branches reaching far into the sky. Be a tree rooted to earth and touching the sky. Know the beauty and contentment of yourself as you stand firm.

Asking Questions

Our spirituality is sometimes best fed by asking ourselves the right questions rather than focusing on the search for answers. Answers often change with growth and transformation, but the questions generally remain the same. We have found the practice of asking ourselves the right questions at the right time to be invaluable. Throughout this workbook we will be posing questions that have been helpful for us to consider, questions women are asking about their spirituality today. We also suggest ways for you to find the answers that are right for you.

Focus Questions

Here are some questions you might ask yourself when embarking on a spiritual journey and at any point in the journey thereafter.

Where am I now in my spiritual journey?

How I am progressing?

Am I moving at a comfortable speed?

What risks am I taking?

Am I realistic in my aspirations?

About Contemplation

Contemplation is a spiritual practice that will help you delve deep inside yourself to find authentic responses to questions and to uncover other information as well. You can contemplate questions, ideas, even images.

When focusing on a question, for example, relax and contemplate the question. Let the question develop in your mind. If you become lost or distracted, return to the original question or to the idea or symbol behind the question.

Consider this metaphor: Your original idea or starting point is like the trunk of a tree. Begin climbing the trunk, but then allow yourself to explore the entire tree; go out on the limbs. Of course, a limb becomes weak the farther you go from the trunk. Your ideas become less powerful, less reliable, when they are too far from the core question or idea chosen for contemplation. When your mind wanders too far astray, bring it back to the trunk, that is, to the original idea.

Contemplation can be relaxing. It is a gentle opening to the unknown. We will suggest using this technique of self-exploration often. Practice it. It is an excellent way of coming to know yourself.

About Mental Imagery

Throughout history and across most cultures, people have used mental imagery to tap new realms of their psyche. This spiritual technique involves intentionally creating dreamlike images in our minds while we are awake and relaxed. We invoke the power of the imagination to create images, even stories. And as we create these images, we also uncover ideas and emotions buried within us.

In guided mental imagery, a general image is suggested to you by someone else. Even with guidance, the specific image that you create is unique to you and holds special meaning for you.

Imagine a crescent moon, for example. (Most people prefer to do mental imagery work with their eyes closed, but it is not necessary to close your eyes.) Visualize the moon in your mind's eye. Let it appear before you. How does it appear to you? What color is it? How do you imagine the sky surrounding it? This is your crescent moon. To fill out the picture, you may use other senses as well. Is your image of the moon accompanied by sounds or smells? Does your image have texture? Can you further develop the image, bringing it into more clear and detailed focus?

The more you develop an image, the more it can teach you about yourself and the more it can inspire and transform you.

At times in this workbook we will suggest images for you to focus on. At other times you will discover your own images. In any case, different types of images will arise. Some will be easily understandable; others may seem illusive and difficult to understand or relate to. It is not necessary to immediately understand a symbolic image to receive the knowledge and healing contained within it.

Keeping a Spiritual Journal

As you move ahead on your journey, you may want to start keeping a spiritual journal to record your progress. A journal can function like a freeze frame or like a zoom lens. Through it, you become witness to your own healing process, your own inner feelings and reactions. As you read your spiritual journal, you replay your experience for yourself to reconsider and reexperience it.

Starting a Spiritual Journal

Begin a spiritual journal, scrapbook, or notebook to record memories and gather mementos of your spiritual healing journey. Work on the exercises in this book in your journal. Choose the kind of paper and the type of book that pleases you and lets you most easily express yourself. You might want to leave space for drawings or photographs or other meaningful pictures you discover. However you choose to record your journey, focusing your energies in this way will help you gain a firm footing on your spiritual path.

About Free-Form Writing

Free-form writing, like mental imagery, is a technique that can help you unearth ideas and images in your inner consciousness.

In free-form writing—sometimes called stream-of-consciousness writing—you write whatever comes to mind. At times in this workbook we will ask you to write in a free-form fashion about different ideas and images as you move through your healing journey. This process helps you find new uncensored ideas that come from a place of deeper knowing.

The key to free-form writing is to write what comes to mind without censoring yourself. Keep your pen moving across the page. Don't change, erase, or edit anything that you write. Don't worry about generating perfectly formed sentences with proper grammar.

Try to let go of any fears you have about writing. Remember that this writing is for you alone.

It is best to do free-form writing for a set period of time. Initially, writing for five minutes at a time is best.

An Exercise in Free-Form Writing:
What Is Spirituality?

Earlier in this book, we presented our understanding of spirituality. In this exercise, you will get in touch with your own understanding of spirituality by doing free-form writing.

Respond to this question: What is spirituality? Draw a picture of it in words. Write as quickly as you can, and do not censor what you have to say;

just let your ideas flow. It is fine to repeat the same idea over again, but do not reread or rewrite. Don't stop the writing process.

Write initially for five minutes. Then stop. Then repeat the process. Do this three times.

Next, take a few moments for integration, looking over what you have uncovered in your writing. Then try summing up your main ideas in a few sentences. Conclude with gratitude for any new information or insight you've gained.

Helpful Hints for the Journey

When starting out on a new path we can benefit from the experiences of those who have gone before, gaining a firm footing as we track the footprints of those who have traveled through similar terrain. With this in mind, we have identified three important issues that seem to occur over and over again in the spiritual healing journey. The first is the need to establish a secure and comfortable space for spiritual practice and healing activities. This can be a challenge. Next is the issue of structure and discipline, how they help, or hinder, spiritual progress. And finally is the all-important need for support, where we can find it on our journey and how we can best use it.

Creating a Spiritual Space

Because our minds and hearts are greatly influenced by their surroundings, it is important to create a spiritual space for yourself. Many people designate a special place in their home for spiritual activity: simply a quiet corner, an altar, or a meditation room. What matters most is that you enjoy being there. Creating a place of beauty in which to worship is a way of honoring your intentions. You are creating an atmosphere where your spiritual energy will flow more easily and more powerfully. You will find that your mind is drawn to this spot, to the colors and objects that you place there. Some women report that simply looking in the direction of their spiritual space produces a feeling of contentment and pleasure. When our experiences are pleasurable, we tend to want to repeat them. Create an beautiful place in which to practice, and you will find that you are drawn to this spot often.

In creating a spiritual space we are drawn to beauty and we are also drawn to order. In a beautiful and orderly environment an attitude of calm prevails, our minds and hearts can come to rest. Although some of us may feel comfortable in an atmosphere of creative disarray, most women with whom we talked preferred an orderly environment in which to practice, worship, or pray. Ordering our spiritual space tends to calm our minds and contributes to an overall sense of peace, helping us to feel less anxious, scattered, or jumpy while we are engaged in spiritual practice.

> *"There was a time when I used my altar for a desk too. I put flowers on it, and my beautiful statue of Quan Yin, but I also would find myself doing things like paying my bills there. I felt it helped quiet my mind to work there sometimes. But then I would leave papers scattered on my altar, pens and pencils, my teacup. Later, when I came to meditate there, things felt different. By not cleaning up after myself, I had scattered the energy. It felt as though I had disrespected my space somehow, that I had disrespected its sacredness."*
> NIA, OFFICE MANAGER, 29

The location of your spiritual space may be important. Consider, for example, the degree of privacy you need. A few women felt they had made a mistake when they put their spiritual space in the middle of the living room. Although very beautiful and attractive to friends, it did not provide the necessary privacy. When they tried to get in touch with themselves, they felt distracted and interrupted. Another woman, who placed her meditation nook near the entrance of her home, found that it served as a spiritual gateway through which her friends and family would pass each time they entered. She received their blessings and good energy each time. One woman told us that she located her altar in her bedroom for privacy but eventually had to move it. She shared her bedroom with her husband, and even though he was not at home when she worshiped, she felt his presence too strongly in her space.

When choosing a spiritual space we think about what we will be doing there: meditation, prayer, chanting, writing, reading, or dancing. Our practices will influence our decisions. For some women, a spiritual space will look similar to a study area: books, writing pads, pencils, and so on being important to their practice. For others, a place on the floor with a cushion, or a simple open area with plants and a few important spiritual objects, will better serve the purpose.

Many of us go out into nature when looking for spiritual space in which to worship. Though such places may not be available to us every day, many women have created altars and sacred spaces outdoors.

"When camping with my kids, I always make sure I get a chance to walk off by myself into the woods. I'm looking for a special place, an energy spot, a place in those woods that speaks to me. I go to that place and make it my spiritual space for a few days. I go there at least once a day alone to pray or just to sit in the beauty and healing power of nature. Sometimes I bring back something like a stone or twig from that place to my altar at home."

ADELE, PHYSICIAN, 41

Creating a Spiritual Space

In this exercise you will begin to create your spiritual space. If you already have a spiritual space, use this exercise to see if you wish to enhance or change it in any way.

Reflect on the following questions, making notes to yourself if necessary:

Questions:

What will I do in my spiritual space?

How much space does that activity need? What kind of space works best for it?

How much privacy do I need?

Now spend a few minutes fantasizing about your ideal spiritual space. Write down whatever you can imagine for yourself. After you are finished, look at your description. What elements of your ideal spiritual space are not possible for you? Note what is possible right now, and develop a plan to create this space for yourself. Consider how you might incorporate any missing elements in the future. Remember, you can change the location anytime if it does not feel right to you. Right now just begin the process of making a safe and comfortable place for spiritual practice.

Another effective way to create a safe and special place is to bless your surroundings. Blessing is the act of making a situation safe and special, taking a moment to honor the special nature of the process. This can be done at any time or place, in any environment. A beautiful nurturing environment can only be improved by a blessing. A chaotic environment can be rendered functional, even supportive, by a blessing. Women who use this practice sometimes feel the energy in themselves and others who are present change when they perform a blessing.

Blessing can also be used as an act of protection. Many blessings are focused on the home. Sacred images can be used to bless and protect one's home. Herbs are sometimes hung in a house to bless it. Blessing and protecting can also be felt from animals. Women who are close to their animals experience them as blessing the home they share together. Listen while women share their experiences of blessing and its benefits in their lives.

"I bought a house for the first time last year. There is an owl who sits at the very top of the redwood tree next to my house. When I hear her hooting sound, I know that she is calling to me, telling me that she is here to protect me and I can sleep a peaceful sleep. She feels like a guardian spirit blessing my dreams each night. Shortly after I discovered her, I went to an art exhibit of beautiful African stone sculptures. There was one especially lovely sculpture of an owl. Although it cost more than I thought I could afford, I purchased it. It sits on my bookcase as a tribute to my guardian owl, as an expression of my gratitude to her."
FILMMAKER, 53

"When I was a kid my parents often said grace at the dinner table. I never understood what was happening, but now as an adult I find myself wanting to honor the meals that my partner and I share with our friends, especially the important occasions. At a dinner party we were giving for our fifth anniversary, I found myself asking for a moment of quiet before we began the meal. Taking the hands of the women next to me I asked for a blessing of our relationship, our home, and our life together. Everyone responded beautifully, wishing us well, each in her own way. Because of that, our energy deepened during the evening. Everyone felt more connected. The occasion became more meaningful."
EARLY CHILDHOOD ADMINISTRATOR, 42

"When I was in a meeting the other day and I felt that my co-workers' energy was low, I spoke about this, and everyone agreed . So I took out my sacred Osha root, which has been harvested and blessed by myself and the other Indian women of my circle. I performed a blessing of each woman in the meeting that morning. We just stopped the meeting, and there in that office building, we blessed one another and changed the energy."
SUBSTANCE ABUSE COUNSELOR, 48

"Before I start my day each morning, I try to bless each person or situation that I know I will be encountering that day. Even if I anticipate trouble, I go ahead with the blessing anyway. I do it with sincerity from my heart as much as possible. When I bless those situations, I feel God's presence entering my body and

going out to the day ahead of me. It sanctifies my path and helps me to walk in peace"
CONSTRUCTION WORKER, 27

Allow the words of these women to awaken your own ways of blessing.

Blessing Your Surroundings

Remembering a blessing. Write in your journal a childhood blessing that you remember all or part of. Perhaps it's a blessing said before going to bed, or a family blessing of a meal. Take some time to read it over. See what you can understand about its meaning. Ask yourself what appeals to you and what does not. If no childhood blessing occurs to you, perhaps there is something you have read or witnessed that could get you started. Now think of someone or something that needs blessing. Bless the situation however you see fit.

The ways I feel blessed. Another approach is to consider in what ways you feel blessed in your life today. You may feel blessed by having a wonderful son or daughter, or a creative and supportive work situation. Let the feeling of being blessed come upon you as you think about ways you feel blessed. This energy is what we endeavor to generate when we perform a blessing.

Choosing Self-Discipline

To remain on a spiritual path, to continue to heal, is not always easy. There can be moments when you feel like taking a vacation for a while, or even giving up. Your inner voice may tell you to slow down, or to quit, or perhaps to head in another direction. Such feelings are normal, well within the scope of what one can expect when pursuing a spiritual journey. Sometimes what you feel will be the voice of wisdom helping you to care for yourself; however, it can also be an old conditioned part of yourself speaking out of fear or resentment. When you sense that quitting or slowing down may be the wrong alternative, it can be helpful to return to a structure. A discipline like familiar prayers or meditations can assist you in times of doubt or confusion. A familiar spiritual practice, easily accessible to you, can protect you and help you to stay connected to your spirituality. In order to utilize structure, however, you need some sense of self-discipline.

Discipline can be a difficult concept to embrace, especially for women. Many of us have been hurt by the abusive use of power and control. In the past we may have followed an unhealthy belief or practice, not realizing we had choices. A discipline or control coming from outside ourselves and our experiences is not self-discipline, however. The kind of discipline we are suggesting here is a self-discipline that comes out of clear choice and inquiry. We suggest discipline only after it has proven to encourage our path of healing and spiritual growth. Carol talks about her use of her daily discipline of tending her altar.

A Story from Carol

Flowers have always been very important to me. Their beauty astounds me. I discovered that placing a flower on my altar helped me to approach my spiritual space with more respect and a reverence, similar to the reverence I have for flowers. Then I got the idea of setting myself a discipline of keeping a flower on my altar at all times. This simple pledge of devotion and obedience has helped me to deepen my spiritual commitment. This discipline helps me to focus more on my spirituality, and to do so with love and appreciation. I don't feel oppressed by the conditions I set for myself. It is simply an agreement I made with myself. I can break it whenever it is no longer helpful to me.

The issue of discipline in spiritual pursuits can be problematic. At this time in history women are questioning structure in organized religion. We are learning to trust our own authority. Some women with whom we spoke tended to reject structure for fear of limitation and control. Others were building their own structure and creating their own ground rules. The questions behind the issue of discipline and structure seem to be, "Who is the final authority? If a spiritual structure or system is not working for me, is it OK to question it?" Rules or guidelines made by ourselves, for ourselves, and derived from our own experience can ensure firm footing on the spiritual path.

Ground rules may simply be agreements you make with yourself, with a group, or with your God. They are spiritual rules for daily living, and you can put them into use when you feel it is necessary. Your ground rules might help you to stay present to yourself and connected to the world around you. An example of a ground rule for daily living is a vow to do nothing that will cause unnecessary harm. Another example is a simple promise to yourself to be honest in interactions with others.

One act involved in creating a helpful structure occurs at the very beginning of your journey: the act of intention. Intention involves knowing your motivation for doing spiritual work, acknowledging it, accepting it, and then committing to it. All healing begins with intention. In the beginning you need to set your mind and heart on what you wish to accomplish. By clearly stating your intention to yourself, you open to a deeper level of willingness. Your energies align with the energies of the universe and with your goal. Sometimes it is helpful to make an intentional statement to your God or aloud to spiritual friends. This tends to reinforce and strengthen your intentions. It is important that the intention be felt in your heart.

Skillful actions naturally follow out of clear intentions. When you have clear intentions, a kind of magic seems to assist you to accomplish what you desire. People around you pick up on this clear and focused energy and support your intention. Possibilities open up that you never could have imagined. The clearer the intention, the more successful the spiritual healing journey. Before pursuing your spirituality further, take a few moments to clarify your intention.

Clarifying Your Intention

Contemplating your commitment. Relax and ground yourself by using any of the three suggested grounding meditations on pages 11 and 12 (or another that you prefer). The purpose here is to come into close relationship to yourself. When you feel in touch with yourself, ask yourself any of the following questions. Choose only the questions that feel comfortable to you.

Questions:

What is my motivation for pursuing spiritual healing?

Am I comfortable with my motivation? Do I accept it?

What exactly is my intention in pursuing my spirituality at this time?

Do I embrace this intention fully?

If I feel the necessity, how can I commit to my spiritual journey more fully?

As answers appear to these questions, trust your reaction to them. Allow more questions to form in your heart and more responses until you feel a sense of completion. End with a sense of commitment that seems appropriate and comfortable for you at this time.

Affirming your intention to spiritual renewal. In this exercise you will use guided imagery to affirm and strengthen your commitment to spiritual renewal. Use this exercise as a model for the process of guided imagery. The bullets indicate appropriate times for you to pause in your reading of this exercise to focus your inner awareness.

First, find yourself a nurturing place to be, where you feel safe to go inside yourself. Lay out your journal, writing and drawing papers, and favorite pens or pencils. Center yourself using one of the techniques presented in the grounding meditations or another method that works well for you.

Feeling calmer and more centered, think about something to which you feel committed, that you are already focused on and your energies are open to. It can be a very little thing or a big thing. For example, maybe it is your commitment to cooking a special dinner tonight, or your commitment to your child, or your willingness to exercise regularly. It doesn't matter what you choose, as long as you feel committed. Check to see if you feel really open and interested in what comes up for you. If not, call up another aspect of your life in which the energy of commitment is flowing strongly.

• • •

When you come up with something you feel willingness about, focus on what you are committed to. What does commitment feel like to you? Can you taste it, smell it, or hear it? Where do you feel it in your body? How does it feel in your body?

• • •

Become familiar with the feeling of commitment and clear intention. Let the feeling grow bigger and bigger, expanding naturally as you give it your attention. With each breath, breathe in a little more of the feeling of commitment. Spend the next few moments enjoying the open, focused energy of clear commitment.

• • •

Now you are going to apply this feeling of commitment to your process of spiritual renewal. Close your eyes and imagine yourself in your process of spiritual renewal, then transfer the feeling of commitment onto it. Allow for the magic of transformation. Allow for the power of intention. Affirm that you are willing to be committed to your spiritual renewal.

• • •

When you feel the meditation is complete, allow yourself to slowly come back to ordinary consciousness. Wiggle your body a bit, and feel the movement. Allow your eyes to slowly open and look around. When you feel ready, pick up your pen and write or draw about this meditation.

At times it may be difficult to stick with the process of spiritual renewal; other activities may seduce you away from the task at hand. Some women find it helpful to set time aside for spiritual pursuits. If you grew up in a home where specific days or evenings were allotted for spirituality, you need to discover whether that timing and rhythm still works for you; if you have no experience of an appropriate spiritual time schedule, this will be a new practice for you.

Take a moment now to define how much time each day or each week you would like to spend on spiritual renewal. As you learn more about your spiritual needs, you will probably revise the schedule. Not all the allotted time will be spent with workbook exercises; some may be spent in meditation or prayer or sharing insights with a friend. We suggest you commit yourself to a time allotment and keep track of how you do. Try not to criticize yourself if you find you are unable to keep to your schedule. Instead, revise it to better meet your needs. Be realistic as you think about your time commitment, and honor your other interests and commitments. When you are enthusiastic, it is easy to set unrealistic goals for yourself.

Time Schedules

Spend some time thinking about your daily or weekly schedule. Look at your appointment book or calendar if you have one. Do you see some time there for spiritual pursuits? Close your eyes and contemplate the questions that follow. Let the answers flow forth even if they seem impractical.

What would be the most pleasurable and easiest times for me to concentrate on my spirituality? How much time in a day or week would I like to give to my journey of spiritual renewal?

Try not to censor responses; just be aware of them. Now open your eyes, and prepare a tentative schedule that integrates your inner responses with the practical realities of your life. When you have settled on a schedule, check again to see if it is realistic. Try out your schedule and revise it whenever appropriate.

Support

When taking on any task, our degree of success is often related to the amount of support we are given. Support is absolutely essential when you embark on the spiritual path or begin a healing process. When we feel supported, we are free to put our energies into personal spiritual pursuits; we are empowered to investigate areas that we might otherwise have shied away from. There also may be times of self-doubt, confusion, and pain, but there is no need to face these moments in isolation. A spiritual friend or support system can make all the difference. By acknowledging the need for support, we do not minimize the need for solitude. We gain strength and support from cherished moments of solitude, times alone with our own inner truths.

Many women we interviewed spoke of their need for support, though they found it in different ways. Some felt they needed the support of a traditional religious setting for their spiritual practice. Although their personal spirituality was not always validated there, these women felt support from the structure and teachings that a traditional religion provides. Some of them felt supported by the members of the congregation; others did not.

Leticia talks about her relationship to the Pentecostal church and her struggles with the issue of support.

"I have this thing that I will say, but I don't know how I am going to say it because I don't say it very often. I have to be careful when I say it. The church I go to I really like a lot because I feel that the Holy Spirit moves there, and I can understand it; it works for me. But sometimes I get very upset because I don't agree with a lot of the things that people say and people do there. There are times when I don't go to church for three or four months because I'm angry with the things people do.

"This is a large congregation with a lot of new people. But there are many people that I've known for a long time. Often when I go to church and see all these people I say, 'Hi, how are you?' and I don't really get a response. Seems like they don't really want to know who I am. To me that's not very Christian. If you're in the same place and all worship together, you might have more caring for one another. I've gone to church saying hello to many people, and I leave there feeling like a stranger. So I've wanted to leave the church after being hurt in this way, but the Lord has not allowed me to leave. It's weird, because although I'm a stranger to all these people, I don't feel like a stranger to the Lord. So I ask myself what I'm going to church for—these people, or myself? I guess I'm going for myself and not for the support of spiritual friends."

Women practicing outside traditional religions can also feel a lack of support for their spirituality. It may be difficult to find people of like mind, or people within traditional religions who are not threatened by divergent points of view. Women on the outside sometimes create circles or meetings to support their own practices. Some attend classes and retreats to support their spiritual journey.

Some women tend not to talk about their spiritual experience, fearing that insights and experiences would be criticized and invalidated. Rather than risk criticism, they remain silent and isolated, drawing support from reading and their individual practices.

Generally however, women want to talk about spiritual experience. They want to share the joy and mystery of their discoveries, to be heard and respected for their particular truths. Interviewing women about the role support plays in spiritual development brought Carol into closer contact with the support she was receiving on her own spiritual path.

A STORY FROM CAROL

Every year I return to the desert. I have been practicing Buddhist meditation with my spiritual teacher and her students for sixteen years now. In a way I feel I have grown up with her. Each year when I return for the women's retreat, I feel I am embarking on a pilgrimage—not a pilgrimage to a saint or idol, but a pilgrimage back to my spiritual self for deepening and renewal. There are others who do the same. Some of these women I know quite well; others I may have seen only once or twice before. I recognize the faces of older students like myself.

The opportunity to pursue my spirituality in a safe and nurturing environment is tremendously supportive to me. I sometimes think that I have no real way of measuring the vastness of the support I receive. When I think about this, I feel a deep sense of gratitude to my teacher and to the women with whom I practice. I wonder if they realize how much they support my efforts by simply being there pursuing their own spiritual healing."

Sources of Support

Make a list of people who support your spiritual growth in any way. Next to each name, write a few words about the type of support that person provides. Now take a moment to look over your list. Ask yourself these questions:

Does the list feel substantial to you? Are you getting the support you need? Does anyone's support feel unhelpful? How?

Circle the name of the person with whom you feel most comfortable receiving support for your spirituality. Now circle the name of the person whom you feel supports you the most. Retain the thought that you want support for your spiritual journey.

Here is a list of places to find support. As you read down the list, ask yourself if these sources of support work for you. Add any others that come to mind.

Friends of similar spiritual orientation
Organized religious groups
Religious institutions
Family members
Spiritual teachers
Spiritual art and images
Spiritual books and other reading material
Spiritual videos and films
Spiritual retreats

Another way to support your spiritual journey is by enhancing your inner resources. We suggest two powerful methods of accessing spiritual support from within: finding a symbol for support and empowerment and working with your inner voice.

Internal symbols are uniquely personal yet powerful connecting points to the spiritual. A personal symbol unique to your own spiritual needs can guide you on your spiritual path and validate the beauty and intensity of your spiritual life. Nature symbols like the rising sun, a snow-covered mountain, or a womblike cave can be particularly powerful for women. As you work with your symbol, the essence of your spiritual life is strengthened.

Support can also come from your inner voice, which is simply a wise and loving part of yourself that may not be constantly available to you. It is your inner sense of knowing. Working with your inner voice involves listening to your heart, availing yourself of the information and support to be found within you.

Enhancing Your Inner Resources

Finding a symbol for support and empowerment. Begin this exercise by establishing your sense of connection to yourself using any of the grounding meditations. With your eyes closed, imagine a symbol of support for your spiritual pursuits slowly coming into your inner vision. Let the symbol develop before you. See its beauty. Feel its power. Let it grow in size and energy until you feel totally supported by its energy. If it's a star, let it shine down on you. If it's a flower, let it enfold you, engulf you in its beauty. Let yourself feel the support available to you. Relax into it. Know that you are cared for and supported in your spiritual healing process.

Listening to your heart. Begin with a grounding meditation. Now slowly focus on your center. This is the part of your body that feels like a central energy point. Many people find their center in their abdomen or in the heart area. Tell yourself you are going deep, to a place of inner knowledge. Gently rest your attention at this area. Allow yourself to relax into a comfortable familiarity with your inner sense of knowing. This can feel like coming home to yourself. When you are ready, ask yourself a question about your spiritual journey. Answers may come in words, symbols, and/or feelings. Take these messages to heart, for they come from a sacred place within you.

Obstacles Along the Way

Embarking on a spiritual path or renewing your commitment to spiritual healing is a special decision; it is a choice to deepen your relationship to yourself and to the world around you. The spiritual journey described in this book is a healing, and healing implies change, which is sometimes accompanied by feelings of loss and renewal. The path may be fraught with difficult twists and turns. You may encounter obstacles along the way, some of them within. You need to learn to recognize potential obstacles, see your blocks for what they are, and understand how they operate within you. You can learn to master tendencies that impede spiritual progress. When obstacles remain unrecognized and unacknowledged, they retain power over you; when recognized, they tend to lose this power. When you understand their universality, you have firmer ground beneath you and an increased feeling of safety and support.

We have chosen to identify four areas of internal difficulty that generally emerge on a spiritual healing journey: attitude, energy, beliefs, self-doubt. Attitude is your general mental and emotional approach to life, the psychic foundation on which your journey rests. Your energy is what can support you in a harmonious and balanced manner. Your beliefs may become obstacles to spiritual progress either when you are not aware of them or when they become too rigid. Self-doubt, the final potential obstacle, is perhaps the most difficult, because it undermines your connection to your own inner wisdom.

Attitude

Our attitude pervades the space within and around us. Progress toward healing and renewal is delayed by attitudes that disturb our minds and hearts. We want spirituality in our lives, we want to heal ourselves, but an inability to deal gracefully with the inevitable difficulties and limitations that arise may hold us back. Anger at ourselves or others for disrupting our lives may agitate our minds and hearts. We may feel frustrated and become belligerent and blameful. We try to push away or destroy what we don't want, and in the process we lose contact with the deeper parts of ourselves.

A most disruptive and hurtful attitude is impatience. Impatience expresses itself by wanting everything and wanting it now. Often it is motivated by the fear of not getting what we need. Part of our motivation for healing may come from a desire to attain more pleasurable states of mind, more blissful moments, and these moments can be ours. However, it is important to let our journey of spiritual renewal move at its own pace. "Pushing the river," grasping too much with our minds and hearts, can only retard our progress.

"As I approach my meditation bench, as I sit before my altar, I feel a grasping in my heart. I want to feel better. I want to have a spiritual experience. It's as though I'm sitting there with my arms outstretched reaching for something or someone, rather than sitting back, relaxing, and just being with myself. I guess it's not really my fault. I'm working so hard all the time, trying to accomplish so much. It's really hard to stop trying to produce results for a while and sit back and just be. I feel that the secret to my happiness lies here in this struggle to be. My healing journey is just about being with myself. But you know, even as I am talking to you, I feel myself reaching ahead, feeling impatient with my own process."
CHEF AT A VEGETARIAN RESTAURANT, 34

"My spiritual practice was beginning to make me feel really down on myself, so much to live up to, so much to attain. I was getting so few results. After a while I just gave up; I got tired of feeling dissatisfied with myself. It was hard to let go, though, because I felt so bad about having failed."
VOCATIONAL COUNSELOR, 36

A STORY FROM CAROL

The other morning I decided to spend time with myself to work on my spiritual exercises. Sipping a cup of tea, I sit down in my favorite chair, book in hand. I turn the page to the exercise that is going to help me establish contact with a deeper part of myself that I had been neglecting. No sooner do I take my first deep, relaxing breath than the phone rings. I respond, feeling slightly irritated at the caller. It's my friend needing my help because her car has broken down.

Later, after returning home from my rescue mission, I settle into my chair again. My mind is drifting, my heart is filling with resentment; I had wanted a calm, free space to do my spiritual investigation. I'm angry at the loss of my spiritual time. I look at the clock—not much time left to relax, I think, especially now that I'm so agitated. For a brief moment I see that I am getting caught up in re-grets and resentments. I see how my selfishness has worsened the situation. I try letting go, but my mind continues down the path of frustration. I fear that I will never be able to find any time for myself and my spiritual pursuits. I am now blocked to myself. There is no space left for relaxation or spirituality. In a few minutes I give up. Wanting to distract myself from this unpleasant experience, I go to the kitchen to look for something for lunch."

A helpful antidote to impatience and frustration is the attitude of open-heartedness. Openheartedness is very powerful because it evokes the feeling of love—love of self and love for others—creating an atmosphere in which we re-main connected even when we are frustrated and hurting. In the act of open-ing our hearts we can feel another's pain and frustration as well as our own. Opening your heart in a painful situation is an act of love and can do wonders for your ability to negotiate the bumps along the road to spiritual healing.

Opening Your Heart

Watching for impatience. Spend a day focusing on your attitude. Watch for the feeling of frustration and irritability. When you feel this way, ask yourself if you are feeling impatient. If so, close your eyes and notice how impatience feels in your body. Watch to see what the attitude of impatience does to im-prove or disrupt your interactions with others.

Later, contemplate this question: How does your impatience affect your attitude toward yourself?

Transforming impatience. Think about or write about a particularly frustrat-ing experience in which your impatience played a part. Then see if you can imagine how you might have been able to change the outcome by using the at-titudes of patience and openheartedness toward yourself or others.

Cultivation of the open heart. Close your eyes, and gently bring your aware-ness to your chest area. Feel your chest rising and falling as you breathe in and out. Let a golden light appear in your heart center. Let this light grow in your heart. As it grows, it warms you and relaxes you. Imagine rays of golden light emanating from your heart center, and feel your heart energy expand, creating a feeling of further relaxation and openness in your chest. Imagine that these golden rays of heart energy are flowing out toward someone else. Allow this to happen as long as you feel comfortable and relaxed. Return to yourself and to your grounding. Then open your eyes.

There will be times, despite our best intentions, when we feel caught in impatience and frustration. There are certainly events in our lives that are unfair and unjust, and it would be inappropriate not to recognize these hurtful moments and feel the pain. We must also take action to move through it. This pain can lead quickly to resentment and eventually to hatred, attitudes that may render our efforts ineffective. When we feel hesitant and afraid to give, cultivating an attitude of generosity can help us move along our spiritual path. As women, however, we face a particular dilemma: we may have developed great skill at giving, yet our motivation for giving can create obstacles to spiritual development.

If giving becomes our only way of securing a positive identity, of feeling good about ourselves, our generosity is then motivated by fear as well as love. This type of generosity is motivated by our need for approval and acceptance. In combating frustration and impatience, it is important to cultivate an attitude of generosity that transcends fear and consideration of the self. This is a spontaneous generosity that comes straight from the heart, from an understanding of the interconnectedness of life. It is an act of love motivated by the desire to prevent suffering. With this understanding comes a feeling of richness and abundance. Fear then recedes as more of life becomes available to us.

Openhearted Generosity

These exercises may help you touch into an openhearted generosity.

Cultivating generosity. Contemplate the word generosity. What past meanings does it hold for you? Write about your associations with generosity. Look it up in the dictionary. Sit quietly for a moment and contemplate generosity as an attitude of abundance. Understand that generosity is a powerful energy that can affect your life. Contemplate this question: How could I be more generous toward myself? Toward others?

Take some sort of action. Experiment with being more generous with yourself. Treat yourself to a special meal. Pay more attention to your feelings. See how it feels to be generous in this way. Now experiment with being more generous toward another. How does it feel?

Giveaway. Take some time to go through a closet or drawer and give away some of the things you find there. Contemplate both the joy you feel in giving and the joy others will have in receiving.

Another powerful antidote to the attitude of impatience is gratitude. An attitude of gratitude focuses our minds and hearts on what we have rather than what is lacking. It helps us to create a world of abundance rather than deprivation. We slow down and appreciate the beauty and fullness of what we have; our needs and desires diminish.

Patience, generosity, and gratitude, then, are antidotes for the attitudes of impatience, frustration, and resentment. It is difficult to feel frustrated and angry at the same time you feel patient and grateful. You have the choice of where to focus your energy and which attitudes to cultivate. When you cultivate patience, generosity, and gratitude, you become more connected to the divinity within you and more in tune with your spiritual journey.

Gratitude

Cultivating gratitude. On each day of the next week, spend a few moments feeling a sense of gratitude for something that happened that day—perhaps a kind word from a friend, a moment of luck, a good idea you had. Allow yourself to appreciate anything beneficial that you experienced. When it feels appropriate, express your feelings of gratitude to someone else. Purchase a small gift, provide child care, or perhaps provide a meal.

We are doing the best we can. This is an exercise in acknowledging your efforts. Four ways to express gratitude to yourself are suggested. Practice the approach that feels most comfortable to you, or try all four, noticing which approach feels best to you. Feel free to adapt these approaches and create new practices to acknowledge your efforts.

1. Send yourself a thank-you card expressing gratitude for something you have done for yourself.

2. Write down some of the things you are thankful for, and post it where you will see it often. When you feel frustrated or impatient, read this list.

3. During a meditation or prayer time, allow time for self-appreciation and gratitude. Contemplate your efforts to do good. Let the energy of self-appreciation fill you. Give thanks for yourself and your life.

4. Practice repeating to yourself daily, "I am grateful to myself for my spiritual healing."

Energy

Attitude and energy go hand and hand. One influences the other. Often women complain of not having enough energy for healing or spiritual exploration. If you have had a particularly hard day, it may be best to go to bed early, for example, rather than trying to force yourself into the spiritual dimension. However, it is important to realize that tiredness may be a form of resistance or avoidance of spiritual practice.

When we start to meditate or perform a spiritual exercise, our minds may feel dense or our bodies heavy and dull. This may be because we haven't yet had enough experience. When we slow down, the mind and body think, "Ah, yes, tiredness, sleep." One way of dealing with tiredness is to test it out. Go for a short walk or do some stretching exercises. Take a drink of water and wash your face. Maybe even eat something. Change your energy, and see what happens. All tiredness is not physical. Some of it is a conditioned resistance to change. It may just disappear!

At other times it may seem that we have too much energy. We feel jumpy and restless. We may find it hard to sit still, we may be easily distracted. Our minds jump from one thing to the next. We find ourselves leaving a spiritually focused activity and sweeping the kitchen floor, or phoning a friend, without clearly having made the decision to do so.

> *"When I first started to set aside time each day for spiritual discovery, I just couldn't focus. I'd find myself off doing things that I remembered all of a sudden needed to get done right then, right in the middle of my relaxation meditation."*

We need our energy to flow, but not chaotically. Physical exercise like yoga or aerobics can integrate the mind and body, and your energy may then flow more naturally. Another helpful clue in dealing with restlessness is to see it for what it is. Agitation is often fed by worry and fear. When feeling the impulse to distract yourself, pause for a moment to take a look at what you are about to do. Then judge for yourself where the motivation comes from and how necessary the interruption is.

Your distractible mind will settle more easily into an environment that it finds pleasing. Think what it feels like to enter a particularly beautiful garden after driving in heavy traffic. Our energy becomes more balanced when focusing on a beautiful environment because we tend to take on the qualities of the things to which we give our attention.

Balancing Your Energy

For the next week, make note of your energy level when you work with the spiritual exercises or as you begin spiritual practice. Make a note describing your energy level in your spiritual journal. Some of us feel too much energy; some, a lack of energy. If your energy level feels unbalanced, work with some of our suggestions to change and balance your energy. Write down any helpful strategies, and use your notes as reminders. You may want to consider enrolling in a movement or exercise class to work with your energy on a regular basis. Energy changes can have organic causes; you may wish to discuss this with your health care practitioner.

Self-Doubt

At times we doubt ourselves. Though a certain degree of doubt can lead to valid questioning, a heavy dose can stop our progress on the spiritual journey. We need to examine how doubt is functioning in our lives. When self-doubt is an old, conditioned voice that overpowers the inner voice of knowing and experience, then it becomes an obstacle, leading us in a false direction and causing us to lose our footing. By contrast, doubt can open up space for authentic questioning and allow room for the divine to intercede. When doubt provides an opening, it becomes an ally on our spiritual journey.

It is important that we learn to discern the difference between the restrictive voice of self-doubt and the expansive voice of questioning. An investigative, questioning attitude can be helpful; an attitude of cynicism or an overactive mistrust of spiritual experience can sabotage spiritual growth. There is never a need to completely accept a doctrine or experience that we do not fully understand. We can deal with doubts by asking questions of our teachers and companions on the path and by paying attention to our own experience.

Some women tell us that when they listen deeply, the restrictive voice of self-doubt sounds different from the expansive voice of questioning. Other women tell us that they can discern the difference when they stay connected to themselves and to the spiritual process. When they listen to a voice, they watch carefully to see where it leads; if they discover that a direction is no longer helpful, they know they can change direction.

Listen to the voices of women grappling with self-doubt, struggling to find their authentic voice. The first story illustrates how the doubts of others can masquerade as self-doubt. The second clarifies how doubt can create space for new growth.

"Sometimes when I am meditating I hear voices in my head saying, 'Why do this? You're wasting your time.' When I pray, sometimes I hear a voice saying, 'Forget it; you're all alone; there's no one there to hear you!' In these moments I have found it helpful to make my doubts the focus of my attention. Instead of trying to chase them away, I listen to the voices of doubt, I listen well. As I focus my attention on them, I realize that they are nothing more than thoughts. They are often other people's thoughts—my parents', for example. They are not any more powerful that any other thoughts. It is in giving them my attention that I empower them."
STUDENT OF MEDITATION, 28

"There are times in my spiritual progression that I feel dry spells. I have come to see that I need these times; they are important. They contribute to my overall growth. Sometimes I need to say to myself, 'I don't think any of this is real; it's all made up.' Sometimes I have to throw everything out 'cause that's the only way to really touch base with myself, touch the primal place in myself where I can create it all over again. Maybe it's the void, the womb of the great mother. When that time comes, I just try to abandon things I have thought, my notions and ideas. In spiritual experience you can never be sure where there might be constructs you have built up by your own associations; they can be mistaken as real. Sometimes I have to question my beliefs. There are also times when I have found myself just doing pragmatic stuff, taking care of business, with little recall of ever having been a spiritual person. I need to take the pressure off myself about it, and then I can just expand back out into that sense of spirit again."
FORMER MINISTER NOW PURSUING GODDESS RELIGION, 42

Questioning Doubt

The habit of doubting the validity of your experience can be unlearned and uprooted. Here are several questions you can ask yourself when you are feeling doubt. These are also questions you may ask your inner voice in meditation.

Questions:
Does this experience feel real to me?
Does it feel safe to me?
Does it provide me with any insight or growth?

Is this experience helping me to heal myself?

Do I feel freer?

Is this experience harmful to me or others in any possible way?

This final question is perhaps the most important. If no harm can possibly come from your experience, then you are on safe ground.

About Self-Image

In confronting our doubts, we must sometimes ask the question, What's so bad about being wrong? Our self-image thrives on success, on a sense of accomplishment. We don't want to appear to be wrong. We want to be better than before or better than others. Our self-image is our "little self," our sense of self as individual.

Keeping a good self-image is necessary but troublesome. Spirituality and self-image are involved in a difficult relationship. Our self-image enjoys spiritual experience if it feels it can grow through it; however, spirituality ultimately transforms our concern with self-image, replacing it with something not nearly as focused on personal concerns: a sense of interdependence and cocreation. Doubts along the spiritual path may therefore be symptoms of our concept of our self-image struggling to survive.

Resistance to a more authentic and developed spirituality may have its roots in confusion over our self-image. A woman's sense of self may not be strongly developed; she may not be fully in touch with her particular needs and wants. But it is not necessary to relinquish ourselves and our needs to follow the spiritual path. Pushing our own needs aside in favor of a self-sacrificing martyrdom is not what is suggested here. Instead, we must work at creating an attitude of balanced give-and-take between ourselves and others. As we nourish ourselves, we strengthen our ability to stand secure in the face of the fears and doubts that do arise.

Unhelpful Beliefs

Beliefs are basically just very strong thoughts. They are thoughts strengthened by feelings, strengthened further by repetition and reinforcement. Eventually our beliefs become a part of us, finding a home in our minds and hearts.

As we grow and mature, we integrate our beliefs into a complicated system of responses called a belief system. Much of our interaction with others is governed by this system. Sometimes we think and act in accordance with these beliefs without much awareness of the process, and that is when our beliefs can cause harm.

Some of our beliefs were formed in response to events of childhood. As adults we may find ourselves acting on the basis of beliefs now inappropriate but learned much earlier and taken for granted now. It is helpful to identify beliefs that hurt you and serve as obstacles to your spiritual healing and growth.

Beliefs strongly influence our spirituality. In pursuing spiritual renewal, you will want to determine what beliefs you hold as a spiritual person and what beliefs you hold about spirituality in general. You may find some surprises.

Elaine describes a belief her mother passed on to her.

"Don't mess with religion, don't change it. This is God's territory, and he is the main honcho and he calls the shots."

She found that this belief limited her ability to set forth on her own spiritual exploration. Jane held the same belief, but she heard the message more vehemently.

"Even though I no longer follow the fundamentalist religion I grew up in, I am terrified to think my own spiritual ideas or to read any spiritual books that have new ideas in them. I was told that other religions are sinful and that I will go to hell for eternity if I look into other religions. I never realized it before, but I have been afraid to test out these beliefs, because deep inside I believed my fundamentalist religion just might be right."

Shirley used to believe that she had to go to church to be spiritual.

"I used to think that there was something wrong with me because I wasn't religious, and I thought that I had to be religious to be spiritual. I used to go church shopping, but some of the beliefs seemed ridiculous. I tried different religions, looking for one that would make me spiritual. It never worked. In recovery, I have found my own spiritual beliefs."

Exploring Spiritual Beliefs

Try any of the following suggestions to get in touch with your spiritual beliefs. These alternatives will help you to come at this question from different angles.

1. Read what other people believe in: mission statements, inspirational songs, religious creeds. Consult spiritual books and articles.

2. Ask someone you respect to share her or his spiritual beliefs with you. Take notes. Read them over later. Notice how you feel about what was said.

3. Try a free-writing exercise. Begin a sentence with "I believe in" and spontaneously complete it. There are no right answers here; this is an exercise in self-discovery.

As you move along in your spiritual journey, you may find you want to discard ideas and concepts that are no longer useful in order to make room for the new. We suggest the metaphor of a compost heap to help you. As in composting, nothing is wasted. Ideas, thoughts, beliefs that feel inappropriate can be placed in the compost bin to be recycled.

Starting a Compost Heap

Imagine that you have your own inner compost heap. Composting is a natural process in which old, useless material decomposes and is transformed into new, fertile soil. Here are some examples of what you might put in your compost heap:

- Any ideas that you read in this book that do not fit your truth
- Any ideas that you were told by others that are no longer helpful

You will want to use the compost heap on and off as you grow spiritually and find a need to discard false or unhelpful beliefs. When tossing ideas into the heap, affirm that through nature's process they will be transformed into thoughts helpful to yourself and humanity.

About Change

A journey of spiritual renewal includes many opportunities for change, which can be a strong ally on the spiritual path, for it brings with it the possibility of healing. Sometimes we resist change simply because we find uncertainty hard to tolerate. With change we step into the unknown, where everything both wonderful and terrifying is possible. However, after all is said and done, change remains our constant companion. Life on our planet is a constant dance. Change lies at the very base of our existence and at the core of our spiritual unfolding. Movement on the spiritual path takes place more easily when we incorporate an attitude of openness to change. Then we can move along the path of our spiritual unfolding with greater grace and a firmer footing.

Healing Your
Spiritual Alienation

I

Introduction

Now we begin the journey back to our spiritual and religious past. The journey begins by focusing on spiritual alienation. We look back to invite a special kind of change, change that is healing and transforms old pain and invalidation into new direction and connection. Whenever we set out in a new direction we are never quite sure where it will lead. It can be helpful to face the unknown with an attitude of openness and interest in the change to come. It can be helpful to reaffirm our intention for spiritual renewal.

This next lap of the journey may feel rocky and steep at times. Pack a backpack or a knapsack to take along with you; fill it with the most precious tools and supports you gathered in "Developing a Firm Footing." Remember, if you feel unsettled you can always return to the exercises and suggestions for grounding and safety. Cultivate an attitude of generosity and gentleness toward yourself.

Feel free to roam around in this section, focusing on what is important to your healing. You might want to intersperse some reading and exercises from the next section, "Seeking Spiritual Connection," with the readings and exercises in "Healing Your Spiritual Alienation." Take a rest when you become tired, some time out if you feel overwhelmed. Take some space when you feel stuck or need new vision. If you ever feel confused, scared, or overwhelmed, remember your inner resources, your friends, and your family.

We look at spiritual alienation so thoroughly because in our interviews and workshops we have sensed lingering pain and hurt from the past, and we suspect that some of women's spiritual inspiration and potential is bound up in this old hurt and pain. We may feel spiritually blocked, stuck, or deadened; that we have lost part of our natural essence as spiritual women. We may feel sadness or anger and a sense of being excluded. We may feel inadequate or fearful about our spirituality. We may feel guilt and isolation when we express our true spiritual beliefs. Or we may feel confused, not knowing how to begin our spiritual journey. We each have our own wounds to heal. We look at spiritual alienation in order to release its grip and to renew our spirit.

> *"I think it is about getting back to your childhood, to that person who accepted everything. We got hurt by that acceptance. But now we can return to the innocence and acceptance and heal the hurt."*

Alienation is disconnected energy. When we are alienated we become lost, disconnected—from ourselves, from our lives, from our friends, from our families. We forget who we are and lose track of what we want. Alienation may feel like subtle discontent and listlessness, or its effects may be more evident. Old pain may turn inward and fester inside us, perhaps resurfacing later in life as self-abuse or self-hatred.

Spiritual alienation starts in childhood when our sacred truths are disregarded and our spiritual experiences ignored. Sometimes alien spiritual and religious ideas are imposed upon us. We become disconnected from our spiritual source and our sense of inner knowing. We can lose touch with life's deeper meaning, purpose, and design. We may feel cast out from the embrace of a divine being.

Much of the alienation we face as women comes from having been ignored and discounted. After a while it can become a habit to ignore ourselves and to give our energy to others. An important part of our healing is to acknowledge and affirm ourselves. One way to affirm yourself is to recall your past and to understand its influence upon your life. So we begin our healing with a chronicling and affirmation of the religious and spiritual facts from our past. These facts will act as a foundation for our spiritual healing.

We begin with a list of questions that address some of the fundamental facts about your personal religious history. As you answer the questions, allow them to spark new questions and new memories. Answer the questions that seem appropriate, and add other questions and facts that help you remember more completely your religious legacy.

Background Questions on Childhood Religion

Did you have a religious affiliation as a child? _Yes_

If yes, what was that affiliation/denomination? _Lutheran_

As a child did you attend church, synagogue, or temple? _____ yes _____

If yes, how often? _____ almost every Sunday. _____

Was that attendance by your choice, or dictated by your parents? _____ by parents

Are you currently identified with the religion of your childhood? _____ No _____

If not, at what age did you leave? _____ around 13 or 14 _____

As a child did you attend religious school? _____ yes _____

If yes, how often? _____ for pre-school _____

Were your life transitions (for example, birth, baptism, bas mitzvah, marriage) acknowledged religiously? _____ yes - every holiday

If yes, which life transitions? _____ birth, baptism, confirmation, graduation

As a child, were you influenced by other religions or spiritualities? _____ yes

If yes, describe how _____ my mother was catholic

As a child a belief in God was (please circle appropriate answer)

VERY IMPORTANT TO ME   (SORT OF IMPORTANT)   NOT VERY IMPORTANT

IRRELEVANT

As a child religion was (please circle appropriate answer)

VERY IMPORTANT TO ME   (SORT OF IMPORTANT)   NOT VERY IMPORTANT

IRRELEVANT

As child was your community related to your religion? (please circle appropriate answer)

YES   SOMEWHAT   (NO)

As a child were you aware of having an inner spiritual life? (please circle appropriate answer)

YES   (SOMEWHAT)   NO

As a child my spiritual life and my religious life were (please circle appropriate answer)

TOTALLY CONNECTED   SOMEWHAT CONNECTED

NOT VERY CONNECTED   (TOTALLY SEPARATE)

Next make a family tree, a picture of your family structure through several generations. Family trees can help you discover family influences and patterns; you usually inherit a great deal from family members in past generations and pass on a great deal to future generations. Religious and spiritual beliefs, in particular, are commonly transmitted through the generations. As you investigate your history it can be helpful to gather information about the spiritual and religious experiences of your parents and grandparents to record on your family tree.

Making a Family Tree

Create a family tree, a diagram that shows your basic family relationships and facts. Most often family trees go back in time to your grandparents and go forward to as many future generations as there are in your family. However, make the family tree as thorough or simple as you wish. We illustrate a sample family tree on the following page.

You can list relevant facts next to the name of each family member. An important fact to include is the religious affiliation of each of the members of your family. In later exercises you will fill in the family tree with more information. You might choose to leave space on this family tree to fill in more facts, or make photocopies of this family tree for use in future exercises.

Finally, we suggest constructing a time line, a chronological record of important spiritual and religious events throughout your life. The time line is a way to preserve memories you encounter as you work through the exercises in the book. See page 48 for an example.

Time Line of Important Spiritual and Religious Events

Start with a large blank piece of paper. Draw a line vertically down the center of the page. Then mark the dates of significant religious and spiritual events in chronological order on the line and describe the event either to left or right of the line. Start toward the top of the page with your birth. You might wish to leave some room above your birth date for events that might have affected your life prior to your birth.

Don't be concerned with filling out your time line completely. This is meant to be a work in progress. Create the format now, and add to the time line as you work through the exercises and remember other significant and

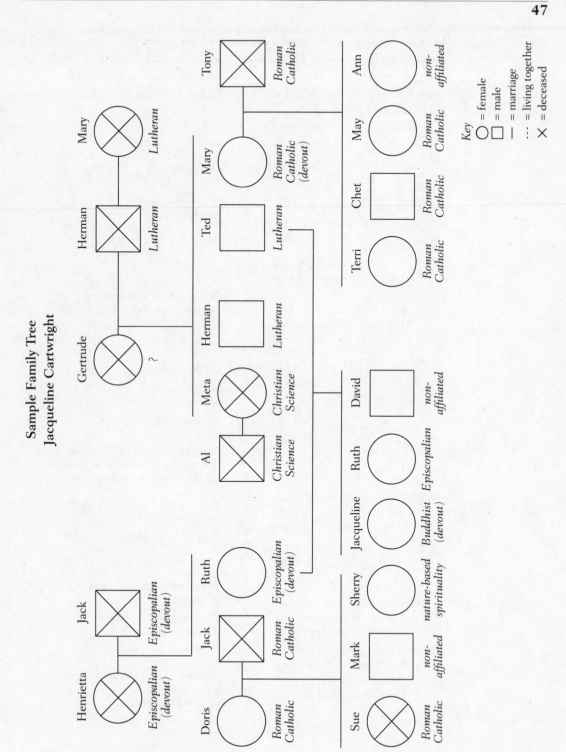

Sample Family Tree
Jacqueline Cartwright

formative spiritual and religious events. Feel free to be as creative as you wish in adapting this exercise. The main point is to have a chronological illustration of the events so that you can see patterns and record your experience. We show some of the significant events in Nelly's spiritual life noted on a time line on this page as a sample.

Nelly's Spiritual Time Line

		The Holocaust
		World War II
My birth	1948	Birth of state of Israel
Meet Barbara, my first spiritual friend	1951	
	1956	"Know" about bomb in sewer
		My intuition affirmed by Mom
Drop out of Hebrew school after attending for a few weeks	1958	
"Freak out" on LSD	1969	Drop out of college
	1972	Move to the country
Participate in women's spiritual circles	1973	
	1974	Move to women's rural community— Womanshare—and live with Carol
		Facilitate retreats and write first book
Begin daily reading of spiritual books	1975	
	1978	Attend first meditation retreat
		Begin daily meditation practice
Dad dies	1979	
	1982	Begin teaching meditation to women
Go to graduate school to study psychology and spirituality	1986	Begin interviewing women about their spirituality
Begin counseling people with AIDS; learn more about death and dying	1988	
Begin writing *A Woman's Guide to Spiritual Renewal*	1989	Complete master's thesis *Towards a Group Model for Feminist Spiritual Direction*

Most of us know about healing; we have healed in many ways. If we have been in psychotherapy, we may have uprooted old ways of feeling and relating and replaced them with new, more joyful and satisfying ways. If we grew up in an alcoholic family, we may find that after remembering the pain and confusion we can shed dysfunctional, unhealthy habits of relating. If we are survivors of incest, we may find that after sharing the memories in a safe and supportive environment, we can reclaim a joyful sexuality and a trust in life.

Healing can be difficult when it entails reexperiencing old hurt and pain, but we may need to take a direct look at the pain to eliminate its influence over us. When the memories reappear, we may feel still as vulnerable as when we initially had the experience. It is important to realize that the injury is no longer happening; it is a memory now. It is important to remember that we are now adults with the ability to care for ourselves.

Working with Painful Feelings

When you are feeling painful feelings, try the following approaches in the order they are listed. If you become more comfortable with the feeling or the feeling passes, then it is not necessary to try each of these approaches. If the feeling hangs on, work your way through all these steps.

1. Describe the feeling. Where do you feel it in your body? What ideas go along with the feeling?

2. Identify the feeling. Ask yourself, What am I feeling? Give your feeling a name—for example, hurt, anger, rage, sadness, guilt, or disappointment. Give your feeling the name that is most accurate.

3. Be with the feeling. Remember, all feelings are temporary, and this feeling will pass.

4. Learn from the feeling. Ask yourself, What does this feeling teach me about my life, about my experience, and about my needs?

5. Be guided to action by the feeling. Ask yourself, Is there something I need to do or change in my life?

When you reexperience alienation, it is important to treat yourself with gentleness and nurturing. When you reexperience trauma, safety and support are essential so that you do not get hurt again. Take some time to think about what and whom you find supportive. Review the exercises on support in "Developing a Firm Footing."

"I have a special place where I go when I do healing work. When I leave this place, I leave the feelings and memories behind."

"I always start my healing work by remembering and sensing my connection to the earth. I feel safe on the earth because she transforms my pain."

"When I am doing intense emotional work, I set aside time to play just as intently."

Remembering Healing

Remember one area in your life in which you have healed from alienation, disconnection, or hurt. (Remember, healing is a process, so you may not feel completely healed.) Some possibilities are

- Healing from a physical illness
- Healing from an addiction
- Healing from a death or loss

Remember how you felt before the healing. Describe how you felt in words or images, letting yourself remember the feelings. Take a moment to think about the healing. Recall the tools and supports that helped you through. What people were helpful? How did they relate to you? What situations were helpful? What thoughts were helpful? When you feel complete for now, write down some reminders of what supports you in healing. Read over this list again if you become discouraged or overwhelmed.

Carol and Nelly both identify experiences of spiritual alienation from their past.

A STORY FROM CAROL

I was raised Episcopalian. As an adult I was unaware of the extent to which my religion of origin was still affecting me, for I never really took to Christianity. As a child it felt like religious responsibilities took up a lot of precious time on Sunday mornings, time I could have used climbing trees and playing in the woods. As a young adult I grew ashamed of my Christian heritage when I saw how many wars had been fought in the name of my religion. I was critical of the Church's lack of support for the needy. I tried to forget that I had been raised Christian. It was only when I was teaching spirituality workshops to women and working as a feminist therapist that I realized the powerful effect my childhood religious conditioning had on me.

As Nelly and I began our interviews in 1986, I took a trip home to visit my parents for the Christmas holidays. It was at the beginning of the process of this book, and I was just formulating an awareness of the influence of my religion of origin. On Christmas Eve my mother and I went to midnight mass just as we had done each year of my childhood. On this holiest of evenings, the church was full. The warmth of the candlelight filled the room, reflecting off the many stained-glass windows. Familiar smells of incense and evergreens opened my senses. The priest moved to the center of the altar to bless the wafer, the body and blood of Jesus Christ. He turned toward the crowd again, inviting us to partake in Holy Communion. Suddenly his appearance seemed to change. His eyes narrowed, his expression very stern. It was as if a dark cloud were hovering around his head and shoulders. As he turned toward me, he seemed much larger than before and very threatening. As I looked around the congregation, I sensed I was the only one who felt this change. I felt dizzy and sick to my stomach. My knees weakened, I thought I might collapse into the wooden pew. I didn't want to disappoint my mother or cause a fuss. The experience lasted perhaps three minutes but left a profound impression.

At first I was unsure what this experience meant. Slowly I realized I had felt spiritually disempowered and intimidated as a child. My authentic spirituality had not been encouraged; instead, something I did not understand had been imposed. I felt inspirational and devotional energy from my mother, which I tried to emulate. But the objects of her devotion felt inauthentic to me. I suppressed my feelings about this for fear of hurting her. My experience this Christmas Eve had revealed the shadow, that which had been previously hidden from me. I realized the extent to which my religion of origin was still haunting me.

This experience guided me to a deeper understanding of my spiritual alienation. I also saw the depth of my connection to my mother and the extent to which she was a spiritual model for me.

A Story from Nelly

As I look back upon my religious past, I am struck by how Jewish I feel and at the same time how little I know about the Jewish religion. This sounds like such a paradox, yet seems to be a common experience among the Jewish women we interviewed. My parents were children of immigrants, and I think, in an attempt to blend into the culture of America, they cut themselves off from the old ways, including the religion.

As a Jew, I sense fear and danger lurking. Though my life has been generally peaceful, I never forget about suffering. The history of my people as Jews is deeply etched into my awareness, a history of five thousand years of cyclic horror and rejection. This remembering is prescribed by the Jewish religion, but sometimes I get angry at remembering, while at the same time, I know that forgetting is dangerous. I was born in the shadow of the holocaust. I keep trying to make some sense of the holocaust and somehow integrate it into my spiritual vision. I believe that every being is intrinsically holy and divine and that there is basic goodness in life and in people. I question where Hitler and the atrocities fit into this vision. Discovering an answer to that question has directed my spiritual journey throughout my life. I have an acute awareness of injustice and a strong motivation to be a compassionate presence in the face of injustice and personal holocausts.

My mother has strong spiritual beliefs that are very much her own. In many ways she is a wonderful model, encouraging spiritual freedom and investigation. In my mother's commitment to my spiritual freedom, she never imposed her spiritual ideas. But without clear spiritual guidelines from her, sometimes I felt somewhat lost and confused. I wish, as a child, I had had a stronger spiritual connection with my mother.

Although my father was more religious, my parents never passed on the Jewish faith to me. I never felt like part of the religious community. I never lived in relationship to or with the support of a Divine Being. We did attend synagogue on the high holidays, but it never felt like a spiritual event, more an obligation. The congregation seemed more concerned with making a showing and with what they were wearing than with authentic spiritual experience. In fact we spent most of our time outside, parading our new clothes. When I did go inside the temple, I didn't understand what was going on. The service was in Hebrew, and I never learned the language. I never understood the religious ritual or felt its impact on my life. Our rabbi was an alcoholic and an ineffective leader. I never felt spiritually nourished, though I think I did hunger for spiritual nourishment.

In my teenage years I spent day after day urgently questioning whether God existed. This was a central concern of mine and continues to be central. I am thankful for the opportunity to reach my own answers and find my own spiritual path. But at times it is hard to define my own path. Sometimes I feel spiritually lonely and lack spiritual community.

Since I became a feminist I have grappled with the male-biased elements of Judaism while at the same time feeling the close cultural ties. I hunger for a *deeper spiritual connection to Judaism. I search for a way to more fully integrate Judaism into my spiritual journey.*

The healing of spiritual alienation will take you on a journey back to the childhood roots of your spiritual alienation. Some old beliefs may need to be eliminated, pulled up by the roots, because they have hurt you and continue to hurt you. Other old beliefs may need to be adapted to fit with what you now know to be truth; the old roots may need to be pruned. You may discover that some of the roots from your religion of origin feed you; perhaps it is time to give them more support, nourish them with renewed energy. Although the healing process may feel difficult at times, the rewards are potentially great— spiritual connection, firmly rooted in your own authentic spiritual path.

The chapters that follow in this section will each focus on different obstacles to spiritual experience, different arenas in which you may have felt alienation.

Where to Focus

The exercises below may give you a better understanding of where to focus your attention. Each exercise uses a different technique for uncovering information.

A checklist. Read over the list of experiences and feelings and check off the ones that apply to you. Then go back over the statements you checked off and change the wording to make them even more descriptive of your experience.

——— I never felt connected to God because he was male.

——X I felt scared and intimidated by God. but closely related w/ my own

——— I felt alienated by the fact that God was personified as white. personified Jesus.

——— I felt closed out in my religion because all the people in leadership were males.

——— As a girl or woman I was excluded from or given secondary positions in religious rituals.

——— What I was taught about religion never made much sense to me.

——— I never had much of a religious background, and that was difficult for me.

——— I was abused within my religion.

——— My life has been so busy that I haven't had time for spirituality.

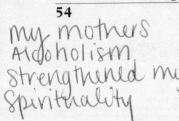
my mothers Aloholism strengthened my spirituality

_____ I felt hurt or fearful as a member of a religion or race or other group that was discriminated against.

_____ Being abused when I was a child affected my spirituality.

✓ Substance abuse, my own or someone else's, affected my spirituality.

_____ I have experienced a great deal of pain and loss, and it has blocked my spiritual journey.

If you checked any of the first three statements, you might want to focus on the chapter on God. If you checked any of the next five statements, you might want to focus on the chapter on religious obstacles. If you checked any of the last five statements, you might want to focus on the chapter on other obstacles.

Clarifying issues. Look back over your time line, and think about your past experiences. Notice any feelings of spiritual alienation that are evoked. What is the alienation about? Does it have something to do with God? With religion? Were there other obstacles? Were you abused? Were you discounted? Then browse the following sections on alienation and see if any of the topics seem to speak to your issues.

Read about alienation and work the exercises in your own way and in your own time. Some of the experiences of the women interviewed will resonate with your own. Others will not. Some will feel like truth. Others will not. Apply what fits. Throw out what is untrue for you. Uncover your own sources of alienation, and discover your own sacred truths. Tell your story. Be heard.

I have felt alienated in the ways that I have come from such a different background, a not so perfect model family, ~~felt~~ I also did not have the ability to act as act as if life were perfect as the woman I grew up with did.

Taking a Look at God

3

In childhood we were taught many things about God. Sometimes we were heartened by teachings like "God is Love." At other times, we may have felt alienated by what we were taught. Some of the images and messages may have fit when we were children but as we grew older became limiting and blocked us from having a vital relationship with God. Some of what we learned about God may even have placed obstacles in our spiritual path. Now is our chance to reexamine what we learned about God and allow our sense of a divine presence to heal, grow, and mature.

Looking at our beliefs about God can be difficult, because concepts about God are presented as absolute truth. We may have been told that it is not our place to question, perhaps even that questioning is sinful or spiritually harmful. Yet for many women the first step in creating an authentic relationship with God is to dismantle old beliefs that are no longer helpful and supportive. Returning to these focus questions can be helpful as you work through your issues about God.

Focus Questions

How can I question teachings from my past, while at the same time respecting teachings that have guided and sustained me?

How can I discover a sense of a divine presence that reflects my experience?

When we imagine ourselves as children again we can better recall the messages we were given about God. It is believed that the nondominant side of the body (the one that we generally do not use for manual tasks) represents our more childlike and forgotten parts.

Messages About God

Messages from childhood. Take out your spiritual journal and a crayon or pen. Then imagine yourself as a child about eight or ten years old sitting in front of this paper. When you are writing or drawing, use the hand that you usually do not favor for writing; that is, if you are right-handed, write now with your left hand. If you are left-handed, use your right hand. Write down any words or phrases that come to mind when you think about God. Write as fast as you can. It is fine to repeat words. Write for about five minutes. You may prefer to work with images instead of words. Allow the images to flow out of you.

Family messages. Using your family tree, think about each member of your family who was in your life during your childhood. Then write one sentence for each family member saying what he or she believed and told you about God.

After completing these exercises, take a look at your lists and see what messages you got about God.

Physical Characteristics of God

"I just couldn't relate to God very much when I was a kid. I imagined him as a man with a long beard looking through the clouds. He seemed very far away and very different from me and my world."

"He was a kind, old grandfatherly kind of man who lived in the sky somewhere. I believed he loved everyone. He was a positive force but very distant."

God is often assigned physical characteristics. This can make it easier for us to relate to God; after all, we are used to relating to other beings with bodies. As women, however, we may find that some of the physical characteristics make it more difficult for us to connect with God: for example, old or distant or white or male. We learn about God's physical attributes in different ways, but perhaps most directly through the images we see. Another way we know God physically is through how God is regarded in scripture and prayer. Before you begin the exercises that follow, go to a safe place, a spiritual space. You might want to bless the place, to reconnect to your desire for healing and renewal.

Images of a Divine Presence

Remembering our feelings about religious imagery. Begin this exercise by spending a few minutes focusing on a spiritual object or thought that you feel connected to right now. As you work on this exercise, keep the object or thought close to you.

Now remember an image of God from your past—perhaps a painting, a stained-glass window, or another religious artifact. Remember the image as clearly as you are able. If you are having difficulty or if you wish to reinforce the memory, you might want to go to a church or temple or to a store that sells religious objects. Make note of the physical characteristics of God from your past. Get a sense of how you feel about that image and, in particular, how you felt connected to that image and how you might have felt alienated by it.

Remembering childhood prayers and scripture. Begin this exercise the same way you began the exercise above, by focusing on an object or thought.

Then spend a few minutes recalling a prayer or scripture that makes reference to God. Speak it out loud. You might want to write it in your spiritual journal. Notice if there are direct references to the physical characteristics of God in the prayer. Do you sense what God looks like? God's gender? the color of God's skin? God's eyes? Allow any images of God to come to awareness. Also notice if you get a sense of the qualities of God.

Now take out your spiritual journal, and make one list of the physical characteristics of God and another list of the qualities of God. Leave the lists for a while. When you return later to your lists, notice your reactions to these physical characteristics and qualities.

Women sometimes feel alienated by images of God as a man or as a father. As girls and women we may not know where we fit into a male model of divinity. Religions with an exclusively male God and male leadership may provide us with few role models for our own spiritual unfolding. Belief in an exclusively male God may reinforce our sense of limited spiritual options.

> *"Without knowing it in words, I knew that men were above women, so it made sense that God would be a male, a father figure. Everybody who was anybody was a male. That was just the way the world was."*

The male God is portrayed as the Creator of the universe. However, as girls we see our mothers and the other women in our lives giving birth to children, creating and nurturing human life. We may question the value of female creation, separating it from divine creation. We may come to belittle the contributions of our mothers and our own potential for creation and creativity.

Carter Heyward, author and Episcopalian priest, stated it simply when she said,

> *"God the Father was really a projection of male values. This God the Father was the icon of obedience and submission, doing what you were told, never talking back to your parents. God kept a lid on me, kept me dispassionate."*

Carter now believes that her spirituality is an enlivening force that encourages her free-spiritedness.

Maggie, who was a Catholic nun for eighteen years, was aware from childhood of the inadequacy of images of God.

> *"I never liked the images of God that were presented. I am not very anthropomorphic about God and wasn't as a child either. I don't get into parent names for God. When I got older and became a nun, I began to realize the patriarchal nature of the church. I got very adamant about how everything was labeled with male characteristics and how everyone in power was male and how God was male. I became very adamant about trying to change this."*

In many religions the supreme being is portrayed as a loving male God, a God we can trust and who will protect us. For some women this is comforting. However, the males in our lives may not model loving, nurturing behavior. It may be difficult to trust in the ultimate love and care of a male God when we have little experience of nurturing male figures.

As a child, Linda was sexually abused by many men. As result of the abuse, Linda became entrapped by addictive patterns. While she finds healing within the Twelve-Step programs, she searches for her own imagery of her Higher Power.

> *"I want to have a better sense of my Higher Power so I can do the work of the program. But I can't use the imagery that has been handed down. I was abused by males. I am not willing to have a Higher Power if it means some other being has control over me. There is a certain amount of surrender required to do this program. I have to look at surrender in a whole different way that does not have to do with giving up power. Because my addictions had such a stranglehold over me, I didn't have any trouble understanding that I was powerless over the addiction. In that context, giving up power was not threatening. But it is threatening to think that I would accept someone else's plan for me or even the universe's plan for me. I am sure this has to do with having had my power taken away from*

me at such an early age, along with my right to consent and the boundaries around my body. I have to think deeply about what my Higher Power is."

Many of us are taught that God is a white man. Women of color may feel alienated from a God who looks so different from themselves and their families. The image of God as white can confuse us into accepting racism as a divine mandate. Our images of God are limited by human prejudice and ignorance.

Angela is now a Presbyterian minister. She was raised Catholic and attended Catholic school during Vatican II, a time when the Catholic church was rapidly changing. When she was in seventh grade, she had the good fortune to see an image of God that more closely resembled her image as an African-American girl.

"When I was in seventh grade, a spunky nun showed me a picture of Jesus who was not blond and blue-eyed but looked like a Jewish Middle Eastern person who had olive skin and dark hair and dark eyes. I was stunned by this picture. I still can see that picture. How many people still believe in the blond, blue-eyed Jesus? I know I had. Now I know it is a symbol. The symbol awakened the humanity behind the symbol. I began to question doctrine. It seemed to me that my God was bigger than I had been told. I began a spiritual quest."

As a child, Shirley was unaware of difficulties with the image of God as white. As she grew older she discovered a God who was not personified.

"As a black child, I remember going to church and seeing pictures all over church of God as this white-bearded man. It was fine for a long time for me that God was a white-bearded man, but when I got older I realized that God was not necessarily a white man; I realized God was not a person."

For many women, relationships are very important; in relationship we discover fundamental meaning and purpose. Understandably we may yearn for a close relationship with God. But some of the women we interviewed told us that God seemed like some guy up in the sky who lived far, far away. His physical distance made it difficult for them to feel a connection; he seemed unapproachable.

As a child Ann yearned for such a relationship with God, but her parents and the people in her church community had a distant relationship with God.

"My parents were churchgoers, though I never sensed that God was a vital part of their lives. As a child I knew there was a discrepancy between what I heard the priests saying about God being in our lives in a daily way and the weekend

churchgoing ritual that I saw around me. When I was six or seven years old, I knew that I wanted a personal relationship with God, and I knew that meant some kind of emotional relationship. Because my parents did not have that kind of relationship with God, I started on my own track."

Although there is no distance from God that is right for all of us, there may be a certain distance or closeness that feels right to you now. As you become more aware of your distance from God, you may be able to adjust it so that you feel more connected.

Distance from God

Think about how you invoke your relationship with a spiritual presence—performing a ritual or saying a prayer or going to a sacred space—then do it. Where are you in your relationship to your God? Are you too far away or too close? Experiment by imagining the distance growing smaller. Bring God close to you or perhaps right inside your heart. Then imagine God moving away from you. Notice what distance feels best to you. Is there anything you want to change in your life to adjust your distance to God?

Qualities of God

As we move beneath the physical images of God, we uncover the qualities of God. These qualities reveal basic spiritual principles. For the most part, God exemplifies the most revered spiritual values; therefore, by learning what impressions we have of God, we can learn a great deal about our underlying spiritual beliefs.

Describing God

Circle the qualities that apply to the God of your childhood:

WARLIKE   LOVING   JUDGMENTAL   ACCEPTING   CRITICAL   WISE
COMPASSIONATE   ANGRY   HOSTILE   COMFORTING   PROTECTIVE
DEMANDING   TERRIFYING   TENDER   RIGID   WARM   WELCOMING
INSPIRING   VENGEFUL   STRICT   PUNISHING   KIND   AUTHORITARIAN
POWERFUL

Add any words you think of that further describe the God of your childhood.

Now look over the list and see which of these words still fit with your sense of spiritual presence.

Some of us feel hurt or deeply intimidated by a punitive, angry God, a God who will punish us if we do not do the right things and think the right thoughts. The punishment might last forever; we might even be condemned to hell. We can become frightened, our natural spiritual inclinations scared away. We can become entrapped by feelings of guilt and inadequacy.

Others learn of a God who is the absolute and ultimate authority; his power is rooted in dominance. This image of God sets up the ultimate hierarchy. We may have deep-rooted feelings of separation and inequality.

"If you didn't believe in God and behave, you were going to die and go to hell, and that was all there was to it."

"It is almost unbearable to be subjected to the kind of scrutiny and criticism that I felt from the God of my Protestant church."

Jackie was in a near-fatal accident that conclusively transformed her belief in a vengeful God.

"I had an experience of nearly dying when I was sixteen years old. It caused me to reject the patriarchal God of my Catholic religion. It made me realize that there was definitely something out there but it was not the scary, wrathful God who's out to get me. I realized there was no heaven and hell. I stopped believing much of what the Catholic church taught me.

"I wasn't without sin as defined by the Catholic church, but I knew that if I died I wasn't going to hell. I stopped fearing God and worrying about whether I was a bad girl. I remember looking down at the priest giving me my last rites, and he seemed insignificant to me; I had no heart connection to him. Instead, I had a very blissful knowingness that I was going to a greater place. I wasn't sad, and I wasn't scared. I had never, ever experienced such peace and calm. I was full of love.

"After the accident, I didn't buy the ideas of the Catholic church about a scary, wrathful God anymore. These ideas were in such contrast to the loving feelings of my own experience. I realized that my spirituality was quite different from what I had been taught."

Marilyn Sewell talks about the difficulties she had in worshiping a punitive male God, a God she modeled on her grandfather. As a child she had difficulty relating to the punitive God of both the Roman Catholic and Southern Baptist churches. As an adult she is a Unitarian minister and has a close relationship with a loving God.

"My mother was a Roman Catholic, and I was a Catholic at first. Then my family split up, and I moved to a small town in north Louisiana with my father, my paternal grandparents, and my younger brother and sister. At age thirteen, I made a decision to leave the Catholic church. I had problems with several things in the church. One was confession. I knew that you had to tell all your sins or you would go to hell, and some of the things that I was doing, even though they were childish things, I didn't want to share with the priest, because they felt like private things. I didn't know if they were sins or not, but I felt guilty. I was getting all bogged down in what was a sin or not a sin and whether I was going to go to hell or not because I picked my nose on Friday or something like that, and that was a heavy trip for me. It had to do with guilt and the feeling that I wasn't accepted and that God was on the lookout for everything that I might be doing that was wrong. That was not the kind of God that I wanted to relate to.

"When I was fourteen years old, I joined the Southern Baptist church. Actually the God of the Southern Baptist church wasn't that different. There was a lot of guilt in that church too. The Southern Baptist church was very Calvinistic, very prudish about certain things. The sins of the Baptist church centered around your fleshly or carnal self. I grew up very afraid of myself sexually.

"My own sense of God was, unfortunately, based on my grandfather. My grandfather was a very patriarchal figure, a Victorian man who ordered other people around. As I look back on it now, I don't think he was very mentally stable. He was very gruff at times. We called him Big Poppa. He was a very big man and very dominant. But he was 'good' in the sense that he didn't do the obvious sins like smoke cigarettes, drink, or chase women. But he was definitely uptight and unloving. But that childhood image of God remained with me for a long time into my adult years. My father was the 'black sheep' of the family. He did drink in a town that was dry, where alcohol was illegal. He did chase women and stay out late and go around with unsavory companions. He was considered the bad guy, but he knew how to have fun. My grandfather didn't know how to have fun; he was kind of mean and puritanical and extremely frugal. He would come and turn out the lights at nine o'clock at night when I was reading because he said he wanted to save on electricity. So connecting my God with my grandfather was a bad mistake. My God was very severe, authoritarian, dominating, rule-making,

unloving. It was the Old Testament, Jehovah kind of God. I felt he was a task-master standing over me. It was very spiritually unhealthy.

"I tried to pray and felt that was important. I had learned that in church—both Catholic and Baptist. But with my concept of God as someone who was so big and powerful and uncaring, it was hard to believe that he did much caring about this little girl. I didn't feel my prayers went all that far."

Marilyn goes on to affirm the ways she felt a spiritual connection within her family and church:

"My grandmother was a very loving person who was also very religious. Every day she would sit there in her rocking chair in front of the fire and read aloud from her big black Bible. I still have this Bible, and I am going to have it refurbished. She would read, 'Bless the Lord, oh his soul, all that is within me. Bless his Holy name.' I titled the novel that I wrote All That Is Within Me. *My grandmother let me know that believing in God and being a person of faith did not necessarily mean being judgmental. She was very sweet and loving.*

"Because my family home was not a very happy place, the church became the center of my life. It was a place where I felt cared for. The church became like an extended family. Some of the Sunday school teachers and choir leaders were loving people and really cared for me. As I grew my own ideas about what God was about, God came to be more a God of love and friendship."

Guilt is rarely helpful. When we feel guilty, we confuse a sense of disappointment about something we did with a self-image of worthlessness. It can be helpful to be specific about what it is that we feel guilty about. Then we can see if there is something we wish to change. Whether or not we choose change, it is always helpful to practice self-forgiveness.

Guilt

Healing guilt. Begin by affirming one way that you feel good about yourself. Then take out your spiritual journal, and think back to your childhood.
  Remember one thing that you felt bad about in the eyes of your God.

Complete this sentence: I felt bad because I _____

_____

_____ and God

would think _____ about it,

and I feared _____.

Then find a new way of looking at that situation.
Complete these sentences:

When I did _____ (the same as above), I was

learning about _____. In the future I will

remember _____.

In the future I hope to _____

_____.

End by affirming one thing about your life that feels good.

Lately I have felt good about _____

_____.

If there are more issues you wish to address, repeat this exercise.

Transforming guilt. Spend the next few days noticing whether you feel guilt. Most of us do. When you find yourself in a situation that evokes guilt, go through the following steps.

1. As specifically as possible, describe what you feel guilty about. For example, "I feel guilty because I have not been completing the exercises in this book."

2. Remind yourself that you are a worthy person. For example, "I know I have lots of responsibilities, and I am doing the best I can."

3. Are there are any changes you want to make? You might change your goals, your assessment of what is happening, or your actions. Be as specific as possible. For example, "I need to reset the priorities in my life; maybe my partner could take the children to school a couple of mornings a week, and I could have that time to focus on the workbook." Or, "I am moving along with the exercises in this book slowly and steadily, and that is really just fine. In fact, maybe there are some advantages in going slowly."

4. Practice self-forgiveness. Repeat these words or words with a similar message: "If I have hurt myself or others by my words or actions, I forgive myself."

Searching and Questioning

As young children we understand the world in concrete terms, so concrete images of God can be helpful. As we grow older we gain the ability to grasp more abstract spiritual truths, opening up the possibility of new understanding.

The search for our own experience and relationship with a spiritual presence involves questioning and evaluating the images and messages passed down by our parents and our religion. Ideally this search is encouraged by the adults in our lives, especially by our families and our religious teachers, though perhaps more often it is discouraged and a rigid image of God imposed upon us. In some religions it is considered sinful or heretical to discover one's own sense of God and the wrath of God is the price to be paid.

Those of us who grew up in homes in which parents were atheists or agnostics were perhaps discouraged from even entertaining thoughts about God and may thereby feel alienated from our spiritual awareness as well as from our friends. Most of the women we interviewed yearned for more support, guidance, and validation in this essential quest.

"I remember one time in philosophy class I was asked to write a paper discussing whether or not God existed. I had a very difficult time writing that God didn't exist, because I was afraid that if I wrote that I might be punished and my life just might not work out for me."

"I would go to Sunday school and ask my grandmother questions about things I didn't understand. She would respond by saying, 'Don't be a doubting Thomas.' I didn't get any answers."

As we search we may encounter doubt. Doubt can be useful when it guides us toward a more complete investigation of the truth. Doubt can get in the way when it breeds bitterness and alienation. One way to know that we are on safe ground when we are doubting is if we can assume a respectful attitude.

Models can help us as we explore new ideas and attitudes. Ann turns to Christ as her model for questioning.

"Christ broke some pretty powerful rules in his time. He spoke to women at a time when a rabbi was forbidden to talk to or touch women. There is a story in which a woman touched Christ. In our culture this may not seem like a big deal, but back then it was an act of pure rebellion. If Christ considered women to be peers and equals, I want to be treated that way.

"Anytime there is a God behind any theology it makes it very hard to question. In churches they present their truth and couch it as 'this is what God said.' If you disagree, you are seen as rebellious toward God. I think that people in power in religion are afraid to question. They fear that if they begin to question, all their beliefs will fall apart. I figure if it is going to fall apart, it isn't worth having."

Ann is a Christian psychologist who guides her clients to deeper spiritual understanding.

"My clients feel so much guilt. Guilt over their own internal questioning. Guilt about not being the way that they were taught they were supposed to be. Guilt over having an independent idea. Guilt about doubting things in scripture. It is very hard for them to understand that they are capable of having insight and a point of view of their own rather than just hearing it from someone else.

"I have recently become a member of the Quaker church because women are very active and people are honored for their sense of searching, inquiring, doubting, and turning things over. People are accepted for their understanding without being belittled. There is a lot more freedom. Although there are problems, it has been a great relief for me. When I talk to men in leadership, I do not feel put down or that there is something wrong with my opinion."

Many women wished they had had more support for their spiritual search. Do you remember feeling a sense of spiritual longing and searching? Was it supported and nurtured? Although we can never change the past, it can be helpful to ask for the support now.

Support for the Search

Appreciate past support. Remember your past and think about people who have supported you in your spiritual search. Consider parents and other family members, teachers, and friends. Then write one person a letter of appreciation and acknowledgment. Tell her or him (and yourself) just how you felt supported. You may find that it is appropriate to mail this letter, or you may not wish to or be able to mail it. That is fine. It is very valuable to you to know and appreciate the support you received.

Ask for support now. Think back and discover if there was a time in your past when you felt the urge to search for your own understanding and relationship with God. Now refer to the exercise on support in "Developing a Firm Footing," page 26, and choose a person who provides you spiritual support now.

Tell that supportive person about the time in your past when you felt the desire to search, and as you tell about that experience, ask him or her to give you whatever kind of support you would like.

The teenage years can be exciting and chaotic, a time when we begin to define our own beliefs and design our own life direction. Unfortunately this natural process can be squelched or controlled. We may become fearful and accept at face value what we are told. In the exercises that follow you will have the opportunity to remember your teen years and to ask for the missing support.

But first join Nelly when she was a teenager. At this age, she sensed that a fundamental element was missing from her life. Passionately she attempted to fill the void with both spiritual meaning and sexual adventure.

A Story from Nelly

Who is this God anyway? I don't know. I seem to care. Now that I am a teenager, I am on my own a lot of the time. My parents are always working. I am in the house alone each day after school. Friends visit 'cause we are free to do whatever we want in my house, no parents to constrain us. I want to explore my sexuality. I want to know who God is and figure out if there is a God anyway.

A few of the boys from the Catholic school come to my house after school. They are different. They are Italian—they are Catholic—they are sexy. Somehow with them I feel free to taste my budding sexuality. But one day it goes too far. They pin me down on the basement floor. There are four of them—there is only one of me. I can't resist them. I am not sure if I want to resist them. I like the attention. It is much nicer than the loneliness of being home alone. But they grab at my body. If feels bad. I scream at them to stop. They finally do stop.

They come back the next day. They apologize. We shift gears, to God, our other shared passion. They are Catholics, so their idea of God seems strangely exotic. The question of whether there is a God is very gripping—just as gripping as my newly emerging sexuality. There's mystery here; it's provoking. I want to know about God. I want to know it intimately. I want to explore the edges and the limits. I explore with others; it's more captivating that way.

It was very exciting when the boys from the Catholic school visited, this stretching beyond the limits of the acceptable. But it was also scary to test out my limits, and sometimes I got hurt. Still, I usually looked forward to their knock on the door.

The Teenage Years

Look for reminders or mementos of your teenage years: photos or journal entries or any memorabilia that you have saved. It would be especially helpful to look at any with spiritual or religious significance, for instance, pictures from your bas mitzvah or confirmation. Allow the memorabilia to spark off memories. Ask yourself these questions: What was my relationship with God when I was a teenager? Did I feel supported in my spirituality? Did I feel acknowledged in my religious community?

Finding an Authentic Relationship with God

As children many of us had a connection with the divine, a connection that may have been before and beyond ideas or concepts about God. It may have felt like a direct knowing and relating to the divine. Most of us lost track of this connection, and with it we lost some of our innate spirituality. Now we can see our original childhood vision of divinity through the lens of our adult vision.

"All the concepts they told me about God never fit. They talk of original sin, but I believe in original spirituality. I have always been connected to my original spirituality. As a child I think I knew that God was inside of people."

"I remember when I was very young I heard a voice speak to me as I was walking down my driveway. It said, 'I am with you always until the end of the world.'"

The Original Vision

The following guided visualization is designed to help you connect with your original vision of a divine presence. Find a quiet place where you feel safe and will be undisturbed, maybe your spiritual space. Allow about twenty minutes for this exercise. Have your spiritual journal open in front of you along with a pen so you can write or draw at the end of this visualization. Begin with a grounding exercise to help you become focused and quiet. Take out a photograph of yourself as an infant or toddler. Become quiet and centered and gaze into the photograph and once again become the young child in the photograph.

Close your eyes and allow the child in the photograph to guide you on a journey, a journey back to your childhood. As you travel back in time, recall a memory of the first time you sensed a divine connection. Notice where you are—are you at home, in nature, in church, in synagogue, or someplace else? Be as specific as you can be. Allow whatever memory comes to you. Don't be concerned about whether it is actually the first memory; maybe it is an important memory. If you cannot remember, then imagine. Trust your images, even if you do not yet understand them. Allow the scene to unfold in your inner awareness using the gift of inner vision. Notice the colors and sounds that surround you. What do you know about God? Allow your early sense of divinity, your original vision, to come into your awareness.

As a young child, ask yourself, Who is God? How do I relate to a divine presence? Where do I find this presence? Is it near to me or distant? Is it within me or outside me? If you cannot remember, allow yourself to imagine what might have been your original vision of God. How does it feel to be in the presence of this God? Notice how your body feels. How do you communicate? Notice if God tells you anything. Is there anything you need to tell this God? Allow yourself to receive a message to remember as you grow older and learn of others' visions of God. Listen carefully.

When you feel complete, take leave of this time in your childhood. Allow yourself to travel back to the present moment, to yourself as an adult. Know that the information you received will remain available to you. Thank yourself and the spiritual presence for anything you have learned. Feel your breath move in and then out of your body. Feel the earth supporting you. Allow your eyes to gently open and look around. Know where you are now. Lift your pen and write or draw in your journal in response to these questions:

What did you know about God when you were young? How did you make contact with God? What did your God tell you? What was your response? Is there anything to remember or to do to integrate this awareness into your spiritual beliefs and practices of today?

As we progress on our journey of spiritual renewal and let go of old hurtful and inappropriate Gods, it becomes important to know with whom or what we are in communion. We grapple with fundamental questions: How do we experience the central or core Spiritual Essence? How do we name that Essence? Where do we find that Essence? What do we do to deepen our relationship with that Essence? The answers to these questions are not necessarily what we were told in childhood; instead, we search for our own answers and an authentic relationship.

Women find the Spiritual Essence in many forms and with many names; women's experience of God is as varied as their life experience. We name God in many ways, often grappling with the inadequacy of words to name the unnameable. Terms for spiritual presence include a vast array of descriptive terms: God, Goddess, Nature Spirit, Creator, Life Force, Divine Being, Divine Pattern, Feminine Divine, and Universal Truth.

Names for God

Take out your spiritual journal. Make a list of the names you have used to refer to your God at different times in your life. Leave the list for a day or so. Then come back to it, and get a sense of which of the terms fit for you now.

Although the Spiritual Essence, or God, is found in many forms and named in many ways, a basic question remains: How do we achieve a relationship? Personal connection can be established in many ways. Our life patterns and personal needs establish the nature and rhythm of the relationship. For women, a vital relationship with God is often one of closeness and intimacy.

Cheryl grew up in the Church of God in Christ. Her entire childhood centered around the church, and many of her waking hours were spent in church activities. At the age of sixteen she left the church and made a decision that she was never going back. Listen to how Cheryl names her God now and how she lives in ongoing communion with her God.

"My God is a large, positive, strong black woman with real strong, gentle hands. Her name is Maat, and she is an African Goddess, the Goddess of all Gods. My image of God is real clear to me. This past year my God became real personal to me. My Mom was not real affectionate, but one of the things she used to do when she was trying to be loving and warm, she would pat me on my knees. Today when I am going through a hard time trying to make a decision and when I finally decide my decision, I can feel that pat on my knee. It is like God allows her to pat my knee and tell me that it is all right; I have done good. I think that is why I picture my God with those loving hands. My God wears a long, flowing red robe, and when I am around red I feel calmed down. I always try to wear something red to stay in touch with her.

"I get up at 5:00 every morning and meditate for half an hour, then God and I go walking together. When I am walking on the canal at 5:30 in the morning, I couldn't get any closer to God than if I were in heaven. When I get in my car,

I offer God a seat, and when I come home I leave the door open for a second for God to come in. Whatever I do, I make room for God. When I water my plants and give them their vitamins, I feel like I am giving back to God what she gives to me. When I am working on refinishing my desk, I take one piece of sandpaper for me and give another one to God. We work on my desk together."

Cheryl's relationship with her God is very close. In her childhood, Cheryl spent a tremendous amount of time in church. Now as an adult, Cheryl devotes a great deal of time and focus to her relationship with her God. Not all women will choose this rhythm and intensity. As we heal we find our own tempo and our own authentic way of relating.

As we adapt our sense of God, we may need to change the ways in which we relate to God. Some of us discover new practices that bring us into closer connection with our newfound sense of God. Many women find a powerful connection to their God when they integrate the spiritual practices of their past into their current spirituality. Familiarity seems to be deeply consoling and connecting. They tap into their spiritual foundation. Often this return involves a reexamination of past religious practices to ensure that they come from a place of inner integrity. For some women prayer, meditation, and quiet contemplation guide them to the spiritual essence. For others, more active processes enliven them into sacred communion.

Angela, a Presbyterian, communicates with her God in a variety of ways, but the general mood is quiet and contemplative, and prayer has a central role.

"My spiritual life is choppy, it is a smorgasbord. I have never been a person who had spiritual habits or routines. My practice is more contemplative, pausing and observing what I am doing. Prayer is important; it is an ongoing conversation with God that is sometimes more focused than at other times. Prayer is when we have a level of awareness that we are offering beyond ourselves. There are different kinds of prayers. There are petition prayers, in which you ask for something; this is done in a variety of ways. We have thanksgiving prayers, acknowledging when we feel good. There is intercession prayer and healing prayer that we can offer for ourselves or for others. It allows you to make it through circumstances that otherwise you would be unable to survive. Contemporary black women writers talk about survival that is grounded in a prayer and in a spirituality that says we are created to be creative beings despite what comes our way. Prayer is a powerful thing. It is not abstract. Prayer is an extremely powerful gift that almost all religions have. It is the miracle piece. It will make something that seemed impossible turn upside down. It is the antithesis of helplessness. My

spirituality goes with me wherever I go, regardless of what I do. It is a way in which I relate."

Bridget looked for her connection with the Spiritual Essence in the quiet, contemplative life but did not find it there. Instead, she found it in the movements of daily life.

"I need my spirituality to be vital, alive, and passionate. This way I describe is similar to that of the indigenous peoples around the earth. I am drawn to Voodoo and African traditions. I am drawn to the dance, movement, drumming, singing. In indigenous cultures spirituality is an everyday experience. It is how you cook your food, how you eat, how you move; everything has a meaning and vitality. I feel less drawn to the quieter, slower way of Eastern religions. The life force is passionate and vital; it is the creative force; it gives birth to form."

Reaching Your God

Allow yourself to become centered inside and grounded. Remember back to your past, and recall a spiritual practice, ritual, or observance that emphasized relating to God. Don't consciously direct your remembering; allow whatever comes to mind to do so. Imagine partaking in this practice or ritual now. See if it still feels as spiritually connecting. Using contemplation, think about a new spiritual practice that might put you in closer relationship with your God. Think about how you might go about doing it.

God: He or She?

In finding our own relationship with a divine presence, we often deal with issues of gender and personification. Is an image of God in human form helpful? Does our God come as a feminine and/or masculine energy or image?

Some women who no longer feel connected to a male god feel fear when they consider other images of God. As Bridget admits,

"Once in a while I feel a very childlike and primitive sense of guilt and fear because I no longer primarily relate with Christ or a male God."

For Women Who Are Feeling Fear

If you are feeling fearful about changing your images or understandings about God, try one or several of these suggestions. These alternatives will help you to deal with your fear from several different angles.

1. Remind yourself that you are just considering ideas and you don't have to change anything. Also remember that you can move as slowly as you wish through this material.

2. Throw on the compost heap any ideas that are not helpful, any fear that is an obstacle for you right now.

3. Remind yourself of people who dared to move away from convention and follow their own beliefs. In fact there are probably models of these people right in your own religion: for example, Jesus Christ, Martin Luther, or Hillel. Are there models in your family?

4. Don't judge your fear. Simply acknowledge it, and know that it will pass.

As we consider the Feminine Sacred, we may confront old disappointments we felt toward our mothers. We may have projected our need for the unconditional love of a Divine Mother on our earthly mother, expecting her to be a Goddess and feeling disappointed or even angry when she proved to be human and fallible. Caught in a world where she is the sole representative of female perfection and nurturing, no mother is able to meet all her children's needs. When you understand the magnitude of her task, the vacuum she has been asked to fill, it may be easier to forgive the shortcomings of your mother.

If your relationship with your mother was very painful, you may have difficulty trusting the Feminine Divine; as you heal that relationship and let go of unrealistic expectations, you may discover more opportunity for a relationship with a Feminine Sacred. At the same time, an awareness of the Feminine Sacred can guide you toward healing your relationship with your mother.

Transforming Disappointment

Work with this exercise to let go of old disappointments. Begin with Grounding Meditation 1, In the Arms of Mother Earth, on page 11. Allow yourself to recall one way you would have liked your relationship with your mother to have been different, one way in which you felt disappointed. Perhaps you would have liked your mother to have been more emotionally available to you; if so, probably your mother did not meet your needs because she was unable to. Spend a little time considering the possibility that your mother was incapable of meeting your needs. Now imagine this need is being met by a spiritual force. Be open to that force in whatever way is best for you right now. Allow yourself to be nurtured by it.

For Angela, who is currently a Presbyterian minister, the question of the gender of God is overshadowed by what she feels are more pressing issues. Angela believes the issues of gender to be more relevant to white women than to African-American women.

"I think God is beyond he or she. I think this issue has been a stumbling block in white feminist theology. From a Christian perspective, if one is just and compassionate, it does not matter what the gender. I think there is danger when you have God look like you. I think there might be other ways to meet the need to birth this thing that looks like you; for example, art might be a better way.

"Historically in black culture God went beyond man or Father. Black theologians speak of womanist thought, which is more community based and is not apologetic or seen against a male backdrop. There is an element of mystery about it."

For others, like Nancy, opening to the Feminine Divine has been healing and has opened up new worlds of creativity and spiritual connection.

"I am more in touch with the Mother, which is the spiritual part of me. I have rejected the Father, though I know that is part of it all. I feel strongly that in these times we need to be getting more in touch with the Mother 'cause the Father has been getting an inordinate amount of energy. I personify the Mother. I think of her as very big, taking up a lot of space. I make little Goddess altars, and as I sculpt them I feel the spirit in me that makes these sculptures."

Carter Heyward, an Episcopal priest, is changing her terminology and images and perhaps her basic theology as well.

"I use the religious terminology of God and Goddess interchangeably, though I know that they really are not interchangeable. I am somewhere between the belief that God is neither male nor female and a tendency to see God in female images. I am beginning to explore more fully the Goddess stories and myths. I am

in a transition. If I have any kind of vocation left in Christianity, it is to some-
how hold together what is most redemptive about that Jesus story with Goddess
reality. Maybe they are the same story."

It can be helpful to try out different terminology for God. In fact, at
some churches and synagogues God is being referred to without male-biased
language.

Experimenting with Reference to Gender

For one day refer your spiritual thoughts and prayers to God using the pronoun *he*. For the next day address your spiritual thoughts and prayers to God
or Goddess using the pronoun *she*. For the next day address your spiritual
thoughts to a spiritual presence without reference to gender. On each day observe your responses and feelings. You might want to write down reactions at
the end of the day.

Goddess

Childhood religion for most of us did not include the Feminine Divine. We
may have been told of saints and heroines, but most likely there was no all-
knowing, all-powerful Goddess ruling our universe.

There is power in knowing that the female body was once worshiped and
the female principle held sacred. To simply know of the Goddess's existence
can bolster our sense of self-worth and enliven our spiritual connection. We
might sense that we hold within ourselves Goddess-like qualities that can be
nurtured into divine expression.

Qualities of Goddess

Listed below are some words that have been used to describe qualities of the
Goddess. Circle the words that seem closest to the qualities that you might
look for in your Goddess. Circle as many as feel right, then put a star next to
the quality that is most important to you. Feel free to add more words to the
list.

COMFORTER   TRANSFORMER   HEALER   CREATOR   TEACHER

WARRIOR   LOVER   PROTECTOR   FRIEND   VISIONARY   MOTHER

PROPHET   CELEBRANT   DESTROYER

For Bridget, discovering a female God was essential. She realizes that her religious background provided her with a foundation of female spiritual empowerment.

"As a child growing up in South America, I experienced the Virgin Mary as having more or equal power to Christ. First there was God the Father up there in the sky. I could never figure out how to relate to him or who or what he was. However, Christ was very real in my life, and the Virgin Mary was his mother. As a little girl I remember being taught very early on 'Maria, madre de Dios; Mary, mother of God.' To me as a child, a mother was more powerful than the son, no matter what age that son was and no matter what his accomplishments. To me, the Virgin Mary was more powerful than Christ. In retrospect I think this made it very easy to make the transition to seeing women with spiritual power and to seeing the Goddess as an entity on a par with a male God. I had already experienced a female figure as a powerful God-like figure who was present in my everyday life.

"It is not only Mary, there were many other virgins as well. Off the top of my head, I can think of three different virgins within a radius of a few miles. Within Ecuador it seems as though there must be about thirty or forty different virgins. All these virgins are the mothers of Christ. I do not know how the Catholic church explains this mystery. To me, the way I have come to understand this is that these are different manifestations of the female principle, in different guises, with different 'jobs.'

"I remember clearly when, as an adult, I reawakened to the Goddess. One day I heard a woman suggest that Christ was a woman. Soon after that I had a dream that I was kneeling at Christ's feet praying, and I looked up and there was a naked woman. That was a spiritual turning point for me. After that I began to try to see God as a female.

"Today I believe that if you cannot see God as female, you can never be whole. In religious teaching they say we are created in the image of God. God serves the purpose of mirroring the state of perfection back to us, our wholeness and our identity. If I look in the spiritual mirror and I always see a reflection of something other that myself, how can I get a sense of myself? If I am always looking to a male figure, how can I be mirrored back? How can I see myself as whole and perfect? I don't think we can be totally empowered, totally ourselves, until we see a female God."

If we look back to past spiritual moments, the Feminine Divine may appear to us. Although she may have been masked and disempowered at the time, she may have been in our hearts and lives. Carter realizes that her imaginary childhood playmate was a trustworthy spiritual guide.

> *"I think my imaginary playmate was my first lively Goddess, sacred presence. She was the one who told me I could be whatever I wanted, and that I should not listen to the strange things they were telling me in church or school about being a girl. She was a very passionate and spirited friend. During the past five years I have realized how to connect to Goddess realities and how that imaginary playmate of mine was an image of the Goddess in little-girl form. She came in the form I could best recognize her."*

Camille discovered the Feminine Divine in the spirit of her favorite horse.

"When I was a young girl I was in love with horses. I had a particular mare I loved to ride. When I was on her back, I felt that we could fly, that she could carry me anywhere. I would daydream often about wonderful adventures we would have together. Now I know that she was my path to creativity and my link to the unknown. She served as guide and protectress. Today I experience her as an emanation of the Goddess."

Do you remember meeting the Goddess? Perhaps if you focus on your past you will discover the Feminine Divine in hidden or unexpected forms.

Revisiting the Feminine Divine

After becoming grounded and centered, allow the following suggestions to permeate your consciousness. After contemplating each question, write any associations that come to mind.

1. Were there any creatures in your life that felt especially protective of you, with whom you had a close relationship? Who were they? What was the relationship like?

2. Were there people in your life as a child, real or imagined, who loved you unconditionally? Who were they, and how did they support you?

End this exercise by expressing gratitude to any loving beings who came to mind.

For some women opening to the Goddess is an entry into new, life-affirming experiences. Because the Goddess is not present and available to many of us, we may need to search for her. The pathways are as diverse as the women who are developing practices and inventing rituals that will lead them to the Goddess. Listen while women describe who the Goddess is to them.

> *"The Goddess's power is about cycles and co-creation—equality and love for all beings equally rather than power over. She holds us all in her lap. She is the power to 'be,' not the power to 'be over others.' To honor the Goddess at this time in history will rebalance and reunite the masculine and feminine principles within us all. The sacred feminine principle is the affirmation of interconnectedness and sanctity of all life. To honor the Goddess would create an important healing for all beings on earth. There would be less war and aggression."*

> *"My idea of the Goddess is that it is the potential within me. We are all our own Goddesses—it is not an enlightened being up in the sky. It's an energy of pure goodness."*

A Story from Carol

There is a cave carved in the cliff by the sea that I visited briefly on my first trip to Puerto Rico. I never forgot the beauty and the aura of this place. When I returned to the island, I made a pilgrimage to the cave to be there for whatever messages might be enclosed within her walls.

Climbing down into the cave opening, I notice a man sitting on a ledge high above me. He does not look at me, but I know that he has seen me. I light incense sticks, placing them at the entrance to the cave as an offering for protection against negative energy. Then, kneeling at the entrance, I silently ask permission to enter. From within my heart, I hear a soft, yet definite, yes.

As I enter, I realize that this is not one large cave but many caves within caves. There are drawings on some of the walls, marking it as an area sacred to the Taino Indians, the original inhabitants of Puerto Rico. The smaller caves surround a circular area in the floor where turquoise water rises and falls with the motion of the sea. There is a rhythm to the waters. They enter her, seeming to pause briefly as they fill her. Then the waters return to the ocean.

I place myself in this pool and close my eyes and listen for a hint of magic or a message about what to do next. It feels like a healing pool, a place for receiving cleansing. Wearing a light cotton shirt and pants, I submerge myself in the waters as they rise to greet me. I lower myself into her depths three times, each time carefully returning to the side of the pool as the waters swiftly withdraw to the ocean. Emerging from the waters, I feel refreshed but also vulnerable, having exposed myself to a healing but potentially dangerous experience.

I lie down in one of the small cavelike spaces. They seem to be made exactly for the form of my body. Lying face down, I feel as though I am lying on my Mother's belly, against her skin. The sand is smooth as silk. As I gently rub the length of my body along her surface, I call to her. I feel myself weeping. I call to my mother, and the being beyond all mothers. She answers by holding me and caressing me and catching my tears as they disappear into her skin. I hear her tell me, "Everything is all right," and I know that she will hold me for as long as I need.

This was my first experience of the Feminine Divine. This experience allowed me to know the Goddess in a very personal and intimate way. She revealed herself to me from within, through my own perceptions and senses, through my own body. After this I could say that I knew her. This was the beginning of my relationship with the Feminine Divine.

A simple, yet powerful way to begin to explore your relationship to the Feminine Divine is to investigate images of the Goddess that are available to us today. Recent archaeological digs have uncovered ancient images of the Feminine Divine. Modern artists are creating new images.

Investigating the Goddess

Images of the Goddess. Search for images of the Goddess that attract you. You might look in bookstores, libraries, crafts stores, or museums. Get a reproduction of a favorite image, and sit with her often. Put her in your spiritual space or on your altar. Allow yourself to gaze at her from time to time, opening yourself to subliminal messages and new understanding. Allow yourself to remember her and what she represents, inside and outside yourself. Write down or draw your experiences in your spiritual journal.

Being with the Goddess. Begin with Grounding 1, In the Arms of Mother Earth. Using guided imagery, allow the Goddess to appear before you. Let her show herself to you in all her beauty and majesty. Take a moment to take her into your consciousness.

Now contemplate these questions: Why you have chosen her? What qualities does she possess that are yours as well? What part of yourself have you chosen to honor as you honor this aspect of the Goddess? Allow for the answers to come. When you feel finished, thank her for being there for you and for us all. Spend a moment in gratitude and self-healing.

Living with God and Goddess

Regardless of the physical characteristics or qualities of your God or Goddess, regardless of where you find your God or Goddess, regardless of how you commune with your God or Goddess, what matters most is that you find an authentic way to live with this force in your life. As you continue to read, more ways of representing and connecting with the divine will be revealed as different women share their spiritual journeys.

You may find that your sense of the divine evolves as you heal and move forward on your spiritual journey, or you might find that what you already experience remains firm and steady. Take your own sense of spiritual presence with you as you work through the material in the next two chapters on other obstacles. Take your God or Goddess with you to guide you to deeper spiritual connections.

Integration

Take a little while to remember the work you have done in this chapter. Think about the ideas that you read about. Remember the exercises you worked with.

1. Recall any important events that came to light while working with this material. Add them to your time line. (See page 48.)

2. Think about the ideas presented, and throw any that do not fit on your compost heap. (See page 38.)

3. Check to see if there is anything else you wish to note in your spiritual journal. You might want to reread some of what you have written.

4. Think about whether there is more work to be done with any of the material. Think about how you might want to do this. For example, you might want to work on the exercises some more later or discuss the issues with a support person, in therapy, or with a support group.

5. Appreciate yourself for the work you have done. Give gratitude for healing and spiritual renewal.

Reviewing Your Religious Past

4

Sometimes we feel spiritually nourished within our religion; a religion with known and familiar rituals, holidays, prayers, and beliefs can be deeply consoling and connecting. However, probably some parts of our religious heritage have felt alienating and have become obstacles on our spiritual journey. As you look at your religion with new eyes, you can clear out the obstacles and find new avenues of connection.

Historically most religions have been biased toward males, both in terms of participation and of validation. As girls and women, we find that our spiritual perspectives are often overlooked and our spiritual contributions minimized. When our spiritual moments go unacknowledged, our religion never deeply touches our heart and spirit.

Growing up in a family without religious affiliation or without a belief in God can provide a fertile environment for our own spiritual exploration or make us feel our spiritual expression is not valid.

An invalidating religious background can make discovering our authentic spiritual path difficult. We may go around in circles, never finding a spiritual center or a focus. The journey can feel lonely because we lack fellow travelers to guide us along the way.

Begin by thinking about ways that you felt invalidated within or in relationship to religion. None of these experiences will necessarily become obstacles. You are the only one who can judge whether or not they are blocking your spiritual journey.

81

My Experience of Religious Invalidation

Check off any of the following experiences that apply to you.

———— I grew up in a family without religious affiliation.

———— I grew up in a family where there was no belief in God.

———— I grew up in a family where people had different religious affilia-tions or significantly different religious beliefs.

———— Because I was a girl/woman I felt invalidated within my religion.

———— As a girl/woman, my role was limited in my religion.

———— As a child I fantasized about being a religious leader but knew I could not be.

———— I felt fearful within my religion.

The experiences that you checked off can guide you toward the focus of your work in this chapter.

Use your imagination to recall moments of alienation or difficulty within your religion.

Returning to Childhood Religion

Take a few minutes to become grounded and comfortable. Then, using guided imagery, close your eyes and take a journey back to a church, synagogue, or religious building from your childhood. Remember the building in as much detail as you can. Remember the colors, the sights, the smells, the sensations. In your imagination, walk into the building, and as you walk through the door notice if you can recall a memory of a time when you were in this building and felt disconnected or alienated. Notice how that alienation or disconnection feels, how it feels in your body and in your heart. Understand the basic issue involved. Get as much information as you can about this issue. When you feel complete, bring yourself back to present time. Allow your eyes to open. You might want to jot down notes about this experience in your spiritual journal.

Before considering hurtful religious experiences more deeply, it can be re-assuring to remember moments of connection as well. Affirming these connections at the start will provide a safer and more comfortable foundation for the healing work.

The women we interviewed had delight in their voices as they described moments of connection related to their religion. These descriptions were rich with delicious tastes, beautiful sounds, and ancient rituals. The context was often the loving and nurturing embrace of family and community.

"There were always seders at my house, and days' worth of work went into the preparation. I have potent memories of my mother chopping the gefilte fish, with the cleaver and the bowl, doing everything by hand. These are my earliest memories of making ritual, of doing something that is meaningful, of following an ancient ritual."

"I lived in a world of magic during Christmas time. I totally believed in the whole fantasy of Santa Claus. I knew that Santa and Mrs. Santa Claus, and the elves had been busy making all these toys. On Christmas Eve, he somehow made it down through my chimney, and in the morning there were presents everywhere."

Religious holidays are the most significant times of the religious year, and our memories of them can give us a great deal of information about our religious experience. Our responses to the holidays are often a microcosm of our feelings about our religion in general.

Remembering the Holiday Connection

Think back to your childhood, and choose a religious holiday that you particularly enjoyed. There are many different ways we connect with the holidays. Did you connect through

The meaning or story of the holiday?
The kinship of family and community at holiday time?
The holiday foods?
The holiday rituals?
The music of the holiday?
The generosity expressed during the holidays?

Think about other avenues of connection.

Now allow yourself to go even more deeply into these feelings of connection by remembering the experience more fully. Enjoy! Is there anything you want to remember to include in your celebration this next holiday season?

During holidays we often have high expectations, and our longings for connection sometimes lead to disappointment. Investigating these disappointments can guide us toward some of the obstacles that may be blocking our spiritual journey.

Investigating Alienation During the Holidays

Listed below are some ways you might have felt alienated during religious holidays. Check the ones that are true for you.

_____ I never understood the meaning of the holiday.

_____ The holiday did not speak to my experiences as a girl.

_____ I came from a family that did not celebrate holidays (or the commonly celebrated holidays), and I felt alienated from everyone else.

_____ I wanted to become more involved in the rituals but could not because I was a girl.

_____ Difficulties in my family made it hard to celebrate.

_____ The holidays were all show. They lacked real spiritual significance.

Rewrite the statements, if necessary, to make them reflect your truth more accurately. If there are other ways you felt alienated, add them to the list.

Lack of Religious or Spiritual Direction in Childhood

Some women grow up in families without a religious affiliation, a spiritual context, or a belief in God. These environments become invalidating when spiritual inclinations and aspirations are ignored, denied, or ridiculed. Appropriate support and guidance need not come from participation in mainstream religions; there are many other sources of support. What is essential is that we do find a context that supports and validates our spiritual life.

Childhood spiritual needs may be met in many ways. For example, a family without a belief in God may have a religious identification or a guiding spiritual belief system. Parents may have their own individual spiritual belief systems; they may pass on ethical and moral principles that guide us through the challenges in our lives. A family may identify with the culture and community of a religion but not the theology. A child may find support for her spirituality in the larger community.

If you grew up in a family outside the religious mainstream, you may find you feel alienated from others with more traditional religious backgrounds. You may, at times, feel different, like an outsider. You may lack a sense of community, or others who join you on your spiritual journey. You may also discover fertile soil for your own unique spiritual perspectives to germinate, not conditioned by the beliefs and needs of others. Part of the healing process involves validating the ways you were spiritually nourished. You may find that you have unique spiritual resources available to you.

Validating Nonconventional Spiritual Lessons

Looking at your family tree, consider ways that your spiritual needs were met in nonconventional ways. Consider each member of your family, remembering spiritual perspectives and lessons that they transmitted to you. Think about aspects you might have previously discounted. Affirm any spiritual resources that you might have previously overlooked.

Zoe was brought up in a home that she described as religiously nondescript and nonaligned. During difficult times in her family she missed a God she could turn to for solace and support. Now Zoe struggles with frustration as she searches for her own spiritual path. She lacks direction and confidence.

"For the most part I felt I missed out on a religious background. When I was a child and went to church or synagogue with my friends, I was struck by the intensity of all these people in one room praying. I knew they were praying to God, but I didn't have a sense of God. I felt the power but didn't understand it. I felt left out, as though I missed the whole experience of childhood religion. There were times I wanted to pray. I wanted to pray that my mother and father would stop fighting, but I felt embarrassed to pray in my family. How would I explain this behavior to my family?

"I remember one Christmas Eve when I was a teenager and walked into a Catholic mass. At first I felt like an outsider, but once I sat down I felt I became part of the group. I presumed that the other people were all having experiences about God, but actually I had no clue as to what they were really experiencing.

"I never got a concrete sense of the purpose of spirituality. It has been hard to find my own spirituality, and it has never been a very solid or practiced discovery. For example, I was nervous about this interview, thinking what the hell was I going to talk about; I have no religious background to talk about. I am sometimes envious of people who do have a clearly defined spiritual practice and frustrated that I don't have one. I question why it is so difficult for me. Is it because I don't make it a priority? Maybe a better way to think about it is that I have to do it on my own. I would like to have a regular spiritual practice but not become rigid about it. I want to hold on to the flexibility from my childhood."

Leila was brought up in a family that was culturally and ethnically Jewish, though a belief in God was discouraged. As a child, her desire for spiritual exploration was stifled. As an adult Leila has returned to her Jewish roots, living an active religious and cultural life.

"I remember having a conversation with my father and telling him I thought I might believe in God. He shook his head and said, 'You don't believe in God.' I felt shame about believing in God and got the message that God was for ignorant people. I know as a child I was blocked from spiritual exploration. In my family you did not talk about being in the presence of something undefinable. Now I realize that this was a loss. Though I wonder if the kids who were more religiously involved came away with a real sense of being in the presence of divinity and of being divine."

Toby always felt a spiritual connection, but she never associated it with her religion. The freedom to search has always shaped her spiritual journey.

"My parents never believed in God, and as a child, I always respected that they didn't say they believed in something that they could not explain to me. I felt different, and there were ways I liked being different and ways it felt really difficult. When I became a teenager, I began to feel crazy and wonder where I belonged and longed for an otherworldly connection. In my desperate search for connection, I tried out lots of different approaches like drugs, pottery, yoga, and meditation. Now I find I make choices that are my own. I trust myself. I do not have to stay within the mainstream. I do not feel locked into any specific system of beliefs. I take from a lot of different spiritual orientations."

Growing up without a belief in God is a different experience for each of us. If you grew up without a belief in God, take some time to recall and understand your experience.

For Women Who Grew Up in a Home Without a Belief in God

Get quiet and centered and remember when you were first aware that your parents did not believe in God. If you cannot actually remember, then allow yourself to imagine how it might have been. How did you find out that your parents did not believe in God? Did they tell you? Did someone else tell you? What did you understand about all of this? How did this feel to you? Now think about your life now. How does growing up in home without a belief in God affect you now? Are there any old beliefs and feelings that are outdated, that you are ready to throw away? Are there new beliefs and feelings that you wish to affirm?

Another kind of dilemma may develop when one parent believes in God and the other does not or if any two influential people in our lives have differing spiritual beliefs. We may feel caught between these people, between these beliefs. When we hear mixed messages, we are challenged to find our own direction, but we also risk becoming lost in the confusion.

Adeline, Nelly's mother, came from a Jewish home in which her own mother was religious, but her father was antireligious. Rather than feeling confused, Adeline took direction from both parents. As you read about Adeline's experience, perhaps you will hear some of the seed ideas of this book, passed down mother to daughter, from Adeline to Nelly—most notably, the value in finding one's own spirituality through life experience.

"My two parents had very different religious beliefs. My mother was saying yes to religion and my father was saying no, so I was forced to figure it out for myself and to find my own beliefs. My mother was always quoting the Talmud, the ethical teachings of Judaism. These are the same ethical teachings that are taught in every religion, like the value in honesty, charity, and doing without. I took these ethics from my mother's teaching; I really believe in them and try to live by them.

"When a Jewish holiday came, my mother would tell us the story about the holiday. Then my father would say that the story was utterly ridiculous, and it could not have happened. He would tell us that it was all a fairy tale. My father's religious views made more sense to me than my mother's.

"I rebel against the way organized religion boxes you in. Like my father, I never believed in a personal God. Even though I do not explain the world and what happens in terms of a deity, I do have a spiritual belief system that helps me understand the world and my place in it, both now and after I die. I have definite spiritual beliefs developed through my eighty years of living."

If you got different spiritual messages from influential people in your life, it can be helpful to sort out these messages and embrace those that reflect your own truth and experience.

For Women Who Got Differing Spiritual or Religious Messages

Begin this exercise by affirming your ability to find your own truth. Consider something in your life now about which you feel quite sure of your beliefs, even though others have differing beliefs.

Now think about the people in your life who have had strong but differing influences on your spiritually. Clarify either in your thoughts or in writing what each person believes and how these beliefs overlap and conflict. Notice which beliefs seem untrue or perhaps even harmful. Throw these beliefs out—you might imagine placing them on your compost heap. Then notice which beliefs seem like truth. Affirm these truths. Notice which of your own truths are a synthesis of these differing beliefs. See if there are ways in which the exposure to differing beliefs has allowed you to come to deeper understandings.

The line between neglect and open-mindedness can become blurry. If you came from a family that did not conform religiously, take a look at your own background and discover for yourself which aspects felt invalidating and which were strengthening. It is possible, in fact, likely, that the same aspects may have been both beneficial and problematic.

For Women Who Grew Up Outside Mainstream Religion

Using free-form writing, respond to the following statements. Write without interruption, writing whatever comes to mind. Spend five minutes responding to each of the three statements.

I felt different because
Being different was difficult because
Being different was a blessing because

After you have finished writing your responses to all three statements, see if you can summarize what you have written in a few sentences.

Invalidation of Girls and Women Within Religion

Most religions are male-dominated and male-biased, and the effects of this bias ripple through most of religious life. Not only is God personified as male, but the more acknowledged and valued persons in the scriptures are also male. Most religious leaders are male, and males usually are the primary participants in religious ritual.

The male bias within religion can limit the options available to girls and women, and we may accept a second-class position in order to belong. We are silenced, our voices drowned out. What is holy is not of woman, so we assume ourselves to be less than holy. We lose track of our innate spiritual connection. We can feel like spectators watching others on their spiritual journey.

In a world men dominate, women and girls can believe that men have a corner on truth. Healing comes about when our truths are heard and validated, so it is important to create safe places where we can speak our spiritual truths and be heard and appreciated.

Speaking Your Truth

Think about something that is spiritually true for you, a truth that you have held for a long time or perhaps something that you learned in an earlier exercise. Now think about a place where you can share this truth. It may be with a friend or family member or perhaps with a group of friends. It may be at a spiritual gathering. What is most important is that you choose a situation in which you will be heard. You might want to set aside some special time to speak your truth, or you might prefer to set your intention and then allow the experience to happen spontaneously—perhaps let it flow out in conversation. Do it your own way! Allow yourself to be heard and appreciated.

Unfortunately the respect for women's truth has not been the norm within religion. In fact women told us over and over again of their experiences of discrimination within religion.

"The discrimination against women in the Christian church is universal. I always resented it."

"Without knowing it in words, I knew that men were above women, so it made sense to me that God would be a male. Everybody who was anybody was a male—the president, the rabbi. That's just the way the world was."

It is helpful to have a clear understanding of what women's role has been within your religion and to consider whether you have experienced male bias. A better sense of your own situation can guide you toward healing and renewal.

Women's Role Within My Religion

There are many aspects of women's role to think about, so take your time in considering answers to the questions that follow. If your religious affiliation has changed, apply these questions to each of the religions you have been part of over the course of your lifetime.

Questions:

Is women's participation in religious ritual limited? Are there any restrictions on women's ability to pray? What is your understanding of the value of women within scripture? Does the religion prescribe women's role in the family? If so, does the prescribed role seem limiting? Are there women in religious leadership? Are there limitations to their leadership roles? Has the role of women been changing within your religion? How comfortable do you feel with the role that women now have?

After thinking about these questions for a while, you might sense a healing response. You need not plan anything, just see if a new way of feeling comes into your heart or if a new way of thinking comes into your mind.

The most conservative sects of a religion are often most blatantly discriminatory to women. Nelly recalls her first realization that girls and women are treated differently in Judaism.

"I remember as a child going to services in an Orthodox temple. The girls and women sat on the upper level of the temple, and we looked down at the service that the men and boys participated in. I was shocked! It reminded me of when I first went to the South in the 1950s, and they had separate bathrooms for blacks and whites."

The discrimination is sometimes more subtle, however. Rituals that girls are permitted to partake in may be considered less important than those for boys. Sylvia recalls how that discrimination manifested in a more progressive congregation.

> *"When they turn thirteen years old, Jewish boys partake in a bar mitzvah. This is a very important ceremony marking 'becoming a man.' About the time I turned thirteen they started having bas mitzvahs for girls in our temple. It seemed like an afterthought, so it wasn't something I wanted to do."*

Sylvia also talks about her disappointment that women are excluded from the minyan, the fundamental prayer group.

Claudia, a Mormon, followed the prescribed female role within her religious community. She now understands just how limiting that role was and has discovered a more satisfying role within her church.

> *"I could not progress in the church. The message of the church was to get married and have kids. I had four kids in six years. The women basically do all the work in the church; they are called on to do 'service.' I could only bake so many pies for church functions before my mind started going down the drain. My husband was very dominating, and I think I had a very crazy idea of who I should be. My self-esteem got very messed up. I ended up in therapy for twelve years. While I was working through these issues, I became very angry at the church. More recently, though, I have found a way to work within the structure of the Mormon church and maintain my personal power and get a sense of satisfaction and connection. They don't reject me, and I don't reject them."*

Claudia now works with a psychotherapist who provides counseling to church members and is paid out of the church tithe.

An awareness of ways that we felt excluded within our religion can guide us toward actions of inclusion.

Healing Exclusion from Ritual

Remember an important ritual in your religion, from either your past or your present life. Then contemplate the following questions: What is your involvement in the ritual? Is this the extent to which you would like to be involved? Are you or were you limited in your participation in the ritual? What is it that limits you? Do you feel comfortable with this limitation?

If you discovered ways that you felt excluded or invalidated, think about one healing action you might take. For example, if you were thinking about a ritual in your life now, you might speak to your religious leader about how to become more involved. If it was an experience from your past, you might share your feelings with a spiritual friend.

In some families, the domination of the husband blocks his wife's ability to fully participate in religious life. Adeline, an eighty-year-old Jewish woman and Nelly's mother, speaks of the limitations her mother felt to participation in the synagogue.

"My mother was very religious, but my father was antireligious. He was angry at religion and rejected it because he thought it was a source of evil. My mother resented that my father never attended services in the synagogue, because if the husband does not attend, the wife is treated as an inferior member of the congregation. My mother was deprived of the ability to practice her religion."

A generation later Jean experienced a similar problem. The influence of her domineering husband discouraged her from following through with her religious inclinations.

"My husband was a very domineering man who didn't want to go to church. I let that influence me, even though I shouldn't have. I feel bad that we did not go to church, because church gives me an inner strength, a sense of confidence. Church would have been very helpful to the children during the time after my husband suddenly died. Church would not have given us the answer, but it might have given us some strength."

Women spoke of other ways they felt untouched by religion, ways that were not specific to their gender. They described rituals that were stale and antiquated, "as old as the hills." Some women felt alienated because they did not understood what was going on during religious ritual; they were bored and uninterested. Some referred to rituals in a language they did not understand, like Latin or Hebrew. Others spoke of rituals that lacked meaning and relevance in their lives.

Marilyn Sewell felt disappointed when she was baptized. She had hoped for a deep spiritual experience but instead felt embarrassed and untouched.

"I joined the Baptist church when I was fourteen. Southern Baptists believe that you are not really saved until you accept Jesus Christ as your savior and receive baptism that is a full immersion. I was fully immersed in a white garment in front of the whole congregation. Then I was lifted up, dripping wet, with all this white clinging to me. I was hoping that this ritual would touch me, but it didn't. I felt kind of embarrassed.

"I think I joined the church because of peer pressure and believing that was what I was supposed to do. Everyone I knew went to the church—my friends, my grandparents. When at a revival they sang the song 'Jesus is tenderly calling you, calling you home,' I felt that I should go down the aisle. There was a lot of psychological pressure. I just did it 'cause I felt that it was what I needed to do to be in with the in-group."

As girls and women, we find that our spiritual journey may be different from the male journey. Some of us find spiritual awakening within the rhythms of our bodies. Male-dominated religions may separate experiences of the body from experiences of the spirit, considering bodily experiences as base and spiritually inferior, a hindrance on the spiritual journey.

"I would ride down those big hills on my bicycle and go very fast. It felt like flying. I was elated. It had an otherworldly, transcendent quality about it."

"When I was a child I went around without a shirt or shoes on 'cause then I felt connected to the earth."

As our sexuality awakens, we may turn to our religion for ethical guidance. Too often our innate pleasure is shamed and we are left in confusion. Many of the women we interviewed spoke of how their natural connection to their body was eroded by the teachings of their church. Annie, who was brought up a Catholic, was terrified as she confessed the sin of masturbation.

"Confession was quite terrifying. You had to go into this dark little room and tell the priest how many times you'd done whatever was considered sinful. I started masturbating when I was very young, and I knew that it was probably a sin. I knew I should confess it, but I didn't know how; I didn't know what to say. I finally told the priest that I tickled myself fourteen times, but the priest never got it; he never asked me what I meant. When I was ten years old a visiting priest came to my church, and he questioned me, 'What do you mean, you tickled yourself?' I told him, 'I touched myself down there.' He gave me extra penance but no guidance whatsoever. I felt very afraid of sex for a very long time."

Marilyn Sewell dealt with similar issues in the Southern Baptist church.

"The sins in the Baptist church centered around your fleshly or carnal self. It was very destructive to my own sexual development. I grew up being very afraid of myself sexually. I began having very strong sexual attractions to boys when I was fourteen or fifteen. I had these warm feelings that ran up my leg when I touched my leg to the boy who was playing trumpet next to me in the band. I thought, 'My God, what was that feeling? I don't know what to do with this.'

"After church the young people would get in cars and go out to the fire tower two or three miles outside of town. People would get out of their cars and go climb this fire tower. It really was a May Day celebration of sexuality and sensuality. It was really late in the night and nobody could see us and all the couples were kissing and smooching. They would have kissing contests to see who could kiss the longest. I was never involved in any of that. I was too goody-goody; I was too frightened to get out of the car. I was afraid I would be punished. I had this punishing God in my mind, and I believed, 'If I go climb that fire tower, I will break my neck.' So I was the one who stayed with the car. I was elected in my senior year as best Christian. I think I was elected best Christian was because I could never get a boyfriend and I was 'sex-free.'

"Now I see that one's sexuality and spirituality are not to be separated at all. Sexuality needs to be handled delicately and with great care because of its potential power. If that power is focused in the context of love and caring and wholeness of personality, it becomes one of the most wonderful and powerful ways to express spirituality."

Sometimes we become entrapped by religious messages about sexuality. There are different ways this can happen. We may internalize guidelines that have outlived their usefulness. Or we may rebel against the messages and do the opposite of what we were taught. It is important that we as adults formulate our own ethical guidelines around our sexuality and commit to following them as much as we are able. As you do this, consider whether your sexuality harms yourself or others. If it does no harm, you are probably on pretty safe ground. As you think about your guidelines, understand they will refine themselves as you learn from your life experience.

Messages About Sexuality

Do these exercises in a safe and protected place. Begin by blessing yourself and the space. Commit yourself to discovering the truth of your own experience. Then try one of the following ways to heal outdated messages about sexuality.

Spiritual guidance about sexuality. Remember one of your earlier sexual experiences, one in which you might have benefited from some guidance. Using guided imagery, imagine that, at the time, you decided to discuss the situation with a leader in your religion. How does this leader respond? What guidelines are expressed? How do you feel during this interaction? Do you leave this interaction feeling clearer about the situation?

If you do not feel completely satisfied with this interaction, try to imagine it differently. You can change it any way you choose. You can go to someone else for this guidance; you can create whomever you like. Then imagine this guide telling you whatever would be most helpful to hear, and in a way that feels healing and clarifying. End by expressing gratitude for healing and by affirming your own innate goodness.

Sexual guidelines. Make a list of the messages about sexuality you internalized from your religion. Write as fast as your can. Don't censor anything or be concerned about whether this is actually what was said. What matters is what you understood or believed. Write until you can't easily think of anything more, and then try to think of one or two more messages. Leave the list for a few minutes or perhaps even a few days.

When you return to the list, make a second list that responds to the first but reflects your sexual guidelines today. Some of the messages on the first list may still be true for you. If so, rewrite them. Other messages might need to be changed a bit; adapt them to fit the truth as you currently understand it. Still others may no longer apply; replace them with what is true for you now.

End this exercise with gratitude and forgiveness toward yourself.

As women reclaim the experiences of their bodies, they often speak of the distinctly female experiences of menstruation and childbirth.

A STORY FROM NELLY

I remember when I first menstruated. It was thirty-two years ago, yet I remember it as though it were yesterday. I had been anxiously awaiting my first period. My best friend and I intimately shared each bodily change of our young budding womanhood; the process seemed so mysterious and extraordinary.

The day my period finally arrived was Yom Kippur, the holiest day of the year for Jews. My family had traveled hundreds of miles to share the holidays with distant relatives. I began to bleed. When my period began, I was quite frightened and quite alone. I felt very ashamed and embarrassed. No one ever talked about menstruation openly, and somehow I got the impression that it was dirty and shameful. I remember standing in the bathroom, plotting where to hide the sanitary napkins so no one would suspect the truth. I kept my passage into womanhood very private and secret while publicly I attended synagogue.

All I cared about was returning home and telling my friend that my period had finally come. I, too, was a woman, whatever that was to mean. As I look back, I am very thankful for this kind of friendship. Thirty-two years later, as I approach menopause, I remind myself to acknowledge this passage. This time I refuse to feel shamed or neglected.

As you thought about the issues of women's exclusion within religion, most likely many memories were rekindled. Was there a time when you felt spiritually connected that went unacknowledged? Take the time now to affirm a spiritual moment in your past.

Affirming a Spiritual Moment

Recall a spiritual moment from your past that went unacknowledged or was not adequately acknowledged. Acknowledge it now. There are many different ways you might choose to acknowledge the connection. Choose a way that feels affirming. For example, you might write about or draw a picture of the connection. Or you might place something on your altar affirming the connection. You might tell a support person about the connection. Allow your imagination to come up with whatever feels right.

Abuse Within Religion

Our religious institutions and religious leaders can hurt us. The abuse ranges in severity from insensitivity and deception to outright exploitation. Many circumstances, including the inequities between the sexes, can create conditions ripe for abuse.

Religious leaders can be perceived as superhuman, as infallible representatives of God. Religious leaders may become intoxicated by their power and greedy for authority. Because their authority comes from God, we may see their actions as not subject to question. Because we long for people we can emulate and trust without reservation, we may forget that they are human beings just like ourselves.

As with all forms of abuse, children are most vulnerable and their wounds most deep-rooted. Children do not have the power to question religious leaders or to leave religious institutions. Even for adults, naming abuse within religion can be very threatening. We want to believe our leaders are ahead of us on the spiritual journey, that they have a higher vision. We may believe that if we question anything, we question the whole religion. We fear losing the parts of our religion that are most precious to us. If we feel connected to the religious community, it can be very difficult to break silence and, with it, break the bonds of connection. Instead we may invalidate and ignore our own truths. One of the first steps in healing abuse is identifying the abuse.

Ann correlates some of the dynamics she saw in Christian churches with what happens in abusive families.

"Think about an abusive family. A certain reality is dictated, and no one is allowed to go outside the family for perspective. The family is very cloistered, set apart. There is a similar tendency in churches. There is an authoritarian structure in which one person is the dispenser of knowledge. Truth is presented, and there is no room for dialogue. The normal, healthy questioning process is cut off; people feel a tremendous obligation to swallow the whole thing. If people make their own choices, chances are, the system will reject them for not going along with the program. There is a cover-up or a scapegoating process whenever the truth comes up."

We expect our religious leaders to model the ethics that our religion teaches. We may feel deeply disillusioned when our leaders behave unethically. Ruth, an Episcopalian woman in her seventies, remembers.

"When I was a young adult I went into an emotional and spiritual upheaval when I found out that one of our priests was going to bed with his secretary and another was an alcoholic. I resigned from the church and looked everywhere for religious answers. When I returned to the church, it was with an individual faith and an understanding that the clergy were people just like me and have their weaknesses."

As a child Cheryl belonged to the Church of God in Christ. She recalls the greed of the minister and could not reconcile it with the generosity of Jesus.

"We were very close to starvation, and I watched my mom give away all this money and food to the preacher. I hated that. The preacher already had two jobs and plenty to eat. I would read the Bible, and Jesus would feed the people. Why

were we feeding the preacher? My mother could never explain this to me. She was the kind of person who did what she was supposed to do."

Sexual relations between a religious leader and a student are always abusive because of the intrinsic power imbalance. Students or laity may have an idealized image of their leader and feel an explicit trust. They may relate to the member of the clergy as a messenger or an embodiment of God. This idealization may become eroticized in the student's mind; however it is the job of the teacher to keep clear boundaries that exclude sex and romanticized love.

It is far more harmful when the student is a child or the sex is without consent. As we know from reports from survivors, the pain can be acute and pervasive and the healing process slow. The injury reaches to a person's very core. If you are not safe within your religion, where are you safe?

The most extreme form of abuse within religious groups is ritualistic abuse, which is more common than previously believed. Cults that ritualistically abuse have been around for many generations and commit terrifying acts of physical and sexual abuse. The abuse often uses religious symbolism and is done in the name of God or Satan. Cult members are cut off from healthy spiritual influences and learn to associate violence with spirituality. Here we see spiritual alienation in its most complete manifestation.

Lily, along with many other children in her church, was ritualistically abused by both priests and nuns. Lily's story may be difficult to read. It was difficult for her to tell. As she spoke she realized that this was the first time she had been able to speak of the abuse without shaking. It is very disturbing that such horrible things are done in the name of religion and under the false authority of God.

Before you read this story, think about whether this is a good time. Especially if you were abused yourself, the story could bring up painful feelings. Read it in your own time and way and with support available.

Lily's story is important for many reasons. For one, it is important that her truth be heard. But Lily's is also an incredible testimony to the power of healing and the opportunity for spiritual renewal. Now her life is rich with ritual, her own healing rituals, which are integrated into the daily activities of her life. As she spoke, she bubbled with spirit.

"I was raised in a very traditional Catholic family. Everything in our family revolved around church activities and church people. My family were alcoholics and very dysfunctional, so the church fulfilled many of the family functions.

"There was a group of priests in my church at that time who were abusing children. My mother and grandmother were so into priests and church that I, of course, followed that modeling and would befriend priests. Pedophiles know the children that they can prey on, and I think I was the perfect candidate for that. I would go and visit the rectory and visit the cook. The priest would befriend me; I would sit in his lap, and the touching would begin, and I would be taken upstairs to be more and more abused. There were other children he was abusing, and he was also abusing the cook. I have remembered the abuse through flashbacks and dreams. I remember screaming and throwing up. I have been working through these memories for several years.

"It was devastating to me. I tried to tell my parents, but they did not believe me. I was told that I was a bad girl and priests do not do those kinds of things and that I was imagining it. I was sick through third grade, and my mother says that they thought I was dying. I stopped eating. As I look back, I think I was trying to commit suicide without knowing it. Later in my life I became depressed and suicidal.

"It is impossible for a five-year-old to separate the person in authority that she sees as God from a man who is a pedophile and has abused her. I know I must have thought that he was God. On one level I knew that he was an authority; on another level, my writings and drawings tell me that I knew that there was something wrong with him. I think there was a piece of me that knew that this wasn't right, and I tried to get out of it and couldn't, so I went under. I felt something very sinister, and I internalized that evil.

"I consider it ritualistic abuse because of the pattern of abuse, the environment in which it happened, and the ways in which it happened. There was kind of a routine. What is happening now is that several people are coming forward who were abused in the same church at the same time. There must have been a nest of pedophiles there at that time. As this ritualistic abuse comes into more awareness, it feels like the opening of an incredible can of worms. I can't imagine the implications. On one level I am scared to death, and on another level I am very relieved. I think they are going to find that there are tons of priests and nuns who are colluding and who have been abused and are perpetrators.

"As I did more and more work on my own abuse, I got more and more angry about the spiritual devastation. How dare they tamper with God's territory? How dare they say they are God and are doing this to us because we deserved it! I went through a period when I was outraged. How dare they distort the God in each of us! God raped me! To heal you have to shovel through and get back to a piece of what feels like God in each of us and then start to build on that again. That takes a hell of a lot of work. The way I healed was to separate the priest *from God at a deep level of understanding. What I know now was that that priest also had God inside of him, but he got really messed up.*

"I made it through, but a lot of people don't. I had to look at how I made it through and what helped me to make it. I must be incredibly strong to have made it. That strength is real connected to my spirituality. They talk about original sin; I think there must be an original spirituality. I think somehow I have always been connected with that."

Luckily most of us don't suffer such severe abuse within our religion. However, there are many different forms of abuse. Take some time to get a better sense of whether you experienced some form of abuse within your religion.

Abusive Experience Within Religion

Listed below are some common forms of abuse within religious groups.

1. Think about whether you experienced abuse within your religion of childhood, focusing on the kinds listed. Blanks are left to fill in other kinds of abuse.

   abuse of drugs, alcohol
   physical abuse
   abuse of money
   sexual abuse
   abuse of influence

   _____

   _____

2. If you are currently a member of a religious or spiritual group, look for evidence of these same kinds of abuse within your religion now.

   abuse of drugs, alcohol
   physical abuse
   abuse of money
   sexual abuse
   abuse of influence

   _____

   _____

If you had any of the experiences listed above, talk to a trusted support person about the situation, perhaps brainstorming about action you might want to take. Before you take any action, be sure to have adequate support.

Lily describes an important aspect of healing, separating the hurt and abuse from her spirituality as a whole. As Lily tells us, this process often takes a while and unfolds in layers. However, the basic process involves differentiating what hurt us in the past from what nurtures and supports us in the present.

Separating Out the Hurt

By working through the following process, you can begin to separate your injuries from the more beneficial elements of your religion.

1. Think about one way that you felt hurt within your religion. Be specific: for example, "The minister was an alcoholic."

2. Allow yourself to understand how that specifically hurt you. Think about how it got in the way of your spirituality: for example, "I tried to avoid him because he scared me when he was drunk. That is why I didn't attend youth functions at the church."

3. When we are hurt, a common response is to avoid anything that reminds us of the hurtful situation. This is protective and helpful, but it can become limiting. Notice if you tended to generalize your feelings about the situation: for example, "I tried to avoid all ministers because I figured they might be drunk too."

4. Examine the generalization, and see if there are exceptions: for example, "I have known many ministers who are wonderful people, inspirational leaders, and who do not abuse alcohol."

5. Don't deny the reality of the abuse, however. Instead, think about a strategy you might use if you run into a similar situation: for example, "If I realize that a spiritual leader is a substance abuser, I will speak my concerns aloud, both to the leader and to others in the church community."

6. Before you take any action, make sure you have support.

Spiritual Leadership

As we progress on our spiritual journey we naturally wish to share our insights and experiences with others, and a natural outcome of spiritual interest and involvement is spiritual leadership. When our truth fits others, they naturally turn to us for guidance. However, in a male-dominated model, our natural leadership skills and inclinations may be stifled.

We may internalize the message that we are spiritually inadequate or unworthy of leadership roles. We may doubt the value of our wisdom, or we may judge ourselves harshly against male standards of leadership. Because we are unaccustomed to visibility, we may fear it. In these ways we hold ourselves back on our spiritual journey.

A common theme of the women we interviewed was the childhood desire to assume spiritual leadership. As children, in play, we naturally try out the positions we aspire to. We can become discouraged, however, when we realize that our fantasies may be unattainable. As adults several of the women we interviewed did assume leadership positions within mainstream religions; however, the struggle for acknowledgment continued.

Andrea expresses her anger and frustration about being excluded from church leadership.

> *"The priest up there was a man. The boys got to be altar boys, and I wanted to be an altar boy so bad I couldn't stand it. My brother and I would play priest and altar boy and take turns. But in actuality he was the one who got to be an altar boy."*

When Maggie played religion as a child, she was always the priest; she felt called to be a priest. However, when she turned her play into adult experience, she found herself limited to the role of nun.

> *"When I was in high school I remember standing in front of a large assembly of five hundred or more students. I asked why women could not be priests. I always knew that being a nun was not the same, and I felt called to be a priest. After I became a nun I continued to struggle with this issue because I felt that I had more skill as a ritualist than many of the priests who were leading rituals. I would plan liturgies for the priests. I felt very angry as the woman behind the man."*

When we dare to assume leadership roles within male-dominated religions, we may meet with discrimination and unjust treatment. Darlene speaks of her experience of being kicked out of her church. Her leadership was not tolerated.

> *"What eventually moved me out of the Pentecostal church was the opening of my eyes regarding what I would now call patriarchy. I didn't have a name for it then. I just knew that I was furious with the hypocrisy and the power-tripping.*
>
> *"I was really passionate in my expression. I was outgoing and had leadership capabilities, so there were some people following. You know how that is when*

someone is willing to take a leadership role, that person gets followed. I can truly say that I was pure in heart, but I was accused of a lot, and it all had to do with the minister's feeling really threatened by someone who is competent, powerful, and a woman besides. There were many accusations, and I was kicked out of the church for things I had not done."

Ann's involvement in religion naturally led her to seminary, where she studied the scripture in search of answers to her spiritual questions. At the same time that she found liberating passages within scripture, she was silenced as a woman.

"I felt no freedom to speak as a woman, and when I did speak my contribution didn't hold much weight. They taught that it was not right for women to be in leadership because Adam had been created first and woman second, and that created a hierarchy. All the passages from the scriptures that describe women in terms of the hierarchy were emphasized, and the scriptures that described women in terms of equality were not mentioned. For example, in one story in the scripture a woman named Priscilla was a teacher and a deacon. She was teaching a man named Apollos. Her name is always mentioned first, as the prominent teacher and person in that relationship. But this story was never mentioned in seminary, and women were forbidden to teach men. It was tormenting to hear this double message, because I did not have a strong enough sense of my own identity to really believe what I was seeing."

Like Ann, many women have studied the scriptures in search of verses that affirm women. You can learn a lot from reading their discoveries.

Women in the Scriptures

1. Go to a bookstore or a library and look in the section on women and religion. Many books have been published recently that explore the scriptures and highlight previously unacknowledged verses and stories about women. Many of the verses that limit women's roles have been reinterpreted. These books have been written by women with different religious affiliations. Read a book that attracts you.

2. Read the scripture and verses yourself, and come up with your own new understandings.

Carter Heyward brought her childhood dream to fruition. Despite all odds, in 1974 Carter was ordained as an Episcopal priest.

"My parents say that from the time I was five or six years old, I was talking about becoming a priest. Women did not become priests at that time. My father told me he was in quandary about my fantasy, because he didn't want to encourage me in something that was impossible, but on the other hand he thought it was a fine aspiration."

Carter went on to realize her impossible dream by becoming one of the first eleven women ordained as Episcopal priests.

"I was ordained in 1974, at a time when the church had not yet ordained women. Contrary to the church's will, I, along with ten other women, was ordained by three bishops. This immediately put us on a collision course with the other church bishops. In this process I got very clear about what I believed in. My alliance could never be with the church institution but instead with other women and people who were struggling for justice. The seminary where I teach is located at the edge of the Episcopal church, and I feel as though I live at the edge of the church."

For Marilyn Sewell, leadership was a natural role to assume, perhaps because circumstance made her the leader in her family. Throughout her life she found herself alternately placed in leadership roles and then denied leadership positions. It took a journey through desperation and a surrender to God for Marilyn to grow into her full leadership potential. She is currently a Unitarian minister at the third largest church in the denomination.

"I was the oldest child of three children, and we grew up without a mother. I was sort of the pseudo-mother of the family. My father was an alcoholic; my brother and sister were younger; my grandmother and grandfather were senile. I was in some ways the strongest figure in the household. I grew up thinking I could do anything. I surprise myself sometimes, because I don't always think of myself as a leader, but I notice that if there is a leadership vacuum I tend to step into it. Other people have always sought me out for leadership roles. It seems to be my destiny, so I have accepted it.

"After my husband and I separated, I found that my relationship to the Baptist church changed. Whereas before I could counsel the kids at the junior high choir camp, now I was told that I could no longer counsel children. I assumed it was because I was divorced, because I was a very good leader. They said that I could chop vegetables in the kitchen, but they didn't want me counseling the children.

"I went through a period of great terror and disillusionment after my divorce. I had some very desperate times financially. I went through two periods of unem-

ployment and agonized about who I was and what the purpose of living was, and how was I going to raise my two kids. I became so exhausted that I passed out while driving and was in an automobile accident. I was tremendously depressed and at the bottom of the barrel. I decided, 'OK, I am not doing so well at running my own life. I thought that I could make it, but I am not making it. So I give myself to you, God. Whoever you are, wherever you are, I want you to use me for the good.'

"Nothing dramatic happened right away, but as things evolved I decided to go to seminary. I had heard of this wonderful school where people were treated with great respect and trust, and you wrote your own curriculum. You could minister in whatever way you were called to serve. I decided to go, but there was a lot of turmoil in the decision because I did not want to take my now almost junior-high-school-age kids with me. I felt that they really needed to be with their father. And I was going with almost no resources out to what seemed like a different country—I had never been to California before. I was still in a physically and emotionally depressed condition, and I knew that I needed to heal. I wept for so many days. Leaving these children was like leaving a part of my body, like leaving my left arm. But I knew I needed to do this, so I did. They are now nineteen and twenty, and they both became fine healthy boys, and we have a good relationship. At this seminary, I found a school that really said yes to the student in a radical way. I found out what my gifts were more deeply—I began writing more in earnest. That program was really wonderful for me because I really came into my own as a writer, a thinker, and a leader."

In many religions the role of women is changing. More and more religions are ordaining women. Attending a ritual led by a woman can be exciting and liberating.

Women as Spiritual Leaders

Go to a religious ritual or observance that is led by a woman. Contemplate or write about your experience. Do you feel open to her leadership? Do you feel comfortable with her leadership? How would you describe her leadership? Were there ways that her experience as a woman seemed to inform her leadership?

Women may have different values about leadership than men. This exercise will help you get a sense of your preferences regarding spiritual leadership.

Leadership Values

First circle the word or words that describe the way you prefer to think of a person in spiritual leadership. Add any other words that fit for you.

LEADER   GUIDE   MENTOR   MASTER   TEACHER   FACILITATOR

GURU   PARTNER

Now read the sentences below about different leadership styles. Think and/or write about how you agree and disagree with each value.

I like a spiritual leader whom I can look up to.
I like a spiritual leader who is like me.
I like a spiritual leader who guides the process.
I like a spiritual leader who tells me what to do.
I like a spiritual leader who knows a great deal more than I
    and can teach me.

What do you understand now about your preferences and needs in a spiritual leader?

Many of us have dreams of spiritual leadership—not necessarily as a profession, but as an important passage on our spiritual journey. Although Carter and Marilyn are both leaders within traditional religions, there are many other forums for leadership. You may already be a spiritual leader in your family; perhaps all that is missing is acknowledgment. Then again you may wish to try a new leadership role. Be bold and daring!

For Women with Dreams of Spiritual Leadership

Take a few minutes to become centered and grounded. Then think about the beginnings of your desire for leadership. Was it as a child or later in your life? Was it encouraged, discouraged, or overlooked? Have you ever been in a role of spiritual leadership? If so, how did that feel to you? Do you have fantasies now of assuming more leadership? If so, is there a small step you might now take toward realizing these dreams?

Although we are not all called to be spiritual leaders, we all need acknowledgment for our spiritual journey. We thrive when we are affirmed and when our unique spiritual gifts are recognized. Each of us has her own spiritual destiny. When you listen deeply, you will hear your call and know how you are to participate in spiritual and religious life.

Integration

Take a little while to remember the work you have done in this chapter. Think about the ideas that you read. Remember the exercises you worked with.

1. Recall any important events that came to light while working with this material. Add them to your time line. (See page 48.)

2. Think about the ideas presented, and throw away any that do not fit. Put them on your compost heap. (See page 38.)

3. Check to see if there is anything else you wish to note in your spiritual journal. You might also want to reread some of what you have written.

4. Think about whether there is more work to be done with any of the material. Think about how you might want to do this. For example, you might want to work on the exercises some more later or discuss the issues with a support person, in therapy, or with a support group.

5. Appreciate yourself for the work you have done. Give gratitude for healing and spiritual renewal.

Hurdling Other Obstacles

5

Obstacles not directly related to your concept of God or the teachings of your religion may block your spiritual path. You may encounter in daily life difficulties within the family, obstruction by community or society—the challenges that seem to be an inherent part of being human.

What is an obstacle for one of us may not be for another. You are the only one who knows what has blocked your spiritual path. Perhaps as you read and worked through the exercises in previous chapters other kinds of obstacles have come to mind.

Obstacles are as inherent a part of the spiritual journey as they are of life. But in our search for a way through the obstacles, we can stretch to new spiritual understanding. What is at first an obstacle becomes a spiritual opportunity.

Focus Questions:

What else has blocked my spiritual unfolding or negated my essential spiritual nature?

How can I be in relationship to suffering so that I neither deny its reality nor deny the goodness in life?

Other Obstacles

Take some time now to examine other obstacles that have blocked your spiritual journey. We suggest two different approaches; each can uncover information. You may prefer one or use both.

Writing about other obstacles. Use free-form writing to generate ideas you were not previously aware of. Remember to write as fast as you can and not censor ideas. Write for five minutes, then take a break. Then repeat the cycle a few times. Address this question: What else has blocked my spirituality?

Obstacles at different ages. Take out your time line. Become quiet and centered using Grounding 1, In the Arms of Mother Earth. Look over your time line. Think about yourself at different ages. What was happening in your spiritual life at different times? As you focus on yourself at different ages, consider any obstacles that blocked your spiritual unfolding. Take time to remember. Honor whatever comes into mind. When you feel complete with your reveries, you might want to add some notes to your time line or your spiritual journal.

Finding a Time and Place for Spirituality

Many of us feel we are busy all the time, with no time to spare for spiritual practice. Days full of appointments and artificial time constraints, focused on material needs and personal accomplishments, make it difficult to tap into a more natural flow of life and allow our spirituality to unfold.

"Spiritual experience is one of the first things to go when my life becomes more organized and less open to the flow. When I am busy structuring my life, it is hard for me to see the natural order."

"I am a single mom and main provider for four children. I carry a heavy load. How can I stay smiling and not take things too personally? I think it is about quieting down and hearing the inner voices. I look toward the elder women as a model. They have endured. They are gentle, not bitter."

The role of women in our society is changing. We are moving into the workplace and taking on leadership roles previously reserved for men. Some of us are raising children alone. Many women complained that they felt tired at the end of a long day and overwhelmed by the combination of work in the outside world, work in the home, and the nurturing of a family. They yearned for a spiritual outlook that might balance their lives but felt too depleted to pursue it. They spoke of the need for new models, models of women who have a satisfying spiritual life within the busy pace of their life.

Finding Models

Take a look around. Think about women in your daily life, women in your workplace, women in your family, women in your community. Look for models of women who are both busy and spiritually nourished. Talk to them; ask them how they do it. Think about women you have read about. Think about women you have learned about in other ways. Allow yourself to learn from the experience of others and to be inspired by their spiritual journeys.

While we learn to integrate spirituality into our busy lives, it is also helpful to find moments of quiet and rejuvenation.

Invoking Inner Stillness

Become grounded using Grounding 3, Become a Tree, on page 12. Then in your imagination find yourself in a place of rest and rejuvenation, a place where you feel completely safe and where there is nothing that needs to be done or accomplished. Envision this healing place in detail. What are the sights? the sounds? the smells? Allow your body, mind, and spirit to be nurtured and comforted by the stillness. If you sense any demands upon you, adjust the environment or the situation so that you feel even more relaxed and renewed. Enjoy your time in this environment, knowing that even a short time can be deeply restful. Find a symbol or souvenir that represents this healing place and your inner stillness. When you feel ready, return from this place of stillness. Know that you can visit it whenever you wish; your symbol or souvenir can help you.

For many of us the beep of the microwave or the computer is far more common than the tones of inspirational music or the sounds of nature. Although the age of information has provided new opportunities, it has also moved us further from the basic realities of life. The technological world can seem diametrically opposed to the traditional spiritual life, but it need not be an obstacle on the spiritual journey. We can use the new and potent tools technology provides for spiritual activities that might look quite different from traditional practices but be just as spiritually uplifting.

Finding Spirit in the World of Technology

Make a list of the technologies in your life. Then brainstorm about how you might use each to further your spiritual journey. Think creatively! For example, your might record your spiritual journal on a computer and print out sections to share with spiritual companions. Or you might form a spiritual support group that communicates by modem. Or you might acknowledge the time saved by cooking with your microwave and dedicate that time one day a week to do a spiritual activity. If you have a VCR, you might check out a movie with spiritual content. Follow through by doing one or more of the activities on your list.

Domination, Injustice, and Abuse

Another characteristic of the world we share is that it is based on a model of domination. A society based on domination considers some people inherently more deserving and powerful, and they rule over the lives of others. When the rule is benign, there may be some benefits; however, the people ruled over may not be able to grow into full empowerment and assume their own authority. All too often the rule is unjust or abusive.

Domination often leads to injustice. We forget our inherent connection and disregard the basic spiritual principle: "Do unto others as you would like them to do unto you." Instead, certain people are considered better than others and are categorically given more status and rights. Other people are considered inferior and are sometimes treated badly, denied basic needs and integrity. These judgments have little to do with the people themselves but instead are based on the arbitrary standards applied to whole groups.

Abuse is the misuse of power, often by those in control. It stems from an unwillingness or inability to meet others with compassion and to honor our inherent connection. It stems from fear, a disrespect for human vulnerability, and a distorted sense of what is ours. Abuse points to a crisis in relationship and in basic spiritual values. Abuse violates and causes tremendous pain, the memories of which become locked in our bodies, minds, and spirits.

Domination separates. Abuse beats down the spirit. Regardless of whether we identify as abuser or victim, domination and abuse hurt us. We no longer trust one another. We close our hearts. We may disbelieve our inherent divinity. We may distrust God and lose touch with the spiritual part of ourselves.

Still, we can heal. The spirit and the heart are remarkably resilient. Our ability to trust, though wounded, lies in waiting for a time when it is safe to come out and test life again, for a time of gentleness and healing. Abuse often takes place behind a veil of secrecy. As it lifts, courageous people embark upon their healing journey. We hear countless stories from women who have transformed adversity into an opportunity for spiritual awakening and deepening, who have transformed themselves from victims to survivors.

Domination, injustice, and abuse are fed by attitudes we are taught at an early age. These attitudes are deeply ingrained and are very difficult to unlearn. For example, most women internalize a sense of being less than the males in their lives. Many of us learn that white people are better than people of color and that members of mainstream Christian religions are better than Jews. Families that have been in the United States for generations generally have more status than immigrant families. Heterosexuals are more deserving than gays and lesbians. In all these ways, we come to believe that others are less important than we are. If we feel unsure of our self-worth, we put other people down in order to put ourselves up. Or we begin to believe that we are inferior to and less deserving than others.

We have all experienced domination, most likely in some situations being the one in control and in others feeling controlled. Regardless of position, we are divided and alienated by domination. Take some time now to consider how you have experienced domination.

The Experience of Domination

Listed below are common kinds of domination, followed by some general definitions. In the space on the left-hand side, check off the categories of domination that have most deeply affected you. A couple of blank spaces have been left to list kinds of domination that are not included and to write your own definition.

_____ Racism: A belief in the inherent superiority of certain races (most generally the white race).

_____ Religious superiority: A belief in the inherent superiority of people of specific religions.

_____ Ethnocentrism: A belief in the inherent superiority of certain ethnic groups or cultures.

_____ Class prejudice: A belief in the inherent superiority of people with more money or from a higher class in society.

_____ Sexism: A belief in the inherent superiority of males.

——— Prejudice against homosexuals: A belief in the inherent superiority of heterosexuals.

——— Age bias: A belief in the inherent superiority of persons of certain age groups.

——— Prejudice against disabled persons: A belief in the inherent superiority of people who are without known physical disabilities.

——— A belief in _____

——— A belief in _____

An important step in healing domination and injustice is understanding how they have affected your life and your spiritual development. When you have insight into how you were hurt, you can find the path of healing. Thinking about categories you checked above, respond by filling in the blanks below.

In my childhood, I experienced _____

_____

and more specifically, _____

_____.

I experienced it directly by _____

_____.

I experienced it indirectly by _____

_____.

It hurt me because _____

_____.

This hurt blocked my spirituality by _____

_____.

We live in a hierarchical society that affords some cultures more worth and respect than others. However, when people of an oppressed culture band together, they can create a deep and essential bond through which they can become strengthened. A shared spiritual foundation then becomes a sustaining source of strength—a basis from which to work toward change.

"In black culture, God was what kept us alive beyond all reason to survive. Prayer helps you reframe your understanding in such a way that what was killing you ceases to kill you."

"As a Jew, I always felt safer with my own people. There is this recognition when I see someone like myself, someone with dark hair and a quick mind that loves to play with ideas. I feel relaxed, like I can be myself."

"My Greek Orthodox religion is wrapped up with my culture. It's about my history, a culture struggling to maintain an identity under Turkish rule. This makes the religion and spiritual practices even stronger. I can't separate my culture from my religion and beliefs."

Because culture and spirituality are so closely connected, when we lose one, we can lose the other. When Bridget immigrated to the United States, her culture was taken from her. It was not until she returned to her homeland and her culture that she found her authentic spiritual path.

"As an immigrant and a Latina I experienced a very subtle kind of racism. I was ten when I came to this country. When I first got here, everyone was very nice but very ignorant about who I was. I was asked how I liked wearing shoes and clothes—this was by teachers who assumed I had never worn shoes or clothes because people from South America were heathens or savages. It was very humiliating and insulting. In school I was given an image of my country as poverty-stricken and my people as illiterate and dirty. Every time I saw pictures, there was some kid covered with mud. I had memories, but you lose those memories in a culture where you do not get affirmation for your memories and everything is eroding, sucking away at the life of those memories. My memories became like mythology; they did not seem like reality. I was pushed by peer pressure; I wanted to belong and be like everyone else. I had been told that something that I was had no value and no reality.

"Although there was a great deal of pressure to assimilate, my family, especially my mother, grandmother, and aunt, were very proud of my culture. They kept the culture alive in the home. The principal at school asked my mother to not speak Spanish in the home, and my mother refused.

"When I finished high school, my mother sent me to South America for three months so that I would know where I came from. It was an overwhelming experience. My sense of betrayal was so profound because Ecuador was so opposite from what I had been told through grade school and high school. I became enraged, and I never believed Americans again.

"The surprising thing is, the awareness of my oppression opened up my spiritual life. In the process of feeling very angry at this country, I entered a crisis of cultural identity. I became very angry at this culture and left this country several times. Returning to South America is what awakened my capacity for spirituality. I lived in the mountains and in volcanoes with indigenous people and immersed myself in the churches. The earth opened up my capacity for female spirituality. In Latin culture, which is permeated with the values of indigenous people, spirituality is part of your culture just as much as language and food. Spirit is embodied in your everyday events. In order to reclaim my culture, I had to reclaim my spirituality. In order to reclaim my spirituality, I had to reclaim my culture."

Many times when we realize how we have been separated by these beliefs, we become motivated to reach beyond these arbitrary divisions. We can become empowered and connected when we reach out beyond our differences.

Cultivating Understanding

Think about someone you encounter regularly whom you perceive as different from you. This could be someone from your church, spiritual group, workplace, or wherever you meet people in your daily life. Contemplate the following questions about your relationship. How do your cultural differences affect the relationship? How do the differences between you alienate you from each other? How do the differences bring more vitality into the relationship? How might you develop more connection? Now do one small thing that might bring more connection into the relationship.

It is a tremendous spiritual challenge to treat all people with basic dignity and respect, a spiritual value professed by most religions. All too often our religious institutions have either failed to take a stand against injustice or have taken a position that breeds more injustice. Carter Heyward, an Episcopal priest, finds support for fighting injustice in the story of the life of Jesus.

"I identify as a Christian. I acknowledge that my own story is in some kind of meaningful continuity with the Jesus story. It does not mean that Jesus is God or the son of God or any more special to God than other people. There is something about the Jesus of Nazareth story that I find compelling, instructive, and

empowering. I feel connected to Jesus' advocacy of the poor and the marginal-
ized and his own defiance of authority, secular and religious. He put a high pre-
mium on friendship and going around with the marginalized folk. I hear that as
a very empowering story. In no way do I believe that story is the center of the
universe or that everybody is supposed to hear that same story and fall to the
ground and worship. I think that flies right in the face of what that story is
about. I know most people who are Christians at this particular time in history
would not hear what I just said as being Christian enough.

"I think, on the whole, the stand of Christianity is appalling with regard to most
of the struggles we are engaged in right now, whether sexuality or the environ-
ment. The churches are either silent or actively the oppressor. I don't see any rea-
son for the church to exist as an institution unless it is going to be an advocate
for justice. We can organize our spirituality in other ways, but where we need
the church is politically, to help show what is really moral.

"The question I get asked most often is why I stay in the church. It is a question
that I can never answer once and for all; the answer always changes. I entirely
understand why some women choose to leave. The church has been part of the
abuse cycle of many women."

Another important step is to take action to change the injustices we evidence. Not only can we initiate change in our own attitudes, we can also generate change within our families and communities.

Taking Action

Do something toward changing a situation that you perceive as unjust. Some
examples follow.

1. Advocate for a policy at work that treats workers with greater respect
   and equality.

2. Organize a new service committee within your religion that addresses
   a need you see in your community.

3. Mail letters to your legislators in support of more just legislation.

4. Speak with your children about an issue that touches their lives.

Carter's words remind us that some people believe their religion has a corner on spiritual truth and that people who follow different religions and adhere

to different beliefs are wrong. Jewish people know only too well the damage caused by the domination of certain religions over others.

Roberta talks about some of the ways that anti-Semitism has affected her life.

"Most of my family died somewhere in Eastern Europe in the holocaust. The Jewish history is the story of old European Jews who spoke seven languages because they had immigrated to seven different countries to escape the pogroms. There is an old saying that the reason that Jews use their heads so much is because if you have to run on a minute's notice that is the only thing you can take.

"My mother didn't simply teach me about suffering; it was more like she breast-fed her pain. But it wasn't only her pain; it was 5,500 years of pain. During World War II her father owned a store in a German neighborhood in Brooklyn that was boycotted. Her family could only afford potatoes and carrots. When I was growing up, she stocked a closet so full of cans of food that when I opened the door, the cans fell on top of me. She was still afraid she was going to starve. I wanted to redeem my mother's unhappiness. I wanted to save the world and myself from injustice, suffering, unreliability, the holocaust, ugliness, sin, ingratitude, guilt."

Roberta personally experienced the effects of domination when she was mugged and shot. She immediately connected the mugging, her Jewish identity, and her sense of God.

"I got mugged a couple of years ago and was seriously injured. The mugging felt like my own personal holocaust. I immediately thought, What kind of God makes a holocaust? I identify with victims, and that has both a good side and a bad side. I think that Jews are a humane, remembering race. We are the social workers, the comedians, and the therapists. We remember to have a heart, and that is because we are not allowed to forget the suffering in the world."

As Roberta sorts out the effects of injustice on her family and her people, she points out the strengths that were honed by adversity. An essential step in the renewal process is discarding discriminatory beliefs about ourselves.

Transforming Harmful Messages

Spend five minutes using free-form writing about the discriminatory messages you remember hearing about yourself, your religion, or your people. Write without censoring, writing down whatever comes to mind. Then burn that piece of paper, and place those ideas on your compost heap. Now write down your truth about who you are.

In the process of correcting inaccurate and discriminatory messages about ourselves, we transform their energy. We discover the spiritual depth that comes from overcoming adversity.

Making Lemonade Out of the Lemons

Look back over the exercise titled "The Experience of Domination" on page 112. Consider the categories that you checked, and contemplate how you have transformed experiences of domination into valuable life lessons. Answer these questions: Did I learn something about caring and compassion? How and where have I found allies and community? What other lessons have I learned? What has had a positive influence on my spirituality?

Some of us experience domination and abuse within our families. Family violence inevitably shapes our spiritual beliefs.

We interviewed several women who had been abused. Although each woman's experience of abuse is different, each went through an extremely difficult period when she believed her life or her sanity was at risk. The healing journey seems to include a period of crisis and a passage through painful emotions. Each of these women in her own way came out of the crisis and found healing. Each emerged with a new relationship to her Spiritual Essence or God.

Randy has always been aware of injustice. She believes that her independent spirit and sensitivity to injustice made her more vulnerable to abuse but also guided her healing. In her healing she draws upon spiritual strength that has been with her since childhood. She understands adversity as a strengthening tool. Randy broke through the veil of denial that hid generations of family abuse. She transformed the anger, grief, and betrayal of abuse into energy to fight child abuse and help children heal.

"I come from a family in which my father was an alcoholic and became violently rageful. My mother was very self-centered and had a hard time seeing anybody but herself. Child abuse and alcoholism have been in my family for generations—generations of physical abuse, sexual abuse, and emotional abuse. There was tremendous grief in my family, which was not expressed but instead acted

out as rage against the children. Although I do not remember any direct incest, there was a lot of sexualized violence. My father would go after me and pin me down in a sexualized kind of way and tickle me while I was screaming and trying to get away. I always felt a catastrophic fear that something sexual and violent was going to happen. I was the oldest child and got the most abuse. There was something about me that really provoked my father. I think it was my independence and unwillingness to be a passive, submissive female. I had my own ideas, and I would argue my point. I argued about all the unjust things he did, and then he would come after me in a rage and hit me. I was always trying to think of places to hide.

"I think I learned to hide in my spirituality. I identified as spirit rather than body. I learned to dissociate, go into trance. Then no one could hurt my spirit, even though they could hurt my body. The lives of the saints and martyrs always appealed to me. They practiced what they preached and helped people. They had survived struggles and intense adversity, and I think that through their suffering I was able to make some sense of the suffering I felt in my family.

"I went through a dark night of the soul caused by a spirituality that was no longer working, the abusive family I came from, my damaged self-concept, and the realization that I was a lesbian. I felt that if I came out as a lesbian I would lose everything—my family and my church. I became suicidal. That was during my atheist period. I was drinking a lot of alcohol and taking Valium in order to suppress who I was. I came out the other side of this dark night of the soul having dropped out of my church. I knew I could not live without being who I was, and that included loving women. I felt that I went through a tunnel and came out the other side. I began a spiritual journey that centered around feminism but had its roots in my childhood spirituality. I would listen inside and get answers. I fought against injustice.

I am a social worker, and I work with abused children and families of alcoholics and drug addicts. I found a great meaning for my life. My family is now accepting of me as long as I am not too confrontational about their issues. I am breaking the silence and denial in my family. I am doing it in a gentle, supportive way. I reported my brother as a child molester. I gave him the chance to turn himself into the district attorney, but I brought the issue out, and it has caused a lot of family problems. I am seen in my family as a crusader. That abused child within me who wanted to be a crusader and a saint has found meaning in my life through helping other children."

As we see from Randy's experience, family abuse that remains hidden and unspoken is carried down through generations. Left unhealed, the wounds of abuse fester. The abused becomes the abuser and causes more abuse. People who have been abused often self-abuse with drugs, alcohol, and self-destructive behavior. The next generation, if not themselves abusers, may attempt to heal the wounds of abuse by absorbing and suffering under the burden of the pain of past generations. However, healing can break the cycle of abuse. There seems to be a connection between a spiritual outlook—that is, a sense of life that is larger than the pain and betrayal of abuse—and the ability to move from feeling like a victim to becoming a survivor.

A first step in healing is acknowledging the abuse, breaking through the veil of denial. At the time the abuse happens, victims often deal with the abuse by imagining that they are somewhere safer, that this terrible thing is not happening to them. This is a helpful response when the abuse is happening but may create problems later in life. It can become a habit to space out the important moments of life. However, this ability to leave a situation and choose another is also the path of transcendence, a powerful spiritual tool.

An essential part of the healing is placing the responsibility squarely where it belongs, onto the action or behavior of the person who perpetrated the abuse. Often people who are abused believe somewhere deep inside that they are to blame. At the same time that it is natural, this is also an inaccurate and unhelpful belief. Holding tightly to that blame can block us on the spiritual path, making it impossible to know our inherent divinity.

Another ingredient of healing is rediscovering a sense of trust. When we are abused, we know in a very deep and absolute way that we cannot trust everyone and everything. This is an important lesson. But it is equally true that everyone and everything is not completely and inherently untrustworthy. As we move from victim to survivor, we make distinctions and find a new sense of trust. For many of us, this includes a trust in ourselves. Now we know that regardless of how painful or difficult life may become, we will make it through. As our trust for ourselves grows, we open up to the life around us and can discover a source of spiritual power that is far more trustworthy than the abusive power that hurt us.

You have probably transformed yourself from victim to survivor in some aspect of your life. It is important to affirm this movement and to allow it to expand into other parts of your life.

From Victim to Survivor

Think of one way that you have moved from feeling like a victim to becoming a survivor. Write it down and read it to yourself at least once a day for the next week. For example, perhaps you used to choose partners who consistently criticized you, and your partner now is respectful. Or perhaps you were always afraid to be alone in your house, and you recently installed an alarm system and now feel safe.

Potent healing can take place when people who have been abused meet together and share their experiences. If you are a survivor of abuse, take an opportunity to share the impact of the abuse upon your spirituality.

Safe Sharing About Spirituality and Abuse

Get together with a few other survivors of abuse. This exercise works best with one to four others. Talk about how the abuse affected your spirituality using the questions suggested below and any others you agree on. We suggest the following ground rules; adapt them or add to them to fit your needs.

Each woman speaks for a period of time without interruption,
    perhaps fifteen minutes to half an hour.
The other woman or women practice deep listening, hearing the
    story through their hearts and with full attention.
There is a predetermined period for feedback (maybe five or
    ten minutes). The woman will define the kind of feedback, and the
    other women respond only with the kind of feedback requested.
During the discussion do not share vivid details of the abuse.
    (Although sharing details can, at times, be very healing, it is
    important that it be done in a very safe way, or it will just cause
    more hurt. Sharing details is usually best done with the facilitation
    of a mental health professional.)

Suggested questions. What messages, if any, did I get from my religion about the abuse? What did I think God had to do with the abuse? What is one way I think spirituality might help in healing now?

Substance Abuse

Substance abuse deeply affects family life, self-image, relationships, and life choices; it has a similar deep effect upon our developing spirituality.

It is no coincidence that alcohol is also referred to as "spirits." Inebriation can mimic the satisfactions and joys of the spiritual life. Some drug experiences may even open the door to a spiritual perspective. However, the satisfactions are temporary and frequently followed by the agony of addiction. It is also no coincidence that Alcoholics Anonymous and Narcotics Anonymous, both very helpful treatments for substance abuse, are spiritual programs. There seems to be an intrinsic connection between spirituality and substance abuse.

As a child, Maggie grew up in a home that was isolated from the community, burdened by poverty, and torn apart by alcoholism and suicide. As a child she was sustained by her spirituality.

> *"I grew up in a family with eight kids, and it felt like an ongoing struggle for survival. My father was an alcoholic who committed suicide when I was twelve. My mother raised the kids on a Catholic teacher's salary.*
>
> *"We didn't talk about feelings at home. When things were really hard, I always had this sense that God knew and understood and helped me through. Jesus was my secret, special friend who always understood what I was feeling. It gave me a framework and a sense of safety in a pretty crazy world."*

Sharon's mother was an alcoholic, and she has spent a great deal of time healing the scars of growing up in an alcoholic family. She realizes that she also learned important lessons.

> *"I was very, very emotionally attached to my mother, so it was very lonely and scary when she was drunk. It became a spiritual quest of mine to try to take care of her and to heal her from her drinking. I would hide the bottles from her. I poured out her drinks so that she would love me, because my mother could not love me when she was drunk.*
>
> *"Throughout my life, my spirituality has always focused on service. As a child I thought about being a nun, even though I wasn't Catholic. I wanted to live a life of service, put aside my own material needs. Taking care of my mother was my first calling to service. There have been different callings throughout my life. Now my calling is through mothering my children."*

Now Sharon uses her awareness to avoid codependent patterns in relationships.

> *"I do it differently now. I transformed my patterns of codependency into service that is truly spiritual. Codependency is not true service or truly selfless but very ego-involved. When I am acting codependently, I give to others so that they will continue to love me. When I am being of service, I practice awareness toward the goal of ending the suffering of all beings. I place myself in this same context and remember to care for myself also."*

Sharon goes on to explain that, despite the codependent elements, she learned important and formative spiritual lessons from caring for her alcoholic mother.

"I got a lot of practice in trying to help somebody and in trying to love somebody and remaining compassionate even though I didn't like what they were doing."

If you grew up in a family where there was substance abuse, most likely it affected your spirituality. Take some time now to consider your experience.

For Women Who Grew Up Around Substance Abuse

Begin by grounding and centering. Recall your own definition of spirituality. Then remember back to a time when you were around substance abuse. Remember with as much detail as you feel comfortable recalling. Now get a sense of how the substance abuse affected your developing spirituality. Did it block you? Did you learn from it? How does the effect of growing up around substance abuse impact your spirituality today? When you feel finished remembering, bring yourself back to present time. Remember one thing about your life right now that is nurturing.

As adolescents and adults, many of us have used alcohol or drugs. Some of us are able to use them in moderation, and they do not interfere with our spirituality. In fact, wine is sacrament in some religious rituals. Others become entrapped in addiction. The path of recovery is one of the most perilous journeys and also can be a journey of tremendous transformation.

Cheryl's sobriety opened up and enlivened her spiritual life.

"I needed a real powerful manifestation to become reconnected with my spiritual self, and I don't believe anything could have been more potent than my sobriety. Being clean and sober allows me to be closer to my God."

Nelly's drug use opened many new doors, some of which she wishes had remained closed. However, she learned essential lessons about fear and commitment.

A STORY FROM NELLY

I first began using drugs in the late 1960s. Marijuana and LSD seemed to open up whole new realms of thought and experience. I no longer felt confined by convention, and life seemed like a big adventure. I guess I got a bit too wild. I took LSD and did crazy things and trusted strangers who betrayed my trust. Suddenly I saw a whole new side of life and became more frightened than you can imagine. Was this what they meant by evil? After that, I did everything I could to avoid feeling that terror and in the process avoided lots of the good things that life had to offer. I sheltered myself from my fears, but they did not seem to go away.

I got scared away from LSD, but I kept using marijuana. I started to depend on it to have a good time and to relax and fall asleep. After many years, I felt really dependent on it. The most difficult times were when I went away on spiritual retreats. You weren't allowed to take substances, but I couldn't abide by the precept. I felt terribly guilty and knew that my spiritual advancement was limited by my addiction. Finally one day I told the teacher that I was breaking the rules and smoking marijuana. He was both very firm and compassionate. He advised me to stop smoking now. He told me I had the ability to walk through my fears. He gave me a poem as a guide. The poem spoke about the power and magic of commitment. I read those lines over and over again instead of smoking marijuana. It ended with a couplet from Goethe, "Whatever you can do, or dream you can, begin in. Boldness has genius, power, and magic in it."

I was really fine without marijuana. The dependence was all in my mind, but those thoughts were very powerful. They had been ruling my life for over a decade. As I moved through my life without leaning on a substance, I felt the sweet taste of freedom. I learned to work with my moods using more subtle and effective inner tools. I never forgot that lesson about the power of commitment. There really is a lot of magic when I commit to my dreams instead of being confined by my fears.

For Women in Recovery

Recovery can be difficult at times. There are often bumps along the way. First clarify how you feel and act when your recovery feels threatened. Write out your "signs and symptoms." Then write out a "prescription" for your spirit. Think creatively about what will feed your spirit other than substances. You might remind yourself to read specific passages of writing that speak your truth. Or perhaps you might write down your own truths and read them aloud when your recovery feels threatened. Perhaps you need to go to a Twelve Step meeting or to church or temple. Remember to follow your prescription when you hit bumps in your journey of recovery.

The Pain of Being Human

Life is difficult at times. Some of us call it pain; others call it evil. However we name it, most of us have experienced or witnessed intense suffering. It is difficult to live with adversity and understand why it exists. These same experiences may turn us toward the spiritual path in search of meaning and resolution. Many religious traditions even have a name for this process: "baptism by fire" or "return from exile."

Ann, a psychologist, grapples with the pain her clients share with her. Though theological answers are no longer satisfying, her own spiritual awareness guides her through the pain and anguish she witnesses.

"I am dealing with evil on an emotional level. Why do human beings encounter and cause so much pain and anguish? I question where God is when we go through all this pain. I know the theological answer for why there is evil in the world, but it does not satisfy me right now. At times the pain and evil does not make sense to me, and then God does not make sense. I have to come back to what I know and trust—which is the existence of Christ. I come back to my own experience of the miraculous and remember that I can't pretend to know what God's purpose is. I do believe that God is compassionate and caring and that our pain is not meant to be a punishment."

As we confront pain and hardship, support is essential; with it, we can transform suffering into compassion. Building support is best done regularly. Take one more step right now to increase your support.

Remembering Resources

List three resources that you can call upon during difficult times. Think about both resources that are within you and resources that are outside you. For example, you might phone a supportive friend and make some time to talk. Or you might remind yourself of your ability to remain balanced in the face of suffering, remembering a situation from the past. You might turn to the teachings of your religion. Look over the work you did in earlier exercises to recall your resources.

Difficult times can nudge us down the spiritual path; at the same time, our spirituality can support us through difficulties.

"When I am down and out and I feel helpless and weak, I know that nothing in this world can give me the strength I need. Only through spirituality can I replenish my strength and regain a sense of my life's direction."

Suffering can arise out of the choices our children make. Darlene is divorced, and her son decided to live with his father.

"This separation from my son is probably the most painful thing I have experienced. I have to remind myself that he is in the hands of the divine and that his path is his and not mine. This is a very deep point of surrender for me, and I use my spirituality as I grieve on a daily basis. You know, when it comes to grief like this, I don't know how people get through it without a spirituality to draw upon."

Perhaps the form of hardship that we share across the human community is the suffering of disease and dying. Although medical technology has advanced, we are not shielded from these basic human experiences. When we face illness, many of us turn to spirituality. Peggy is a survivor living with AIDS. When she was diagnosed as HIV positive, she immediately turned to a search for spiritual meaning. As Peggy faces death directly, she is guided by a deep inner strength and a firm spiritual foundation.

"A little over two years ago I was diagnosed with leukemia and as HIV positive. From the very minute that I got my HIV diagnosis I was afraid, but I was also very curious as to what spiritual lessons were to be learned. I knew right away that I had choices, and I asked my doctor what lessons I was going to learn from this. The doctor thought that was a weird question. I told the doctor that I knew this was an incredible opportunity. Afterward I questioned whether this spiritual attitude was denial, and I think that in part it was. There have been many moments when I have not been in denial and I have been very angry and thought that if I could hold on to my spirituality I would not have all these feelings and I could ride above it all. But I knew that part of my spirituality is about feeling what I feel and being who I am. Part of who I am is an angry woman who hates this virus.

"Right after my diagnosis I was so focused on the spiritual that I did not give enough thought to the practical issues and ended up taking some treatments that I did not feel very good about. Now I am totally on an herbal program and doing better healthwise than I have in three years. I have learned what is best for my body. I have learned what I need spiritually to get through.

"Being infected with HIV has been one of the most important facts in my life. It has given me the opportunity to change. It gave me an excuse to confront my fears about mortality and to find out what I really feel and believe spiritually. It's been a real kick in the butt. I do not know how much longer I have in this dimension; this false sense of having all the time in the world was grabbed out from under me. Since there is a chance that I am going to die next month, I have to know how to deal with that and not wait until it happens to deal with it. So I started thinking about what I believe. I realize I believe in my own inner energy and its connection with all energy. I began to realize the difference between being around positive energy and negative energy and the great effect that other people's energy has on me and on my health and my level of anxiety. I realize I needed to develop my own inner energy to balance the times when I was around other people whose energy was not real positive, because I don't want to live in a bubble. I had to really work to learn how to balance my spiritual energy in a similar way to how I balance my physical energy and physical output.

"I think having AIDS has totally clinched in my mind and my soul and my being that this life is just part of the journey. I now believe in reincarnation. It is very obvious to me that this life is just one of the opportunities I have to learn and grow and to become more connected with my spirituality."

Certainly Peggy's spiritual convictions have been tested by adversity. A few weeks before the interview, Peggy faced yet another test. She responded to her granddaughter's death with strength, love, and empathy. Her spiritual beliefs were affirmed by her actions.

"My granddaughter was an hour old when she died. I will never forget when my daughter told me the baby was dead. This was a real test for me. There was no time for planning; it just happened totally unexpectedly. Usually when someone dies you have some time to work through your feelings. Instead, this perfect-looking baby was suddenly gone. I could have really framed this in a negative way, and at first I thought, Enough is enough, why more death and illness in my life? Then I realized this is not about me and that I have a lot of strengths that I can give to my daughter now. I had to pull out every bit of spiritual energy I could draw on. I had learned to focus on what is important to me; at the time of my granddaughter's death what was important was to be loving and empathetic and compassionate and strong. And also to realize that it hurt very badly and it was horrible. That was the first time my spiritual strength was there right from the beginning, and I thought that was a measure of how far I have come spiritually in the past two years since I have been diagnosed HIV positive. I had been working on these issues and it sounded good when I talked about it, but my

beliefs had not been tested like this. I had never been that close to death before; I had kept it off to the side before. I feel a connection to my granddaughter; I felt her presence in the room. I believe she was here as long as she needed to be here. She had an incredible impact in the hour she was alive. She created a lot of change in the family, drew so many family members together. She gave my daughter and her husband an opportunity to grow and come closer to each other. I knew that it was not the quantity but the quality of life that matters. That really helps me deal with my sickness.

"I believe that I put myself in my family in order to learn my lessons. I picked Catholicism because I needed to develop my own inner strength and go beyond Catholicism and connect with a much more positive spirituality that was true for me instead of beliefs imposed from the outside. I have learned that you don't have to suffer. With AIDS there is a lot of suffering in connection with the illness but not because the suffering itself is the way to get closer to God. I have learned to feel the pain and that actually experiencing the pain reduces the pain. I think that the pain is ever-present, but I have so many other things to think about. I look at the pain as a guide to see if my life is out of balance."

When faced with the greatest tests in her life, Peggy developed an explanation of suffering that moved beyond the Catholicism she had learned as a child. Some of us will find that the teachings of our religion will support us through stressful times. Others will need to adapt the teachings to give meaning and support in times of turmoil and adversity.

Making Meaning

Begin this exercise by affirming one way that your spirituality or your religion helps you through life. Then consider the teachings of your religion about pain and adversity. First think about the religion of your childhood. If your religious affiliation has changed, also think about the teachings of the religion you are affiliated with now. How is pain explained? Is there responsibility placed for adversity? If so, how and upon whom? What does misfortune mean? Are there guidelines for living with adversity? Are there guidelines for alleviating suffering? As you think about these questions, consider whether the answers seem helpful and reflect your experience and understanding.

Peggy immediately reframed her illness as an opportunity for spiritual growth. Sometimes the spiritual deepening potential of a difficult situation is obvious. At other times, we need to search for it.

From Challenge to Opportunity

Remember one difficult experience from your past. Choose an experience in which you sense a healing has already occurred. For example, perhaps you went through a divorce or had an illness. What was your experience? Think about what you did. How did you feel and think about the situation?

Did this experience build your self-trust? your courage? your compassion? What about other inner resources? If you feel some regret about how you dealt with the situation, take some time now to clarify how you might deal with a similar situation in the future. Remember, it is always easier to know the best course of action with hindsight. Practice forgiveness toward yourself or toward others if you have lingering feelings of resentment. Affirm the strength and spiritual direction that guided you through this experience. Remind yourself that you can get through difficulties and that difficulties can deepen your spirituality.

How do we live a spiritual life in a world riddled with domination and abuse? How do we maintain energy and hope in the face of pain and suffering? How do we find time for spirituality in a busy, scheduled life? These are questions you must answer for yourself. Remember, this is the work of a lifetime. Be gentle yet committed. In that gentleness you are in partnership with yourself and with your spiritual journey.

As you read on, you will explore the areas of spiritual connection in your life. These moments of connection may answer some of your lingering questions. As you continue forward on your spiritual journey, you can create a future that is spiritually nourishing and joyful. You will find more and more opportunities for spirituality in your daily life.

Acknowledge the work you have done to heal spiritual alienation and to transform spiritual obstacles. For most of us, this is the more difficult work and the reading and exercises to follow will be more pleasant. However, the work you have done has paved the way for greater spiritual connection. Acknowledge your efforts and your willingness in whatever way feels best to you.

Integration

Take a little while to remember the work you have done in this chapter. Think about the ideas that you read about. Remember the exercises you worked with.

1. Recall any important events that came to light while working with this material. Add them to your time line. (See page 48.)

2. Think about the ideas presented, and throw away any ideas that do not fit. Put them on your compost heap. (See page 38.)

3. Check to see if there is anything else you wish to note in your spiritual journal. You might also want to reread some of what you have written.

4. Think about whether there is more work to be done with any of the material. Think about how you might want to do this. For example, you might want to work on the exercises some more later or discuss the issues with a support person, in therapy, or with a support group.

5. Appreciate yourself for the work you have done. Give gratitude for healing and spiritual renewal.

Seeking
Spiritual Connection

II

Introduction

As you revisited the past, remembering times of spiritual alienation and exclusion, most likely you also recalled experiences of connection, when you felt spiritually in touch and validated. These are the experiences we wish to bring forth now. Highlighting these experiences will increase awareness of your authentic spirituality. Celebrating these moments will foster a reconnection to your spiritual gifts.

This lap of the journey is often enjoyable. When a woman connects with the truth of her spiritual experience, there is a sacred moment of recognition. Energy flows. Sparks fly. New possibilities are born. People come together and things get accomplished. The path beneath our feet feels welcoming and supportive. We notice beautiful sights and pleasant sounds along the way. We spend time in communion with others. We travel through a deep and powerful channel. We are going home.

For some, spiritual connection occurs within the context of religion. Probably all religions, at some point, touch the core of spiritual truth. Rituals access deep feelings through engaging our senses; the sound of ancient music, the pungent smell of incense, colorful robes, the reflection of candlelight. Religious observance often creates a feeling of connection. This feeling may foster a supportive bond between members of the same religious community. If a family has practiced similar religious observances and ritual for centuries, a spiritual connection may be felt with one's ancestors.

For others, spiritual connection happens outside organized religion: moments of deep communion with family or friends; moments spent in harmony with the earth, the sea, the sky; creative experiences in which we give birth to the unknown and unformed; moments of deep inner knowing.

133

Sometimes memories of spiritual connection have been temporarily forgotten. At the time they occur we feel their power and meaning, but often with the passing of time their importance is diminished. In some cases this is due to the context in which they happened. There may have been a feeling of shame connected with the experience if it occurred outside our religion of origin and didn't conform to the teachings of our parents. Or we may simply have been embarrassed by the intensity of feeling induced. All too often our experiences and insights were discounted and belittled by others as well as ourselves.

Connection is the experience of being in relationship; it implies being in a state of rapport, feeling an affinity. Connection feels good. We feel warm inside; our breath deepens; we can feel the life force moving through our body. When we feel connected, our life seems to have greater meaning and purpose. We become empowered. This is not the power of dominance. We move beyond self-interest into communion with the world around us.

A deep sense of connection can be felt with anyone or anything. Connection can be an opening to our innermost self, to one another, to God/Goddess, or to life itself. What seems to be essential is the desire to intimately experience another person, or another reality. As we connect spiritually, something happens that words cannot adequately describe. Seemingly by chance we are touched by a power larger and more encompassing than ourselves. We connect with our innate spiritual wisdom. We become greater and more beautiful than we were before.

As we move forward on our spiritual journey, let us consider which connections we wish to deepen. What direction do we want our spiritual journey to take? Which pathways do we want to explore? This part of the workbook will help you uncover and recover images, tools, and practices to support your ongoing spiritual journey.

Nelly shares her special connection to the Passover holiday, as a child and then again in her adult life.

A STORY FROM NELLY

Passover 1958. *We are gathered around my grandma's large oval table; the setting looks both beautiful and familiar. The food is on our red glass Passover dishes, which are only used during Passover. I love to hold these dishes before my eyes and see the world cast in rosy hues. I am encircled by the ritual Passover foods, each with its own symbolic meaning. I am told this year and every year why these foods are on the table and why we celebrate Passover. I am once again told the story of Passover, the story of the liberation of the Jews from slavery.*

I look around and see some new, unfamiliar faces at the table. These people are dark-skinned. My grandma explains, "On the holidays, we welcome all Jews to our table; no one need be alone on Passover." My life is usually filled with people who look more like me. I am curious and excited to share this holiday with people so different.

Passover 1984. A hundred or so people gather in a large hall for a women's and children's Passover celebration that my Jewish friends and I have organized. The mood is festive as the kitchen fills with many different potluck dishes—special ritual foods like matzo, hard boiled eggs, and horseradish—and everyday foods like chicken soup and salad. Passover is the celebration of spring and the story of the Jewish people's liberation.

We have rewritten the Haggadah, the book used for the Passover seder ritual. We adapt the ritual to make it meaningful to the women who gather, women from many different religious backgrounds. I feel a deep connection to my sisters as we read the traditional stories and imbue them with new interpretations. The story of Passover makes meaning out of pain and suggests a path toward freedom.

After the ritual dinner, the celebration moves into full swing. I lead the group in circle and line dances. I feel exhilarated as I jump and twist to the minor tones of Israeli and Yiddish music.

Passover 1993. I celebrate Passover this spring as I have each year. This year it is small celebration. Passover is an opportunity to share my culture with my partner, who is Italian and was raised Catholic. Just like many Jews, I work to maintain my cultural and religious identity within an interreligious and intercultural relationship.

This year, my two-year-old friend is the honored guest. Jewish children have a central role in the Jewish seder. At two years old, she is not yet able to read the four traditional Passover questions, though in her own way she asks why this night is different from all other nights. We tell her about her Jewish roots.

I feel chills running up and down my spine as we read from the Haggadah and interpret its relevance in our lives today. "The story of the Jews leaving Egypt means that each of us must break the shackles of narrow-mindedness that bind us to ignorance and hatred." I suggest that each of us contemplate the ways we feel shackled by narrow-mindedness and our vision for liberation. In this way we support one another to move forward, out of our own personal enslavement.

A STORY FROM CAROL

As a child I spent much of my time playing outside in the woods behind our house. It was a magical place for me. I felt so empowered in the woods. I could be my own person. My friends and I built forts with secret hiding places among the scrub oak and blackberry bushes, where sometimes I hid out, talking to the squirrels and birds. My favorite pastime was playing "hero." My friends and I would imagine that we were under the threat of some impending doom. I always knew what to do to save the day. I would receive a secret message of what to do to guarantee our safety. My plans for escape could come from the animals, "voices" in trees, or messages in the clouds as they passed overhead. I don't know if I had heard of Joan of Arc at that young age, but thinking about this today I see similarities: her heroic temperament and the messages and direction she received from her Voices. I was so open that I could see signs everywhere, in the swarming of bees and the flight of a bird. I would perch myself high in the apple tree and survey the surrounding area. Then after I had thoroughly contemplated the situation, I would go charging off, my little friends behind me, to a secret cave or a magical grove where no one could touch us. It was wonderful to feel so connected to my environment. There was always the possibility that anything could hold meaning.

Getting Started

In order to bring yourself into clearer connection with your spirituality, we suggest you try the following exercise. It can help in making your transition from disconnection to connection and enliven some pleasant memories.

Take a few moments to become grounded and comfortable. You may wish to use Grounding 3, Become a Tree, on page 12. Remember a time when you felt your spirituality. This can be anywhere, in any circumstances. Hold the memory for a moment. Feel the energy of the connection to yourself and something beyond yourself. When you are ready, gently let it go and return to yourself.

Ask yourself the following questions and contemplate your responses—now, or whenever you have the time. Your answers will provide clues to new directions for your spiritual journey.

What were the conditions that allowed for the connection?
Exactly what was I doing at the time it occurred?
Did the connection I recalled occur within or outside organized religion?
How would I describe the feeling? Is this feeling something I would like
  to experience more often?

As you journey to unearth and revive moments of spiritual connection, you will be nurtured by your efforts. In your remembering, you create the conditions for spiritual connection to be rekindled. However, because each of us is different, we will open to our spirituality in our own way. Spirituality can be thought of as a many-faceted diamond, each facet reflecting the authentic, yet unique, spirituality of each of us. Connecting with our spirituality, we become more fully who we are. Being more fully who we are leads us to an infinite variety of possibilities. The inherent beauty of each soul is reflected by her quest.

Read through the narrative, stories, and exercises in your own way and in your own time. Some pathways to connection will feel familiar. Begin where you feel most comfortable. Each section is an opportunity to explore your spirituality from a different perspective. We offer you the opportunity to stretch yourself and to attain deeper grounding in that which is already familiar.

Experiencing Nature

6

"There was a time in my life when I was quite unhappy. There were nights when I didn't sleep well. I would wake up early, just before dawn, and take my troubles with me down to the lake.

"I remember standing quietly at the water's edge waiting for the sunrise. There was a special stillness in the air. It was so quiet. And then the light came, subtle, almost colorless at first. Soon soft feathers of yellow and pink were streaking across the horizon. The air began to stir, making patterns on the water, rustling the leaves. I felt myself coming alive, as my heart opened to greet the morning. Soon my problems seemed to lose their power over me."

Gifts of Nature

The quiet serenity of nature, the awesome beauty, the profound mysteries—we begin our journey of spiritual connection with nature because the natural world is a place where girls can feel whole, safe, and nurtured and a place where, as women, we can return for spiritual sustenance and inspiration. How often have we said to ourselves, "If I could only get out into nature for a few days?" to avoid the distraction and confusion of man-made priorities and systems. We go to nature in search of a more natural approach to life, a way of being in the world that is calmer, more centered, an approach that will help us reconnect with ourselves and with our essence. In a setting of natural beauty we feel appreciative, even in awe of our surroundings. Our mood is elevated. It is as if a power greater than ourselves surrounds us. After a time spent close to nature we often feel refreshed and renewed.

When asked about moments of spiritual connection, women recount experiences in nature, stories of relating intimately to Mother Earth. Women describe how their spirituality is awakened and continues to grow through their relationship to nature.

Angela remembers living close to a natural setting that provided her with the tranquility she needed to connect with her spiritual self.

> *"When I was a child I lived near a creek. Being with the creek was a powerful piece of my spirituality. When you are outside, in nature, your body changes, as does your consciousness. Sitting next to the creek, I learned how to be quiet. As an adult, I now have the ability to be quiet and to hear what is really going on around me. If you spend some time with nature, it allows for an awakening about the mystery of life."*

When we are young, there is sometimes an older person who helps us connect with our spirituality. Annie learned to love and respect nature through family values imparted to her by her mother.

> *"I spent a lot of time in the big persimmon tree out in my front yard. The tree was my getaway place, where I could be alone and contemplate life. Mama taught me how to sit in the boughs of the tree without hurting them. She didn't allow me to build a tree house, because she didn't want me to hurt the tree by putting nails through it. She taught me a reverence for nature at an early age that never left me."*

Janice's spirituality was awakened on long walks in the woods with her grandfather.

> *"Grandpa loved the earth. He taught me about the sacredness of nature; I guess you could say I'm a nature worshiper. My first deep connection with nature was our mushroom hunting together, walking quietly through the woods searching for what he called 'nature's little treasures.' It seemed a miracle to me that these amazing forms could pop up from nowhere overnight, appearing in the middle of a vacant field or on the side of an old rotting log. I think it was then that I began to truly appreciate nature's gifts. Grandpa taught me which mushrooms were edible, which were used for healing, and which ones people admired simply for their beauty. They came in so many different shapes and colors: bright reds, deep chestnut browns. The more I observed the mushrooms and learned their names and qualities, the more I loved them. This experience really opened my heart to the natural world."*

Nature has been described as the controlling force of our planet, providing a structure, a system on which our existence is based. Rhythms and cycles of nature are sometimes felt on a very deep level within us. It has long been known that the ocean's tides are the effect of the moon pulling on the earth. Is the moon not pulling on us as well? Often we feel ourselves responding to nature's rhythms, whether it be the phases of the moon or the changing weather. Have you ever felt the effect of the changing cycles of the moon? These patterns in nature can bring order and meaning to our lives.

The power of nature to create beauty, to heal, and to destroy is beyond the control of human beings. The destructiveness of a hurricane or a flood leaves many in awe. Farmers are aware of the life-sustaining power of nature as she brings rain to a land threatened by drought. We see nature's creative potential in the regeneration of a forest destroyed by raging fire.

A personal experience with the power of nature can affirm our connection with spiritual reality. Through her cycles, the earth never allows us to forget the inevitability of change. The earthquake of 1989 in San Francisco encouraged Bridget to focus more intently on her spiritual journey.

> *"As I relate to the recent earthquake, I am reminded that the earth is a living entity. After this natural experience, I realize I need to take time to relate to my inner experience of God and the earth."*

Although not all of us have had opportunities to experience nature out of doors, almost all of us have had some opportunity to know her mystery. Watching a seedling develop into a plant in a pot on the kitchen windowsill, for example, or watching kittens being born are experiences with nature that can open the door to spiritual connection.

A STORY FROM NELLY

As a young child I remember spending what seemed like endless hours staring at patterns of dust swirling in the air. I was mesmerized by the dance of dust as it glittered in the sunlight. What was I searching for in these patterns? There seemed to be a natural order there. I looked carefully, with all my attention. I felt consoled by the sense of order. I also felt a deep inner longing. I wished my body could move with the same abandon as each dust particle. I wanted to know that order in every cell of my body. Staring at those patterns, I came into harmony with the wild yet orderly dance of the dust.

When I think about my experience with the dust patterns now, it seems like a perfect metaphor for my understanding and relationship with the spiritual. I believe the spiritual realm is always visible, but only when I have the time and attention to look. My God is the cosmic order and pattern found in nature. My spiritual practices put me in touch with that pattern. My deepest longing is to feel at one with this cosmic pattern.

Ruth grew up in New York City in a small apartment. She describes her family as a working-class family with little time or money for excursions to the country.

"Life in Manhattan was busy; family life was hard. We really had to keep moving to survive."

At the age of seventy-seven, Ruth explains the formative influence nature had on her in her youth.

"I remember when I was eighteen and graduating from high school. I went on a camping trip in the Canadian wilderness. We actually carried our canoes from one lake to another. We caught fish in the streams. I had never done anything like this before. It was thrilling. The deep silence, and then the occasional night noises—the hoot owl. But mostly I remember the stars, especially the shooting stars. I had never seen the stars like that. In the complete dark they seemed so close. There were millions of them.

"I was from the city, thinking that I knew a lot, but I realized my insignificance and my ignorance before that vast starry sky. It felt like I had passed a milestone in understanding. I wasn't the same afterward. I saw things through different eyes.

"I never had a room of my own, or a place to get away from everyone. I never had any personal things of my own. In the vast expansiveness of nature I was inspired to move beyond my limitations. If there was so much more out there than I had ever known, then maybe there was more to me."

Zoe's early childhood relationship with the earth was an embodied experience. Although managing to maintain a connection with nature throughout her life, she remembers a challenge to that relationship bordering on censorship when she was a child.

"When I was young, I was with the earth as much as I could be. I climbed trees. I would run around without my shoes. I went around without wearing a shirt because it helped me feel closer to the earth and in tune with nature. I remember being angry when I was six years old and was told I had to wear a shirt. If I

had been a boy, I could have run around without my shirt for the rest of my life! That pissed me off. It didn't make sense to me."

Zoe grew up in a home without a religious base and as a teenager discovered an earth-based spirituality. As an adult Zoe continues to remain close to nature through her work.

"I spend a lot of my time working with trees. I was a tree planter and now I am a tree pruner. When I was a tree planter, I spent periods of time living close to nature far out in the woods."

Although Zoe now lives in a city, she is in close relationship with nature.

"I prune the city trees. Even when I am driving around during the day, I am looking at the trees. Trees are my work and my inspiration."

To reexperience and deepen your connection with nature we suggest beginning where you are. Slowing down to simply look at what you are actually doing can be the safest, yet most fruitful exploration. Often reestablishing connection is about looking carefully at what is, and nurturing it. We have provided a guided exercise to help you in that process.

Where I Am Now

You may want to begin with Grounding 2, I Am My Breath, on page 12 to bring you more deeply into yourself. After watching your breathing for few minutes, go for a walk inside your home. Look for evidence of your connection with nature. Notice pictures on the walls, objects on shelves and tables. Which ones are images or objects of nature? Do they feel alive and powerful? You may want to rearrange them, or even discard something if its meaning is lost to you.

Choose one image or object of nature with which you would like to deepen your connection. It could be a photograph you took and especially liked or a shell you found at the beach. Place it in a central location where you will see it often. Make a promise to yourself that you will spend some time with it each day.

If you feel a lack of nature's presence in your life, you might want to consider adding an important object of nature to your home environment. Anything will do, as long as you feel it speaks to you personally. Here are some suggestions:

A poster or graphic
A large plant
A stone or rock
A weaving

Nature as Healer

"Nature is my healer. She renews me spiritually and feeds my soul."

Why is it that nature serves as an easy entry point to spiritual connection for women? Perhaps it is because nature carries a healing quality within her. We are truly mothered and provided for by nature. When the apple tree puts out fruit, we are nourished. As the sun rises each morning of our lives, we are reassured and made hopeful. Mother Earth has protected and nourished us since the beginning of existence. Women look to nature as a spiritual friend who can be there in our hour of need.

For Darlene, her relationship with nature compensated for the lack of physical closeness in family relationships she felt as a child. She felt as if nature physically enfolded her body,

"Much of my nurturing came from nature. I lived with my grandparents, who were of a generation when people didn't show affection. My mother was taught that too much affection would spoil me. I knew that she loved me, but there wasn't much of a physical enfolding. It was only when I was out in nature that I felt held. It was as though the trees and bushes surrounded me with their physical presence and I relaxed into their arms."

Helen grew up with a lot of adversity, her family poor, her father an alcoholic. She was sexually abused by her priest. As Helen struggles in her healing process, she notes the power of the natural world to move her beyond personal issues.

"I remember the feeling of awe as a child watching the stars and being fascinated by the shapes of flowers. These experiences put my life and feelings in perspective. Today I still have a tendency to take myself too seriously. I can get easily jerked out of shape. When I experience awe in nature, my personal concerns just don't matter so much anymore."

Linda was sexually abused as a child. She looked to nature's patterns and predictability for comfort when people were inconsistent and hurtful to her. She found trustworthy companionship in the natural world.

"When the whole world would seem topsy-turvy to me, I would look at a tree and at the ground. All those things that a tree is and does are real and solid. You can trust a tree to continue to be a tree. The cycles of the seasons and the moon—they are all reliable when the rest of the world isn't."

Picture a time when you felt down and something in the natural environment lifted your spirits. Think of a time you felt moved by the beauty of your surroundings. These experiences were moments of healing. However brief they may have been, they altered your state of mind and supported your sense of well-being.

By putting our caring for the natural environment into action, we deepen our connection with nature. As we care for a plant, for example, we come into intimate contact with the plant and its healing energies. And as we nourish it, it nourishes us.

Sylvia has a very nurturing and giving relationship with nature. She also feels a need to protect her.

"My spirituality deepens through spending time alone in nature. I take daily walks in the hills to renew my spirit. I have learned to open beyond the boundaries of my physical body to nature. At these times I feel I am nature. A few years ago my partner and I bought a large piece of land in the country. I feel that we are the caretakers of this land and all the creatures living there. I take care of my land, and the land takes care of me."

Nurturing Our Environment

Create a relationship with a plant outside your home by giving it some special attention. Talk to it when you walk by. Send it love from your kitchen window. Maybe buy it some fertilizer, or give it a good pruning. Make sure it's watered.

Pay attention to the relationship you are developing with the plant. As you care for this plant, do you feel you get back anything in return? You might write about this experience in your journal.

The healing power of nature rests in our ability to understand and connect with nature in deep ways. The energies and patterns we see in nature, we can also feel within ourselves. Healing is often about coming to honor the natural cycles and rhythms we discover within ourselves. Healing is being who we really are, coming into contact with our true nature, making space for ourselves, allowing ourselves to be. It is about having the faith to trust that who we really are is basically good.

Being with Our Natural Cycles

Contemplation. Contemplate the rising and setting of the sun, nightfall and dawn. Contemplate the changing tides, high tide and ebb. Think about the ever-changing winds. In what way are you like them? How is your energy right now? Is it more like sunrise or sunset? Remember that feelings and events come and go. Feel how you are connected to the patterns of nature. Feel the natural cycles of your life. Here are some activities that can help strengthen your connection to your natural changes.

Activities to try:

1. Mark the cycles of the moon on your daily planner or calendar.
2. Chart your menstrual cycle.
3. Watch your daily energy pattern and see if you are a "morning person" or an "evening person."
4. Take your temperature every morning before rising. Notice any changes.
5. Try letting your appetite decide when you will eat. When are you usually hungry?
6. Trace your moods in your journal. Notice how they come and go.

There are places in nature that can hold the key to spiritual connection for us. For example, there can be a calm familiarity about the land or elements of the natural world in which we grew up. Tina was raised in the woods of the Midwest, and generations of her family have hiked in those woods.

"Walking in the woods was part of my upbringing. I meet my spiritual needs now by walking in the woods."

Even though Tina now lives near the coast, she never grew accustomed to the ocean.

"I am afraid of the ocean. I have never gotten used to all that power and all that water. I still prefer to hike the mountain trails."

Andrea made a conscious decision to return to live in the natural world of her childhood, an aid on her spiritual journey.

"Part of my spiritual path is about the Goddess and learning to love the earth again. My deepest memories and metaphors of the earth are from my childhood: the way the land looks, the hillsides, the oak tress, the Spanish moss. I came back home to the country where I grew up and in doing so got more in touch with my spirituality."

Making a pilgrimage to the land where we were raised or returning to special places that inspired and supported us spiritually can strengthen those memories and reinforce them in our consciousness. Whether we really return to these places or travel only in memory, we can take with us the lessons learned from the natural world and integrate them into our daily lives.

Canyon Sam, writer and now student of Buddhism, made a trip to Asia in search of her cultural roots and a deeper spirituality. She shares an inspirational moment during a trek up the Rongbuck Valley in Tibet that leads to Mt. Everest, or as it is properly called, Chomalungma, Mother Goddess of the Earth.

"As I moved into the valley I stopped talking much; my mind got clear and light, like the lapis sky opening up above the high desert plateau. My consciousness became quiet like the soft, whistling wind that blew down from the Himalayas. My body felt brown, solid, grounded like the ancient, weathered cliffs above me. As I walked my heart was full and satisfied like a day when the bird songs were happy and clear, and the yak bells tinkled through the pale purple dust, letting everyone know that the mountains would sleep well, and we could too."

Diane Mariechild, spiritual teacher and author of *Motherwit*, makes a pilgrimage to a large wilderness reserve. There in the meadows she encounters the powers of Mother Nature in full expression. As she opens herself to the forces of nature, Diane moves beyond her individuality to a feeling of connecting with all that is.

"I go to the woods and ocean of Inverness to meditate often, to be closer to Mother Nature. On one visit my friend Sharon and I walked Pierce Point Trail. It was during the tule elk mating season. We spent several hours sitting in the

meadow watching the elk from less than sixty feet away. There was a herd of fifty females presided over by one huge bull with a great rack. The mating call is intense. It's loud and deep, bearing a slight similarity to a horse's neigh but more primal. When the elk bellowed, the sound vibrated through me with such intensity that I became that sound. My attention was riveted to the herd due to the intensity of the energy exchange between the females and male. I became so focused, the world dropped away. I was aware of my own body and looking through my own eyes, but neither my body nor my eyes belonged to me anymore. They opened out to include the whole world. It felt as though Sharon and I were in the center of the herd, part of the whole scene, the wind, the sun, the golden grass, the blue water of Tomales Bay below us. We lay in the tall grass among the thistles, totally absorbed."

Your Place in Nature

Begin by doing Grounding 1, In the Arms of Mother Earth, on page 11. As your relax into the earth and feel supported, imagine that you are actually in a place in nature where you have connected in the past. Look around. Use your senses to fully experience this place and the feelings of sustenance it brings you. What images are before you? sounds? smells? End your meditation in gratitude for this experience with nature.

Is a place like this accessible to you in the area where you live now? If not, it may be possible to find a place that evokes the same feelings. Make a plan to discover and visit such places.

Activities to try:

1. Get a map of your town and plan a short visit to local parks and recreational areas. Pick one each weekend.

2. Note the trees and birds present within a block of your home. Become familiar with them. Learn their names.

3. Consider investigating your spiritual relationship with nature in an atmosphere relatively untouched by human intervention. Plan a visit to a national park or wilderness area. Our national park system provides many examples of nature's power and beauty. If possible, plan a visit to the site of a particularly strong manifestation of the power of nature—a volcano, a waterfall, a canyon.

4. If appropriate, take a trip to the place you grew up. Rediscover feelings of connection with nature you knew as a child.

Animals often become our natural companions and spiritual teachers. Annie, who was raised on a farm, has always felt a deep connection to animals and is trying to sustain this connection in the city.

> *" I am happy living in the city. I just cherish the animals that I live with now. I find that I cultivate very special relationships with them. I feel I can communicate with my animals and that they understand me on a very deep level. My sense is that animals are here to serve us, to help us see more clearly, to help us love ourselves. They are emissaries of unconditional love."*

Sometimes nature's creatures surprise us with their presence, adding beauty and inspiration to our lives. When Kim moved from the city to the suburbs, she and her husband chose a house with half an acre of land behind it rather than a small plot. She is glad they did, because she is thrilled to find that the animals come to visit her.

> *"I am particularly moved by the deer. They come after dusk to sleep and to feed on the tall grasses. I love it that they feel safe on our little hillside. At night I think of the deer outside sleeping peacefully, and I feel safe too. In the morning when I'm out watering the plants, I find their forms traced in the grass, their sleeping places from the night before. I saw a doe and her baby deer as they left very early one morning. Even after they'd gone, I still felt the blessing of their presence."*

Julie Wester, a teacher of Vipassana Mediation and Buddhism, talks about what it means to her to "live in the world of the spirit." She discusses her trip to the Monterey Aquarium to visit the jellyfish.

> *"These translucent creatures, which before I had only seen collapsed in heaps where they had washed up on the beach, here can be seen floating in their full grace and beauty. The aquarium is a very busy place full of hundreds of people dashing around looking at fish. But there in the midst of the rush I found myself transfixed, kneeling on the bench placed before the jellyfish tank. I felt that I was in a temple, in a sacred place, in the presence of the most amazing simple being, whose whole life seemed to consist of breathing and floating. . . breathing and floating. . . reflecting the inhale and the exhale, taking in completely, and then letting go in total relaxation.*

> *"The jellyfish has become for me a reminder of the possibility of relaxing into the simplicity of life, in which there is nothing more important than to breathe and float, in the midst of the changes."*

Finding Your Nature Image

Begin by using Grounding 2, I Am My Breath, on page 12. When you are ready, ask your inner guidance to show you an image of an object in nature or an animal that is sacred to you. Allow some time for the image to present itself. Ask yourself if you feel comfortable with what is presented. If you do, spend time examining it closely. Notice the feeling quality of your experience. When you have completed the meditation, contemplate the idea of strengthening your connection to nature by bringing this object or animal more into your life today.

Activities to try. If the object was a stone, for example, you might search for a similar stone to keep on your altar or in your pocket. If your animal was an elephant, you might go to the zoo to visit one or find a powerful image of an elephant to keep nearby.

Experiencing the elements—fire, water, air, and earth—can provide a deep spiritual connection. Carol tells of her investigation of the water element and the God she discovers within the waters.

A STORY FROM CAROL

When I was a child the sea was my confidant and adviser. I would sit on a cliff above the bay staring out at the water with questions in my mind. Sometimes the sea would offer wise and helpful advice.

As an adult I have a more distant relationship with the sea. I am aware of her dangers as well as her gifts. Often she seems wild and forbidding. Once at the seashore I asked in prayer for help with a problem. As I stood there in the waves, a Portuguese man-of-war emerged from her depths and stung me badly. I remember feeling hurt and confused as I tried to put meaning to this painful incident.

A few months ago I was walking on the beach at sunset. As I gazed out at the receding waters, golden light revealed images in the rocks. I saw the body of a woman traced in one of the stones. It felt like a gift, a renewal of my connection with the sea. I took the stone home and placed it in my garden.

While in Hawaii recently, I swam out to greet a family of dolphins that had come to play in the bay. As I swam I noticed that the sea felt gentler and softer than usual. I relaxed, feeling the ocean as I moved through her, feeling my body glide through the waves. The sea became a vast and powerful entity—surrounding me, supporting me, keeping me afloat. I let go of lingering fears and swam effort-lessly toward the dolphins.

As I experience the different energies of the sea, I experience the many faces of the Goddess. She holds me within a reality where apparent opposites come into relationship with one another and with the whole. For me, she comprises all that is natural and sacred.

The Four Elements: Contemplation

Contemplate the four elements: air, earth, fire, water. Visualize them before you. Which element feels the most interesting to you? What are its qualities? What it is that draws your interest?

Activities to try:

1. Sit outdoors one afternoon and watch the patterns of the weather change. See if you can notice changes in the drops of the rain or in the light from the sun. Look for changes in the winds and clouds.

2. Get to know the earth on which you walk. Dig up the earth. See how many rocks you find. Notice if there are creatures living in this earth. Hold the earth in your hands; notice the texture of the soil. Is it moist or dry? How does it smell? Contemplate the idea that you are holding Mother Earth in your hands.

3. Sit quietly before a campfire or a fire in a fireplace or a wood-burning stove. Open yourself to the warmth of the fire. Let it penetrate your being.

4. During your morning shower, feel the warm water as it comes into contact with your body. Contemplate how it soothes your muscles. As you rinse off, feel its cleansing power. Feel the water washing away your tiredness, preparing you for the new day.

Hallie Iglehart Austen is a teacher of women's spirituality, and author of *WomanSpirit* and *The Heart of the Goddess.* Her connection with spirituality comes through what she calls the Goddess or the Sacred Feminine, and much of her spiritual experience reflects an intimate understanding of and connection with Nature. Hallie talks about the threat she feels to the earth and her spiritual commitment to protect her.

"In the mid-1970s I met with a Hawaiian woman kahuna. She gave me an assignment, and it's still with me over fifteen years later. I am still practicing this and trying to pass it on to other people. She told me to go to three different places in the islands and listen. One of these was a very large banyan tree at a fancy hotel in Honolulu. I found the hotel and sat under the banyan tree. I was dressed in white yoga pants and a white top. Even though I felt conspicuous, I sat there with my hands on this tree and my eyes closed. Soon a group of men came by. They started laughing at me and making nasty jokes and comments with an ominous tone to them. I could hear them very clearly even though I was trying to listen to the tree, which was something I had never done before. I was feeling threatened by these men, but I just persisted. I kept focusing on the banyan tree, remaining open, listening to the tree, and letting the threats remain on my periphery. After about fifteen minutes, one of them said to the others, 'Oh, just leave her alone, we have to get out of here.' I realize that was a test of my ability to focus in the face of fear. It was a good learning experience."

Years later Hallie finds that her connection to nature has deepened. She spends many hours listening and interpreting the voice of the earth, the voice of Gaia, the Goddess who personified Earth for the Greeks.

"Recently what I have heard Nature saying is a cry for help. I started hearing this in the mid-1980s when I moved to Point Reyes—a 60,000-acre national seashore. I started to go out and sit on the land. I would just sit and listen. Eventually, to my surprise, I really did hear a distinct voice. It was not a voice outside of me but a voice that came through me. I heard the voice of the earth, what I now call the voice of Gaia. I now call this practice 'listening to Gaia.' I heard her tremendous cry, her great cry for help from the sea, from the air, from the earth. I was very deeply moved by this. It really propelled me to enlarge my focus from empowering women to empowering anyone who can help the earth. This is the crucial thing we need to do now. After this experience I started to listen to Gaia more, asking her what I should do. Following her guidance, I started encouraging and teaching other people to listen to the earth as well. It is not easy to get past mental chatter and the busyness of our everyday lives—even our fantasies of what the earth has to say. It is important to know that we can all come to hear what we recognize as the authentic voice of the earth, which for me is the voice of Gaia."

Try watching for the influence of nature in your daily life. Discover whether you feel a connection to the natural elements and how you might experience that connection.

Nature in Your Daily Life

Here are some suggestions that may help foster a deeper connection to nature and your spirituality. Try the ones that seem most interesting to you.

Activities to try:

1. Visit places near where you live—a river, a stream, the seashore. During your time there you might want to use Grounding 3, Become a Tree, to help you make yourself more fully present to the experience of your spirituality in nature.

2. Plant a tree or a small garden.

3. Ask yourself what you can do to for an animal that may be close to you. Do the birds in your yard need feeding? What about any squirrels or raccoons that may be nearby? Living in a city does not mean that a raccoon won't be living under your front steps or a stray cat waiting at your door. Open your heart to the possibility of caring for the birds, animals, even insects in your environment. See where this leads you.

4. Try reading a book or renting a video about something in nature that has always captivated you.

5. Investigate the programs of environmental protection groups. Think about which environmental issues seems most important to you. Consider taking some action in support of the earth and your natural environment.

The practices of Native American spirituality often involve nature and the earth. Teresa is a Mexican-American woman of Indian descent. Her spiritual journey includes practices Indian people have shared with her since she was a child. In this story, Teresa describes her special healing relationship to nature. She had moved from New Mexico to California and felt uncomfortable about the move.

"I came out to California, and I felt homesick, like I didn't fit in. I was off balance, I felt dispirited."

This situation worsened, coming to a crisis point, and even though she could usually heal herself, she now needed someone else to come and work with her. On this day she met with an Indian couple who were to help her heal spiritually. Notice the emphasis on Mother Earth in her healing story.

"We met out at the Indian village on a Monday morning, early. It was pretty chilly, it must have been in November or December. This is a beautiful, spiritual place. It's just so peaceful there. You don't have to be with anybody. If you go early enough, as I did, the deer are real close to you—you can hear the birds and the mist, because there's always fog in that area. As you drive up, you know are entering a spiritual place, a place of prayer and of thanksgiving."

Teresa goes on to describe her healing experience in nature.

"The three of us sat down at a picnic table. I looked deep into the woman's eyes—it was a really intense connection there—and I said what I needed. I asked for healing for myself and my family. She suggested we go looking for a pepperwood tree. I use sage for my cleansing rituals; the people from this area use the pepperwood leaves and angelica roots more as their herbs for cleansing.

"What I was told on the spot was, 'You've been here all these years in the Bay Area, but have you asked permission to be in the area of the spirits, of the ancient ones?' and I said, 'No, nobody's ever told me such a thing. I've felt lonely and I've prayed to God and I've cried about that but never felt that I had entered a place without asking permission.' This was a whole new way of thinking for me. So she stayed with me and told me to walk with her some more.

"As we walked, she said, 'You appear to be of a sincere heart; I have some medicine for you.' This is God-given spirit or healing. As we walked, we gathered pepperwood leaves. That's the first time I got to experience working with these things. She said it was OK to gather them because they were being used in a good way. By then her husband had started a fire in the Roundhouse.

"This is the first time for me in a round house. I've been in tipis and gatherings in open spaces in the country and in hogans, but I had not been in a round house—it's a real experience, because they are underground. Even a sweat lodge is above ground. I believe sometimes they're made with mud on the riverbanks or with a willow tree, but here the round house has been put together halfway underground—it's a hole in the ground that's been covered with poles, and skins or canvas, and then mud and grass. When I first saw the round house, it looked like a little hill—I didn't know that underneath there is a complete room, a complete gathering place.

"As soon as I walked in, I was told I was to address the four directions. She did a prayer, acknowledging their traditions—she's Pomo and Miwok Indian, I think, and he's full-blooded Miwok. But the minute we stood by the fire in the cold, my *sense was, I am home. I did not understand what that meant exactly, but I was crying, not incredible sobbing, but just that stream of tears that, for months, I had not been able to let out. I wasn't crying for what was happening to me or my family, I was crying tears of joy, tears of coming home. Then I was told I could take my shoes off if I wanted to (the Miwok dance in their bare feet). I was feeling so at home, so relieved, that I just took my shoes off. I remember the earth was cold.*

"This is actually quite healing. It's real spiritual. It's a real touching way, a healing way. At my first sweat, I experienced a healing similar to this. You see, many years back, my mother abandoned me. At that time I thought I did not need mothering. But in the sweat lodge, I experienced Mother Earth holding me. I could feel my need for mothering, and I was grateful that the earth could provide what my mother could not. There in the Miwok Roundhouse I did not connect exactly in that way—it's just later on, through talks and the many times of going back to the Roundhouse, that I realized what I was feeling. It was the mother, Mother Earth, holding me again. My understanding of my abandonment is being healed by walking on this earth, by recognizing and acknowledging it. My healing and comfort in the Roundhouse came in standing on the earth, the place of prayer, where other people have left their prayers and their gifts. I felt I was home. They prayed for me with the pepperwood leaves and cleansed me, and we set the leaves to the fire to take our prayers to the creator.

"At the end, both of them asked me to do a blessing for them, because they knew that I carried prayer. Initially I thought, 'But I've been so shattered, so weak, so away from feeling my centeredness, how could I possibly?' But the minute I quieted down and asked for strength from the earth and from the Great Spirit, the words came. My healing was complete."

Teresa and Hallie both made a journey to a sacred place for healing and spiritual insight. Making a pilgrimage, or devotional journey to a sacred place, may be something to consider for yourself. If you are struggling with a question or a decision you must make, sometimes it is helpful to go to a powerful spot in nature. In a natural environment it can be easier to connect with your inner voice. You could make a trip to a place you knew as a child or a spot you feel called to in your adult life. Such a journey usually takes careful thought and preparation. Often it is done in consultation with a spiritual friend or teacher. Wherever you choose to go, approach your journey with an open heart and a willing mind.

A Spiritual Pilgrimage

Activities to try:

1. You may want to ask for blessings or offer a prayer as you enter the area.

2. Seek inspiration for a special affirmation you can use when at home again to connect you to this place and to your power.

3. You may find an object to take home as a reminder of your journey.

4. When you leave, you could offer gratitude to nature for your experiences there.

5. Leave time at home afterward to share your journey with family or friends.

6. Write about your feelings and experiences in your spiritual journal.

You may want to pause for a moment to integrate your experiences.

Integration

This exercise will help you to clarify the role nature has in your spiritual life. You may want to write out your response.

How has nature played a part in my spiritual journey?

Do I feel inspired to spend more time with nature? If I had to say what my favorite natural setting was, what would I choose?

What is one step I want to take to integrate nature into my life in a meaningful way?

Experiencing Beauty and Sensuality

7

"Is it not comforting to realize that beauty can provide a connection to the spiritual life, and that spirituality is not gained only through suffering or difficulty?"

We do not have to suffer to know the face of God. We can be spiritually uplifted by appreciation of the beauty in the world around us. In fact, much of our attraction to nature is caused by her breathtaking beauty and the feeling of happiness it brings.

We experience the beauty of our world through our senses. The melodious song of a bird, the smell of home cooking, a friend's smile, freshly fallen snow; these sense experiences are pleasing to us. When we like what we hear, smell, or see, we open to these sensations, and in doing so we open to the beauty of life. If our feeling of pleasure is strong and compelling enough, we may be transported to another realm of existence, expanded. Hearing beautiful music at a concert may open us to appreciation not only for the music but for the friends with whom we share the experience, the weather at the time, or whatever we encounter as we leave the concert hall. This blissful feeling may even extend to the belligerent taxi driver on the way home. As we allow beauty rather than ugliness to rule our lives, we expand our consciousness. We develop a sense of well-being, a more optimistic outlook on life.

All too often however, we find ourselves preoccupied, missing the beauty of our surroundings and sense experiences. We may jump into the shower in the morning in such a hurry that we hardly feel the caress of the warm water or the smooth, pleasant touch of the soap on our skin. To experience beauty in our lives all we have to do is be there for it.

When beautiful moments occur, try to acknowledge them. Next time you see a beautiful flower or feel the warmth of the sun on your skin, take time to smile to yourself. Take the time to acknowledge happiness as your birthright.

As healthy infants we are born with a natural appreciation and interest in our surroundings. Our world is filled with feeling and sensation. Take a moment to recall the face of a child as she stands before a thing of beauty, eyes open wide in wonder. How many experiences like this have we had that, although now forgotten, laid the basis for our connection with the world? These feelings encouraged spiritual connection. They created a love of life. Sometimes childhood moments of awe and wonder remain with us, reminding us of our ability to feel pleasure and experience beauty in our everyday lives. We experience this beauty through our five senses—the doors through which beauty enters.

Smell and Taste

Although perhaps not considered primary by some people, our senses of smell and taste influence our lives to a great extent. Can you remember the smell of the air in the place you grew up? or the taste of some special dish your mother made for the family?

These two senses may hold the key to pleasurable memories and experiences that produce feelings of wholeness and connection. Debbie grew up on Long Island about a mile from the bay, and after school she often rode her bike down to the water. She recalls the smell of the salt air, and how it still affects her today.

> *"After school I would ride down to the bay to renew myself. When I reached the top of the hill, suddenly I could smell the sea. What is it about the smell of the sea on the East Coast? It's so full, so much the sea. I could smell the clams and the mud you dig for them in, the fish swimming in the ocean, and the seaweed drifting on its surface. All that was contained in one breath, my one inhalation at the top of the hill. Today when I take off from work in the afternoon I often find myself heading for the coast. As my car turns that last corner on to the beach road, I begin to smell the sea. As soon as the salt air hits me, my whole body relaxes. My mind slows down. My consciousness changes, and I connect to myself again."*

Religious holidays provide wonderful opportunities to appreciate the sensual quality of our spirituality. As children, many of us experienced a pure and simple sensual joy when exposed to the sights, smells, tastes, and sounds of religious holidays. These memories can be sought out, relived, and reincorporated into our adult spirituality. Bridget's spiritual background includes much exposure to the sensuality of religious practice: places of worship of extraordinary design and color and strong spiritual images. Here she remembers her childhood church in Equador.

> *"We went downtown to the main cathedral where everyone from the town went, including the indigenous people. I loved it. I have vivid memories of being in church on All Souls' Day, among brown-skinned people with candles and incense. The indigenous people all talked out loud to God and the saints throughout the mass. They brought offerings of fruits and even doves to church."*

Bridget is also influenced by the great variety of smells and foods. For Bridget, going to the market was a sensual experience that deepened her spirituality.

> *"My grandmother spent hours choosing from mountains of vegetables and fruits that were in every phase of ripening. As a child, I was always underfoot where the crushed vegetables and fruits had been discarded. With my nose closer to the ground, my senses were permeated by the smell of rotting fruit. In the meat section the animals were whole and had the expression of their death. I could taste the blood in the air. We always ended our trip at the flower section, where we were washed clean by the aroma of thousands of flowers. For me, the marketplace was a spiritual experience of life, decay, and death."*

Today Bridget works at a mental health clinic in the United States. She incorporates the sensuality of her religious background into her work.

> *"I have the Virgin Mary up on the wall in my office, and my images of saints are there. Once in a while I put on my Indian music and sage the whole office. It gives me a sense of well-being"*

Appreciation of Beauty

Smell. Go to a store where incense and essential oils are sold. Sample the oil smells. Smell the incense through the wrapper. Identify the scent that smells most pleasurable to you, the one to which you are most attracted. Take it home and burn the incense ceremoniously. Sit quietly by and see if the scent has an affect on your mind. Rub a little of the oil on your skin, and see if during the day the scent has an effect on you.

Taste. Take a moment to think of any foods that you consume in a ceremonious manner. Here are some suggestions that you may or may not relate to:

> Vegetables grown in your own garden
> A special wine for a special occasion
> A roast pig
> Hot chocolate on a cold winter's afternoon
> Your mother's special dish at the holidays
> Challah bread
> Marshmallows at the campfire
> A wedding cake
> Chicken soup

Does the taste of these foods ever heighten a feeling of spiritual connection for you? Does the taste of food ever contribute to your sense of well-being and spiritual community?

Remember the Beauty, Guided Imagery. Close your eyes and allow your mind to drift back to a time you were particularly moved by a spiritual experience. (This can be related to your religion of origin, or apart from it.) Contemplate this moment. Can you feel a sense of awe and wonder? What is it about this experience that is most captivating? See what beauty is there; touch the objects if you can. Now take a moment to hear the sounds, tastes, and smells. When you think you have participated in this experience to the fullest, return your awareness to your breath. When you are ready, open your eyes and respond to the following questions. You might want to note the responses in your journal.

1. Circle the sense that provided you with the best connection to the experience: SIGHT SMELL HEARING TASTE TOUCH

   Put check marks next to the senses you also used to experience your spirituality.

2. Were there images and objects that you connected with? What were they? What was it you liked about them?

3. What was the general *feeling* of your experience: peaceful, exciting, happy, stimulating? How would you describe it? Begin with the words "I felt . . ."

Sight

"When the world looks truly beautiful to me, I know I am seeing it through the eyes of the Goddess. It's at these times the part of me that is her grows a little."
LIBRARIAN, 63

The pursuit of beauty can be a path to expanded awareness, especially when we participate in its creation. We experience beauty by engaging with it, and we bring our impression of the experience out into the world with us.

The allure of color and shape inspires Tina to create stone sculptures. The different colors and shapes of the stones draw her to them and to a deeper place within herself. Opening to the urge to touch them and then to arrange them together, she feels deep pleasure and appreciation. The creation of beauty enlivens her senses. She connects with a spiritual part of herself that provides insight as well as gratification.

"I have a new thing that I do with the stones that people brought me for my birthday. I keep all the stones in a big glass bowl together underwater. The water makes the color stand out and brings out the detail in the stones.

"I have another very beautiful shallow bowl that I have filled with sand. This is where I create my sculptures. After gazing at the bowl of stones for a while, I take a few of the stones out of the water and put them in the sand bowl. I choose the stones by what colors and shapes I happen to be drawn to or who gave them to me or whatever thoughts come at the time. Today I was really drawn to the deep red quality in some of the stones; on a different day it will be something else that will catch my eye. The stones can raise questions for me. It's a little meditation piece that I live with for a while until I'm ready to change it. Every time I play with the stones, I am surprised by the immediate gratification I feel. As a child I wasn't taught that pleasure and gratification were accessible."

For Helene, religious holidays were a time of beauty and sensual appreciation. Helene loses herself in the sensual experience of the beauty of the lights at Christmastime.

"I remember all the lights at Christmas and how they affected me as a little girl. When things around our home would get really hectic, I would lie down under the Christmas tree and gaze up at the lights and reflections of the decorations. Everything sparkled so. Sometimes I would lie there for a long time creating a world of my own, a world of beauty and light."

Later, Helene's use of her sense of sight increased her appreciation for life.

"As I grew older I remember gazing at the sun's rays coming through the trees and the brilliant reflection of the sun on the Colorado River. Whenever I do this, I feel transported to a more peaceful, happy place. This special connection to light is often with me. I notice the effect of light in my environment all the time. It's a source of spiritual inspiration to me."

People moved by spiritual feeling sometimes create visual images and objects as an expression of their religious experience. Bridget is visually stimulated by her memory of attending religious services in Equador.

"There were a lot of traditions, so much to see and experience, I'm not sure where they all came from. I remember one I particularly liked. On All Palms Day, the holiday before Easter, I saw people weaving the palms into baskets, birds, and all different kinds of beautiful objects."

Annie recalls the spiritual connection she felt in Hawaii while looking at religious paintings.

"There is a little church in South Kona; they call it the Painted Church because the entire inside of the church is painted with beautiful religious images and stories. Looking at these images, I connect with the joy and reverence of the people who worshiped there. During the service I feel the paintings help me to open to these qualities within myself."

Seeing Beauty

This exercise is designed to heighten your response to the beauty around you, to experience pleasure and beauty through seeing.

Choose an image that you find particularly beautiful. Sitting before it, empty your mind of extraneous thoughts. Open yourself to the beauty of this image, its color and form. Notice any details that make it particularly pleasing. Allow a feeling of appreciation to fill your heart.

Touch

"If there is one spiritual concept that has stayed with me from my days in the Presbyterian church, I would have to say it's the idea that our body is the temple of God."

KRISTEN, HOMEMAKER, 27

Sensual experience is the base from which some spiritual practices are derived. The body serves as the medium through which the spiritual connection is made. Movement, dance, music, rhythms, all evoke energy that can be used for worship. Some women talk about "moving with the spirit" or "blending with God through heavenly song."

Alice recognizes the spirit of dance and movement in her life, and the part sensuality plays in spiritual celebrations in her culture.

"A friend of mine who is a minister showed me a film he had made in Africa of women doing ritual dances. Watching the film I realized that some of the rhythms and body movements were similar to what I do when I dance or am in motion, or when I'm in church. I remember telling him I recognized the same god or the same spirit. I could feel it all the way from Africa, a different place, different time, but the same kind of rhythm and movement—the same kind of spirituality, same kind of connection that you know deep within your body. I can feel that today when I dance."

Ronnie first learned tae kwon do to defend herself after she had been attacked on the street. As she worked with the movements and the discipline, it developed into a spiritual practice that saved her life.

"I remember when I began practicing my moves, I felt a powerful energy I had never felt before. The more I practiced, the clearer it got, and then I noticed I wasn't afraid anymore. Soon I would just go work out to feel better about myself and to keep centered in my attitude toward life.

"When I'm in tune with myself and my routine, there's no stopping me, I'm out there kicking and swirling . . . it's a timeless feeling like I'm all alone with myself and the energy. Since I took up this practice, I have been attacked again, and it was the same feeling; I was moving in a vortex of energy, my consciousness focused only on my moves. I believe that's how I survived."

Sensation

Here is a meditation exercise designed to help you come into closer conscious contact with your body. You may want to try this while sitting at your desk or even while waiting in line somewhere. It can help you come back to yourself when you feel distracted or confused. The long-range benefit is clarity of mind and the ability to remain present to the world around you.

Close your eyes and feel your breath. Let your awareness be with the rising and falling of your chest. After a few minutes focus your awareness on your feet; feel the touch of the floor. Then beginning with your feet, slowly move the focus of your attention up your body, ending at the top of your head. Note any sensations as you move along. There will probably be areas of the body where you feel little or no sensation. That's perfectly normal. You may wish to spend a little extra time there. (If this seems too difficult a task, you might try focusing on one particular part of the body where you are feeling sensation at the time, like your shoulders or neck, for example.)

Whether we touch with our lips, our fingertips, or the soles of our feet, sensory perceptions send messages of pleasure and pain to the brain continuously. Some of the sensations are very enjoyable; some border on feelings of ecstasy.

Darlene is a minister. She has experienced the voice of God coming through her. While preaching she feels the presence of God throughout her body.

"You know, when I was a kid we used to march around the church with tambourines and sing, and it really felt good. I remember that some of my mother's friends used to accuse her of being a thrill seeker, because she had so many sensual experiences through religion. They said she engaged in religion just to have those experiences, but I have come to realize that those experiences and feelings were her way of reaching God.

"You know, in the old days when women worshiped, they were hot, they really tore it up at that time. So I took my cue from them. When I became a pastor I really spread my wings. It was my chance to speak in church. I learned how much I love to speak. It's a really powerful spiritual experience for me, in terms of sensing the presence in my body and feeling that something is occurring that is beyond me."

When we connect deeply with our body and its movements, we are sometimes transported to unexpectedly high states of consciousness. Carol shares the story of her unexpected encounter with the Goddess through an experience of movement and dance.

A STORY FROM CAROL

Near the end of my years in Puerto Rico, I participated in a trance dancing session where I feel I went beyond the boundaries I often set for myself in my spiritual explorations. I reached a level of surrender to Spirit that was deeper than most of my previous experiences. The session was led by an experienced teacher, whom I trusted, who taught trance dancing as a path to divinity and ecstatic experience. After a short demonstration by the teacher, the drumming began. She danced among us, starting each of us off individually in our dance. As I twirled out into the dance area, my body felt light and very fluid. As I danced I was aware of the others dancing around me, but I did not feel them individually. They were just part of THE DANCE, like very small particles of an atom moving in time and space to a divine rhythm. I was not dancing—someone else was dancing for me, inside of me. Someone was giving me signals when to turn, how to move.

It was wonderful to let go and feel the divine pattern within the dance and to know I was part of it. I felt the joy of having arrived, of having found that for which I had been searching. I was dancing with "The Lady." And as she danced through me, I became her. I felt physically changed, stronger and more graceful. I felt the experience of joy I had never felt before.

I don't know how long it lasted, but it seemed an eternity, and when it was over I remained exhilarated. I was soaked to the skin. My shirt clung to my body. My hair hung in ringlets. Since then I have learned that there is a great tradition of women's sacred dances, pathways to touch the Goddess and celebrate her joy and ecstasy.

Exploring Your Sensuality

As these women have done, you may want to deepen your relationship to your body by exploring its potential to serve as a vehicle for spiritual experience. Here are some exercises that can help further this connection.

Free-form writing. Use free-form writing to help you assess how you relate to your body and its sensuality now. Try responding to these questions: What activities encourage my sensuality? Do I consider myself a sensual being? Why or why not? Let your feelings and thoughts about your sensuality flow out on to the page.

Sensual activities. To help you get closer to your body and its sensations or sensuality, try any of these suggestions that appeal to you. You may wish to both revive an activity from the past and experiment with something new.

1. Try a "Swedish sauna." Sit in a hot sauna for as long as you feel comfortable and then immerse yourself in a snow bank, a barrel of cold water, a cold shower.
2. Take up a sport, any sport.
3. Go for a complete physical exam.
4. Go out dancing more often, or take a dance class.

5. Consult with a licensed naturopath, homeopath, or doctor of Chinese medicine. These health care practitioners use what is called energy medicine. They can help you connect with energy patterns in your body.

6. Change your diet.

7. Choose your favorite type of exercise and do it often.

8. Go for a full-body massage. During the massage try to remain attentive to the sensations in your body.

9. Go for a walk in the rain without an umbrella.

10. Sleep on a bed with silk sheets, or go to bed in silk pajamas.

11. Walk around nude on a warm summer night.

12. Go skinny-dipping.

Contemplation. Begin by contemplating each of these thoughts. Spend a few minutes on each, then write about the images and ideas called forth in you.

My body is a temple of the gods.

My body is the home of the divine spirit.

Through our sensuality we experience the power of desire; we desire that which is pleasurable. Perhaps you can remember "falling in love with" a beautiful face, wanting to possess a beautiful but expensive art object, or traveling thousands of miles to a site of natural beauty. These are attempts to be closer to beauty. We may desire to touch it, to hold it, even to possess it.

"You know I've tried a lot of spiritual paths and attitudes, but after all is said and done I've come to realize, if I'm ever to know God, I have to want God like I want my lover."

LEANDRA, MASSAGE THERAPIST, 32

Diane understands desire and sensuality as spiritual energy, as a path to the Divine. In this case she transforms her desire to make love into an experience of spiritual connection.

"The energy of desire filled my body as I sat before my altar. I begin to silently repeat the Padmasambhava mantra. Instantly in the air above and in front of me, Padmasambhava appeared seated on a lotus with his consort. The experience was both visual and kinesthetic. I knew I was his consort. The feeling was the

same as the most intense sexual energy I have ever experienced. I felt the pleasure of our union spread from my genitals throughout my body. Padmasambhava rose and stood full length. Although I remained seated, it felt as though my cells were vibrating, my whole body sparkling. I experienced incredible bliss. I knew without words that the meaning of this experience was this: There are incredible reservoirs of bliss available to us. We do not need a physical partner to experience this. This powerful sensation comes from letting go of all attachments. The heart must be open and vulnerable. The delightful sensations continued, and I wanted to see Tara. Immediately the twenty-one Taras appeared in the air above my head. I could not distinguish myself from them. Again the experience was both visual and kinesthetic. We were dakinis dancing and making love in the sky. The bliss expanded out into a feeling of great peace that lasted for four days without wavering. There was no tension within my mind. There was no desire for sex or wanting anything outside myself."

Hearing the Music

The world of music has long been used to honor the gods. There is a vast, well-developed musical tradition in most religions, from the drums of Africa to the harpsichord and flute of early Europe. Church bells ringing out over the hills of France for the celebration of Marie Mother of God, the sound of the gong at the Buddhist temple summoning the people to meditation—these are the sounds of a spiritual call, a reminder to stop what one is doing and reconnect with the spiritual realm. There are hymns of praise and appreciation of the divine, songs of inspiration and spiritual illumination.

For some of us certain tones or pieces of music can elicit a healing response. We feel that energy has moved within us and that we are somehow different, clearer and more whole. Some sounds particularly appeal to the senses, raise our spirits, and trigger a spiritual mood. Chanting is an example of a practice based on music and song that is specifically designed to elicit spiritual feelings and insights. Most of us have been exposed to some sort of spiritual musical tradition even if that exposure was minimal. Spiritual music has a way of staying with us, of permeating the heart. In thinking back on our religious experiences, we may find that we responded emotionally to certain songs or hymns. Christian hymns, Jewish songs, and Buddhist chants are specifically designed to induce a spiritual feeling.

Hearing

Ask yourself, What sounds are pleasing to my ear? Do these sounds ever contribute to a feeling of spiritual connection? Are there sounds that relax me, sounds that make me smile? Here is a list of sounds that provide a connection to spirituality for some women. Check any that have worked for you:

Spiritual music
Popular music
The sound of a bell
A child's laughter
A foghorn
A bird's song
The voice of a friend on the phone
A thunderclap
The howl of a wolf
The sound of a drum

Pick a sound that particularly appeals to you. Listen for it during the day.

As a child Randy had intense spiritual connection with the music of the church choir. She describes how music and song transport her to a higher spiritual dimension.

"I had transcendent experiences in church. One time the choir was singing and it began to sound like angels singing, and I saw all this light and felt an intense inner experience of rapture, love, and light. Once it happened when I was thirteen, and it probably had to do with hormonal changes and not eating for hours, but of course that is what saints will do to have those kinds of experiences. Other times it didn't seem connected to something biological. I had a profoundly deep sense of spiritual connection."

Camille developed a deep appreciation for Christian ritual and tradition through her connection with sound and sensual experience. Although somewhat alienated from her Christian background today, she still feels connected to the music and the spiritual feeling it evokes in her.

"The music was very important. When I couldn't stand what was being said, I would think about the music. I liked the discipline of the music, learning the

music, the choir. The music seemed 'higher,' it got me closer to something. I liked the way I felt when I sang. I liked that the choir stood closer to the big altar in the middle of what was happening. I loved the lighting of the candles; the vestments were beautiful colored materials from another era and gave me contact with the past. They connected me to something that came before me and would come after me. Today I still feel moved by church music."

Lullabies are sung to put babies to sleep. They create a mood of relaxation and invoke trust, so that the child can let go of fears and gently drift off to sleep. Often they include inspirational and ethical messages. These may have been the first profoundly moving and reassuring musical sounds and messages we heard. These tones came from the same person who, if we were fortunate, provided for our needs. As the mother sings the lullaby, we feel taken care of and protected by an entity much more powerful than ourselves. In this way, for some of us, the lullaby was perhaps our first spiritual song. Looking at lullabies sung to us as children, we can see strong spiritual influences. Carol remembers a line from a favorite lullaby sung to her by her mother.

"'Baby's boat's a silver moon sailing on the sea. Baby's boat goes sailing out, then hurries back to me.' This song was often sung to me and my sister at bedtime from the time we were babies to maybe three years old. It's curious to me that I remember this line so well. I feel happy and loved if I sing it to myself. I feel a spiritual connection through the imagery. The moon and the sea are strong spiritual images for me today."

There are inspirational songs sung in nursery school and at home that inspire spiritual feelings in children. They may be teaching behavior and values at the same time. "Swinging on a Star" is an inspirational song for children, offering hope for a good life and the possibility of success. It teaches the value of getting an education and being clean, polite, conscientious. Inspirational songs may inspire children but at the same time admonish them by presenting the unfortunate consequences of not behaving correctly. Were there songs in your childhood that inspired you but also made you feel unworthy?

Emily remembers feeling very confused by the song "Swinging on a Star." She felt inspired by the possibility of swinging on a star and doing magnificent things, but was not sure that she could live up to all that was required of her.

"It was strange when my Mom sang that to us kids. I could never tell if I was going to get to carry moonbeams home one day or not. What if I wasn't a good little girl like the song suggests? My spirit sometimes felt troubled after we sang that song together."

Reexperience a Childhood Song

Allow yourself to reexperience a favorite childhood song or lullaby. See if you can recall the words. Try writing them out. Sing it to yourself several times silently or out loud.

How does it feel? What does it say to you today? How do you feel singing it? Is it inspirational, comforting? Do you feel particularly reassured or taken care of when you remember this song? What implication might this song have for your spirituality today?

Some music has an especially inspirational quality. In the passive participation usually called music appreciation, we sit back and listen to the messages contained in the music, which takes a certain skill and openness. In the active creation of music in honor of God, we can send out a call to the divine by shaking a rattle, ringing a bell, or conducting a symphony. Alice feels a strong connection to gospel music and the hymns of her childhood religion. Listen as she talks about how this creative connection to music has become a spiritual practice that has carried her throughout her life.

"Music has a very spiritual connection for me. Sometimes when I get up in the morning I spend some quiet time, do my morning meditation, and when I take my shower I sing different songs. A lot of these songs I grew up in church with when I was a little girl. They have stayed with me, and they are uplifting. There's one in particular that I sing in the morning. It's called 'This Little Light of Mine.' When I sing it I feel a glow, like it's that light inside of me that is coming out to shine. I actually feel it as I go about my day. Songs and music have a lot to do with my spirituality. It's how I feel a healing. I take time out during the day to do this. I know my neighbor sometimes says to herself, 'Oh, there she goes again.' She's told me she can sometimes hear me. I hope she doesn't mind too much, because I feel good, and that's what matters.

"There are other songs that work for me too, depending on what mood I'm in—'A Motherless Child,' for example. Sometimes I feel like a motherless child because I am a motherless child. It's like a grieving when I sing it. It's OK for me to sing it because it feels nurturing. It takes me through that mood and that period in my life. I would be in a low mood, feeling alone. When I sing this song I hold myself, and rock myself, and work through it. Afterward I feel OK again. I look at it like a healing experience. I think for African-American people as a whole, song had lot to do with how we kept strong. Look at the struggles we've been through, coming from slavery, being captured and brought against our will to America.

Sometimes I think the feeling and the emotions behind the music are still the same today. The people back then sang about struggle, like when it was raining and it was a harvest and you didn't expect the crops to come through, and then when they did you were real happy, and you had inspirational things to sing."

Sometimes we have a favorite song or piece of music that stays with us so much that we feel a special connection. For Alice, such a song is "Amazing Grace."

"I feel a special connection to this song because I feel like my life is covered with a sense of grace. I have been at the valley of the shadow of death four times in my life. It's a confirmation to me that if I weren't protected by God's amazing grace, the outcome of these situations could have been a lot different. I get more humble when I sing that song. Grace is a feeling of protection. It's like a covenant. When grace covers my life, I get this spiritual tingle. I feel very sheltered. I feel ready to do what God has in store for me each day even if I wouldn't necessarily feel like that before. I feel like I'm here to be used.

"Music can also make me feel disconnected. I used to sing the blues a lot, but the blues can make you kind of down, sort of depressed. I used to listen to a lot of Billie Holiday's music. She was a great singer, but a lot of her music can make you feel alone and disconnected.

"There's a song I heard recently in a movie called 'I Feel Like Going On.' It's a newer gospel song. It's a song of a person in recovery. It says the 'storms may be high, but I still feel like going on.' It's not a real uplifting song, but it's a song of hope and growth. There is a spiritual sense to these songs. Singing them keeps people going on, doing the motions of getting through the day. Having that contact of singing is a way of taking care of myself when I'm struggling. Like in the song 'Old Man River,' there is still the hope of just rolling along, no matter what, just going on like the river."

Music as Spiritual Connection

Introducing music and song into our lives is a way of accessing our spirituality. Here are three activities to try that may deepen your connection to music and song.

1. Pick a popular song that appeals to you. As you listen, ask yourself if you feel a special connection. Do you feel inspired or energized when you listen? Do you feel spiritually uplifted and supported in any way? If so, find a time each day to listen to this song.

2. Try humming or singing an inspirational song to yourself during the day or at times when you feel a little down.

3. Circle the instrument that most appeals to you: PIANO   DRUM   TRUMPET   GUITAR   HARP   FLUTE

  Listen to a piece of music that highlights that instrument.

Music meditation. Choose an inspirational song or a favorite religious piece of music. Arrange yourself in a relaxed, comfortable position for listening. Placing your attention at your ears, close your eyes, and be with the music. Be aware of the sounds as they enter your consciousness. Allow for any feelings or images that might occur. When your mind leaves the sound, gently bring it back. Practice this for the length of the selection you have chosen.

Adornment

Much religious experience traditionally uses adornment as a mode of spiritual expression and connection. Spiritual leaders have traditional ways of dressing that convey their degree of spiritual attainment. Practitioners also dress to convey their relationship with the divine. Special garments are worn for specific rituals or holidays. Think of the white dresses worn by girls for their First Communion in the Catholic church, the use of choir robes, or the saffron-colored garments worn by some Buddhist nuns.

When we adorn ourselves, we discover what is beautiful and pleasing to our senses—a color, a material, or a piece of jewelry, for example—and we incorporate it into our way of dressing. We combine beauty and sensuality.

We suggest making time to explore how you might choose to connect with your spirituality through adornment. You may find that what is pleasing to your senses can also be pleasing to the gods.

The Spirituality of Adornment

1. Experiment with color. Choose colors that invite you. Dress yourself up in a splash of color. Notice how bright colors affect you, how soft colors affect you. Go through your clothes closet looking for "spiritual garments." Spontaneously choose a couple of things to lay out on the bed; look them over; maybe try them on. Consider why they feel spiritual to you.

2. Before attending a spiritual class, retreat, or ceremony, pay particular attention to how you wish to adorn yourself for the occasion. What are the colors, garments, and jewelry you will choose for this occasion?

3. Notice how you feel about the dress of a particular spiritual leader or teacher. Ask yourself why that person might be dressed in a particular fashion. You might even ask him or her why a particular garment was chosen.

Make a commitment to open more to your senses. When in a beautiful and especially moving situation, remember to open to your full ability to experience the moment. Spend more time in appreciation of the beauty around you.

Affirmation

Create an affirmation to repeat to yourself to help you open to the beauty of life. You may use one of the suggested affirmations or create your own.

I see the beauty that surrounds me.
I appreciate the beauty in my life today.
I walk through my life in beauty and grace.
The beauty inside me touches the beauty that surrounds me.

We are often inspired to create beauty as well as to appreciate it. Crafts such as writing, making music, dancing, sculpting, provide opportunities to create and experience beauty. As we participate in these endeavors, we move beyond ourselves. There is always the possibility that we will touch our spiritual center and bring back a poem, a painting, or perhaps a creative dance. Spiritual connection through creative expression is open to all of us, whether or not we choose to make a home for ourselves in the creative arts.

Using Your Creativity

8

"Creativity is born in the heart, from an intense desire to know what is just beyond our vision, just beyond our grasp."

To create is to bring into existence. To create we reach beyond the limits of the known; we connect with unformed ideas and breathe life into them. The act of creation moves us into the uncharted waters of the nonmaterial world, where anything is possible.

There is an energy that comes with being creative, a curiosity, a love of life and experimentation. This is the energy that drives us forward in our endeavors, sometimes despite great difficulties. Particularly creative moments, or breakthroughs, when we get new ideas or inspiration, feel special, set apart from ordinary life experience.

Creativity in Childhood

Creativity involves the willingness to imagine. It first blooms in childhood along with our spirituality. We invent games filled with imaginary people, places, and wild adventures. We build tree houses, play houses, or hideouts. We make up dances, invent silly rhymes, and play practical jokes. Although seen as child's play, these activities include elements of artistic expression: acting, storytelling, songwriting, and creative dance. When we create a house with our building blocks or a new game or story, we bridge the gap between form and spirit. Our childhood imagination takes us beyond ordinary life experience.

173

Creativity seems to come naturally to children, but, as we take on the responsibilities of adulthood, we find it increasingly difficult to find the time to access our free creative spirit. Eventually we may come to believe that creativity is given to only a chosen few; we may tend to feel intimidated by its expression. Women have found that one path to deepening a connection with spirituality lies in exploring and reaffirming their creativity. Celebrating your creative potential may provide unexpected opportunities for spiritual renewal.

As a child Marie used her very creative imagination to make up stories and invent invisible friends. Today the characters she imagines appear in her novels and screenplays. Sometimes they come to her as spirit guides, offering wisdom and spiritual direction for her life.

"Today there are still a lot of characters around me, be they spiritual guides or the characters I create in my novels and scripts. I have never actually seen these guides, though sometimes I see a flash and sense that a guide is near. I would like to be able hear them speak. Now I hear them in my heart.

"Right now I am writing a book with a young girl as the central character. I feel she speaks for the child within me. When I write her dialogue, and especially when I read it, I feel strengthened, even healed. For me this type of writing is a spiritual act."

Through writing, we can experience spiritual connection. After writing a letter, we may sometimes notice that it contains a philosophical or spiritual message. This is true for Roberta. She uses her writing to develop her personal moral philosophy.

"I got mugged a few years ago and seriously injured. The mugging felt like a holocaust in my life. Although I realize my life should not claim such importance, my thoughts immediately went to 'What kind of God makes a holocaust?' However, a better measure of God might be the drought in Ethiopia and the holocaust for infants. I wrote a lot of poetry about people and gods who were unjust—anger and then forgiveness."

Even more simply, the act of putting thoughts to paper can create a spiritual connection. Roberta talks about the altered state of consciousness she experiences when expressing her feelings about injustice and human suffering.

"I started writing poems at nineteen. This is where I took the risks and paid the sweat, blood, and tears to advance spiritually. When I wrote I would hit into holocaust energy and utopia energy. Holocaust energy in the sixties was about

civil rights and the war in Vietnam for me. As a poet you would touch the wire of a national psyche hoping the currents were not too violent to bear. If they were too violent, you might end up committing suicide as did many poets of my generation like Ann Sexton, Sylvia Plath, and John Berryman.

"I am now doing meditation. This meditation cultivates Buddha-mind, which is similar to the mind state I reached when in the course of writing a poem. It was a state of mind absent of struggle, a point of sheer vivid seeing, an acceptance of things as they are."

Many forms of writing all hold the potential to connect to the spirit.

Writing

Types of writing. Here is a list of types of writing. Circle any that you already use: ESSAYS STORIES CARDS ARTICLES POEMS LETTERS REPORTS NOTES TO YOURSELF JOURNALS. Add others yourself. Ask yourself, Do I feel especially connected to any of these writing experiences? Which forms of writing seem to come most naturally to me? Put a star next to any that you might like to explore further.

Contemplation. Ask yourself, What have I written that has meaning for me? Now take a moment to remember that bit of writing. Feel the energy of what you expressed in it. Understand that this was an expression of spirit, and allow yourself to see your writing in this way. Do not judge your work. Ask yourself how you might use writing to deepen your connection to your spirituality. Write down any ideas that come.

Tina, a photographer, remembers that her childhood experiences of creativity started early in life, with an activity common to many of us.

"As a kid I just loved to take my crayons and just color, color, color. I was passionate about it. It reminds me of how I now hand-color my photographs. What I like about it is that it allows me to get my conscious mind out of the picture and do whatever comes up. I can trust that it's going to be right because it's easy to change. Hand-coloring my photos feels spiritual in that I am giving a lot of energy to one image. I may sit for four or five hours, taking in everything that is there. I'm finding there is a lot more than I realized. I'm putting all this energy into the image, all this affection and love and excitement. The color becomes charged. Later, I can feel the energy emanating from the photograph. When I was younger, I didn't dare alter reality so much. Today, sometimes, it feels like I'm playing God."

Coloring

Choose an image to color or paint. You may use the image on this page or anything else you might like to color. Arrange the colors in front of you, noticing how each affects you. Take your time as you start to color, and see if you can feel a sensual connection, a pleasure in what you are doing.

drawing by Annie Hershey

*"It takes a lot to pull good ideas out of the cosmic consciousness into reality.
It takes the power of spirit and a willingness to go where the gods live."*

Cassandra makes a connection between creativity and spirituality in her life and in her art. She lives in the woods in a cabin she built. She says her drawings are an expression of her devotion to nature and a reflection of the quiet life of a woman living in relative isolation.

> *"The openness I must feel in order to create as an artist is the same openness I would use to meditate or pray. Creativity and spirituality can be expansive, freeing, stimulating, beyond definition. It is about trying to define the undefinable. Creativity and spirituality are both about silence—inner silence—leading to awareness. Both are about faith—for example, a belief that the process will lead to enlightenment. Both require an inner strength and guidance, a direction, and the desire to follow a path, to go somewhere unknown."*

For Nancy, spirituality was the entry point to her creativity and later a byproduct of her sculpture. In her first sculpture class the instructor incorporated ritual to invoke the muse or creative spirit within.

> *"My spiritual connection was through those classes I first took. The teacher came from a very spiritual place. She did rituals with us before each class. It was a whole education for me. We were not just technically learning how to make a doll; there was a spiritual process involved. She had an altar wherever we did our work. We would do a guided meditation before class. Sometimes we constructed the altar together. We placed meaningful objects on the altar that were related to our creative process at the time. I have come to realize that creativity is to me what religion is to some people. In a way, creativity is my religion. I am very thankful that my direction in art was through classes that incorporated spirituality. I guess I was led there. My Higher Power must have gotten me to that place. It was really a wonderful opening for me.*

> *"Right now I am doing sculptures. Sculpting puts me in touch with the Great Mother; working with clay is working with the earth. For me, it's a sensual experience. I feel the presence of the Great Mother when I make these little goddesses. It feels like her spirit is inside me as I create.*

> *"I sculpt little ridges into my goddess figures where I later place gifts—like feathers, shells, things from nature. Each time I change the gifts and offer something new, the ritual creates a spiritual connection for me with the Goddess. I made the first one with her arms down. With each successive Goddess I made the arms go farther up, until she was reaching for the sky. Eventually wings began to grow from her arms. The open arms gave me a joyous feeling. The wings were about*

letting go, taking off in a new direction with my life. The creation of these god-desses is a spiritual healing practice for me. I love my little goddess altars. I've placed them all around my home. They are helping me to create a very comfort-able, safe space for myself."

Working with her creativity helps Tina accept and even value her fears. As a child, Tina learned that fear was a warning. She was taught to stop whatever she was doing when she felt fearful. As a creative adult, Tina sometimes experiences her fear as a signal that she is doing exactly the right thing.

"There are times in the creative process when I don't know where I am going. I'm working on my edge. As I learn to live with my fears, I develop self-trust. There may be a feeling somewhere in my body that I'm going in the right direction even if I'm scared, but I'm not sure why. I couldn't explain it to anyone if my life de-pended on it.

"My creativity is spiritual in that my best images feel like they come through me. It's not like I'm making them. It's like being a channel for the creative force. I get the feeling this is an image that the world needs and I'm available to execute it, but it does not feel like mine. There's a certain point in making a photograph, when I need to get my ego out of the way. My rational thinking needs to go, and I just act. It's in that moment that spirituality and creativity come together for me."

As we heal and open spiritually, our creative juices begin to flow into our art, as well as other daily activities. Opportunities for creative expression abound. Although the ways we use our creative energy will vary, each of us be-comes a creator. Nancy describes her entire life as a creative process.

"I can see creativity in everything now. I try to live in such a way that I feel a creative connection to everything I do. I guess you could say it is a spiritual way of life. My fundamental way of relating to people has changed. Before, I was on a quest to connect with another through a sexual relationship or marriage. That urge has been transformed into relating to people in a creative way. My creative energy goes into making something that manifests an inner aspect of myself that I give to others, like writing a letter, dressing myself in the morning, or cleaning a room. When I clean and rearrange my home, I am working toward creating a kind of divine order. I may not be thinking of this at the time, but if the work I've done makes me feel peaceful and nourished, I know I've touched into some-thing spiritual."

As we come to realize that most activities in life hold an opportunity for spiritual healing and growth, we may experience our spirituality in unlikely situations. As women, we find that most of our waking hours are spent working, either in or out of the home. If we discover a spiritual connection to our work, we create yet another area in which our spirituality blooms. Our workplace can become the canvas on which we paint our personal masterpieces.

Elizabeth writes proposals to funding agencies and institutions. She requests large sums of money for what she believes to be important social service programs. Although she does not practice her spirituality in a religious context, she has found a powerful and creative outlet for her spiritual feelings through her work.

"I really enjoy the creative challenge of writing requests for funding and developing a new program. I think about the benefit it will provide to the community as well as the opportunity for meaningful employment it provides. So far, this is the best use of spirit I have found for my life—to channel my talents into this kind of service. I feel really blessed that I can be of service in this way and that I am successful at what I am doing. When I'm doing this writing, I feel a spiritual connection to the program I create and the community I serve."

Nancy is a nurse working in a stressful and demanding hospital setting. She attempts to provide spiritual connection between herself and others.

"My creativity goes into my job. I use my creativity to enrich the feeling of spiritual connection I have with people. Each interaction is an opportunity for connection, an opening from myself to another person. I find creative ways to enhance the feeling of connection. For example, I take more time. I pay attention to my patients. It comes through a lot if I'm touching them—when I wash someone's feet, or do a dressing. I feel my energy flowing out to them; it feels like healing energy."

Take some time now to focus on the activities of your daily life; this may be where spirituality is most available to you.

Daily Life

Make a list of some of your daily activities. As you look over the list, ask yourself, Which of these activities do I feel have potential for creative spiritual connection? See if one activity stands out as having a particularly spiritual feeling to it. Imagine how you can use it as a tool for spiritual development.

We can more fully discover the spiritual lessons intrinsic in the workplace, when we set our intentions in this direction.

The Workplace

Guided meditation. Begin with a grounding meditation. See yourself in the workplace performing a helpful service. How does that feel? Now see yourself in a moment when you are very connected to your work, very focused. Again ask yourself how that feels. Now sit with the suggestion that there is a spiritual feeling about what you do, and see what images appear to you.

Free-form writing. When you are ready, pick up a pen and do some free-form writing about what came up for you.

Spirituality at work. Dedicate one workday to remaining alert for spiritual opportunities. Begin the day with a ritual, affirmation, or meditation that spiritually dedicates this day. Before you begin, possibly on your way to work, think about how you might experience your usual tasks from a more spiritual perspective. When you come home from work, take some time to write about your day and think about how you might continue to integrate some of the perspectives you practiced.

Creation of the Self at Birth

"Is it not a creative act to take our first step or to say our first word? Were not each of these acts little miracles? Think of all we created for ourselves in our first years of life."

Birth is a door through which we all pass, marking the beginning of our journey on Earth. As we emerge from our mother's womb, that first breath we take is perhaps our first creative act, for in it we affirm our life. With that first cry we assert, "I am here, I exist." We make the decision to be, to connect with life. It is unfortunate that most of us cannot remember this moment of joining with life, for it must have been of high spiritual power and connection.

Saying Yes to Life

Use the gift of imagination to remember the moment that you said yes to this life. Imagine saying, "Yes, I want to be me, I want to live this life." What must that have felt like? Reflect on the spiritual qualities of faith and trust that might have come into play as you made the decision to embrace this life. Here are some affirmations that might nurture this feeling within you. Try saying them silently or aloud for a few minutes each day. See if they work for you; if not, create your own.

> I embrace my life with love and enthusiasm.
> I say yes to life.
> I trust that life provides for me on a daily basis.
> I live my life fully with appreciation.

Giving Birth to a Child

"To create is to enliven, to breathe life into form, shape, and color. One way I judge a piece of art is to ask myself, 'Is it alive, does it live for me?' This is where the artist becomes a god, in her ability to give life. An artist births her work very much as a woman gives birth to a child."

As women, most of us will give birth at least once in our lives. We will participate in the miracle of creating a new human being from the substance of our own bodies. Often women describe giving birth as their ultimate creative and spiritual act. For those of us who have given birth or who have been present at a birth it is difficult to deny the spirituality of this event.

In order to give birth, the mother must be willing to move from the world of the known into the world of the unknown and unformed. She must slip back over the threshold of life into the darkness where the child waits to be awakened and guided out into the light of awareness. Implicit in every birth is the possibility of failure, that life will not triumph over death, that something will go wrong. There is risk involved, possible danger to be faced. When mother and child succeed in completing the miraculous journey together without mishap or injury, joy fills the hearts of those present in the delivery room. There may even be a moment of grace or spiritual illumination felt by those present, an ecstatic recognition of the life force. Seen in this way, each birth is a celebration of the triumph of life.

Camille expresses our special connection to the birth process and her frustration at having that experience taken from her while giving birth to her son.

"I was awake and pushing hard, and the baby was in distress. The doctor told me he was going to do a caesarean section. I remember feeling very disheartened. This was my experience, mine and my baby's. I wanted to keep trying to push the baby through the birth canal. Giving birth was a spiritual act for me. It was something I had always wanted to do. I didn't want to give up.

"My husband was there. He consulted with the doctor, and they just sort of went ahead with the operation. I'll never forget this. I felt so disempowered. To this day, I still believe I could have done it myself. At least the decision should have been mine—I feel I was robbed of one of my greatest spiritual experiences. Based on the first, my second birth was a caesarean also. An important part of my creative power was stolen from me in the delivery room. I feel they took part of my spirit from me; I'm still trying to reclaim it."

Tina compares the creative process of her photography with giving birth to a child.

"I think my first awareness of feminist spirituality came when I started attending people's births and saw babies coming into the world. I had a real strong experience of their spirits. I really experienced another person's entry into this world when the baby was born. This realization reminded me of feelings I had before, when I gave birth to my own children. I remembered feeling their spirits entering their bodies and my own part in their creation.

"I felt what I was seeing and feeling at these births was important, so I began photographing births. I feel the world needs these images. They are images of women as creator, as the source of life. I think it is difficult to look at these images and deny the power of women. I see myself as an instrument that gets the photographs taken, works with them, and believes in them enough to put a god-awful amount of energy into them. I care for these images; I get them out into the world. It's like being a priestess. This creative process often feels very much like giving birth."

Tina goes on to talk about the relationship between the creation of new life and the experience of death.

"I had a very clear and simple spiritual insight watching these infants come into the world: People come into this world and people leave. This was the closest I ever came to a friendly feeling about death."

Tina deepens her understanding of the connection between birth and death as she contemplates the death of an old friend. Septima Clark was founder and leader of a grass-roots literacy training program that was part of Martin Luther King Jr.'s Southern Christian Leadership Conference. She was an inspirational teacher and role model for Tina when they worked together in the civil rights movement.

> *"I had the experience of sitting at the bedside of Septima Clark when she was in her eighties and soon to pass over. As I sat with her she would be with me and talk, and then she would drift away. Septima was coming and going between the two worlds, just as a pregnant woman does. When one is pregnant it feels like the connection between this world and the spiritual world is very close. When I was pregnant I felt very close to the other side. I experience pregnant women as being very sensual and spiritual. They are the bridge for humanity to enter this world. What higher creative act could there be?"*

Lauren works and also volunteers at a hospital. By participating daily in the human cycle of birth and death, she awakens to her spiritual feelings. The miracle of creation provides her with spiritual insight and connection.

> *"Working in obstetrics I get in touch with the omnipotent power. It seems like a miracle to me that a child is born, develops, and comes out perfect. How does this act of creation happen? I get caught up in the emotions of it and cry right along with everyone. Then I go back out on the floor to be with people who are dying. I find I am participating in life and death at the same time. This feels very real, very grounding. When I volunteer, people sometimes ask, 'Why are you here? You're not getting paid.' It's because I feel good helping people. I feel good when I feel I made a difference. I get moments of spiritual insight working in this field; I just have to be open to it."*

Birth

Choose any of these exercises to connect with feelings of creativity and spiritual connection through birth.

Contemplation. Seek out and contemplate a small example of the process of new life entering the world: a seedling pushing through the earth's cover, a butterfly emerging from its cocoon, a chick bursting through its eggshell.

Guided imagery. Begin with Grounding 2, I Am My Breath. Then gently let yourself drift back to a time when you were pregnant or giving birth.

Imagine or recall the sensation of carrying life within you. Relive the birth process. See if you can recall the moment your child came into the world. How did it feel to have your child presented to you after it was born?

Birthing creativity. If you have not given birth to a child, perhaps you have given birth to a project or an idea. Recall yourself at a moment of creative breakthrough, when things were suddenly flowing and you felt connected and inspired. Allow yourself to feel the full extent of your creative potential at these times. Discover to what extent this was a spiritual experience for you.

Attending a birth. Consider attending a birth. If there are no pregnant women in your family or among your friends, perhaps there are some pregnant animals. Before attending, cultivate an attitude of openness to the miracle of creation.

You may want to pause for a moment to integrate your experiences.

Integration

Contemplate these questions. You may want to use free-from writing to explore your responses.

> How has creativity played a role in my spiritual journey?
> How much of my journey involves the use of my creativity?
> Am I satisfied with this? Or do I want it to change in some way?
> What is one step I want to take to integrate creativity into my life in a new way?

Developing Rituals

9

"When I perform an elaborate ritual, it feels like a party I am giving for all my friends with God as the honored guest."

Childhood Religious Ritual

Rituals are prescribed methods for spiritual practice. They are participatory events designed to open our minds and hearts to our spirituality. When a ritual works for us, the actions we take and the words we say feel compatible with our inner truth. We feel safe while performing the ritual. Spiritual rituals are as diverse as the people who perform them. Their effect on us can vary greatly. We may feel energized, or comforted. Rituals can be used to bless, to heal, to protect, or to give thanks.

A central ingredient in ritual is repetition. Some rituals have been practiced in exactly the same way for centuries. By repeating a ritual over and over again, we deepen our relationship to it, and its effect becomes more powerful. To understand how repetition functions within religion, consider the power of repetition in your everyday life. Can you remember repeating your position in an argument until it was heard? Have you had the experience of repeating words of a foreign language over and over to yourself until you internalized them?

Whether traditional or personal, ritual practice does demand a certain amount of trust. You learn to trust a ritual form in the same way you would trust a recipe, a dance, or a set of physical exercises. Those of us whose experience with ritual has been part of an oppressive religious experience may feel unsafe with ritual. The idea that there is a prescribed form for spiritual practice may feel scary to us. What are the guarantees that this seemingly foreign activity will speak to us? How can we be sure we will be nurtured and protected if we open ourselves in the prescribed manner? We may need to start with a clean slate by discovering whether ritual has a place in our spirituality at all. We may want to invent our own rituals, discovering which elements further our spiritual connection and which do not. Some of us will find rituals of childhood spirituality that endure; by practicing them, we can open up a pathway to a spirituality we may have forgotten.

For Annie, spiritual connection through the use of ritual was motivated by childhood experiences within Catholicism.

> *"I remember coming home from church with my girlfriends and playing 'mass.' Girls weren't allowed to help on the altar, so we would take turns being the priest and the altar boy. We wore long-sleeved shirts. For the communion we poured grape juice from my mother's fancy vinegar bottle, pretending it was the blood of Jesus. For wafers we had crackers, and we even had bells to ring. By acting out this ritual, I felt much more connected to my spirituality than I ever did during mass in church."*

Annie's story illustrates the close relationship between creative play and spiritual experience. In this case, Annie was creatively acting out a spiritual ritual that she had seen performed many times, a ritual that held meaning for her and had inspired her so much that she wanted to take part in it, to experience what she felt altar boys were experiencing.

Annie takes what she learned as a child about the spiritual power of ritual into the realm of performance art.

> *"I have always enjoyed acting out my experiences. Right now I am involved in a play about women and cancer. It's helping me heal unresolved grief from the deaths of my grandmother, mother, and aunt from cancer, as well as some of my friends. I see myself as a vehicle for healing energy through the medium of theater and ritual. I'm also in an improvisational acting group. We use the ritual of performance to transform our pain. This has become a 'spirit healing' practice for me."*

In her youth Sharon had to leave the Protestant church in which she had been raised and move with her family to a new city. Deprived of the childhood spiritual rituals to which she was accustomed, Sharon uses her imagination and creativity to bring spirituality back into her life.

"There was a year when our family had moved to Los Angeles and we were in between churches; we didn't belong anywhere at the time. I was nine years old, and I became very religious. I read this article for kids about bringing spirituality into your own life and about how you could set up an altar. I created a special place for myself. I set up an altar in my room. My father had made me a doll altar. I covered it with a cloth and got two pieces of wood and made a cross and put my Bible on it, and I would sit at my altar every day and think about spiritual things and talk to God. This was my own personal ritual. I did this all on my own. No one in my house did things like this. But I wanted to be in touch with God and spend time thinking about things that are important. I felt really in touch with something bigger than I was, and that was very positive. Objects and order are still very important to me. They affect my moods profoundly."

Repetition of ritual fosters spiritual connection only when we perform the ritual from our hearts. It can be difficult to connect with words and actions prescribed and created by others. If you find yourself mindlessly repeating the words or having trouble maintaining a schedule, you may need to reconsider your relationship to the ritual. Ask yourself where you feel disconnected. You may want to combine traditional ritual practice with newly discovered personal images and activities. You can develop private rituals that correspond more directly with your individual spiritual growth and challenges. Your practices need to reflect who you really are.

Jackie was raised a Roman Catholic. For the past seventeen years she has lived on rural land in close relationship with herself, other women, the Earth, and her God. Although she has rejected her religion of origin, she has incorporated some of its rituals into her spiritual life today.

"I was raised as a Roman Catholic, and although I have rejected that religion, there are some rituals that I have adapted to fit my new women's spirituality. For instance, I wanted to acknowledge the Harmonic Convergence in a big way because I believed it was a time of significant change and transformation. For years as a Catholic I had always given up something for Lent. As a symbol of openness, I wanted to give up something important to me for the Harmonic Convergence, something that was going to have a big impact on my life. I decided to give up smoking marijuana. Since giving up marijuana, my life has definitely changed. I feel clearer. I have more energy and more self-esteem. I feel better about myself because I don't have something ruling my life.

"Another way my religious background influences me is in a desire to confess when I feel disappointed in myself because of something I have done. I want to use that sacred way to tell someone else about what I have done. I find myself

saying, *"Bless me, Mother, for I have sinned." As I do this, I see an image of a spirit guide, and I confess to her. My spirit guide just pops out of me. She is at my side, and I talk with her. I then feel I have gone through a process that holds me accountable for what I have done. Afterward I get a feeling of peacefulness."*

Jackie has replaced prayer with her personal affirmations, but she finds that her experience with repetitive Christian prayer still helps her.

"I use my early Catholic training and apply it to my affirmations. I say them in the same way and with the same feeling. I affirm, 'I love myself and approve of myself exactly as I am.' I can do this easily while walking down the street. I think this is partly because I have had so much practice saying ten Hail Marys, ten Acts of Contrition and three Our Fathers as a way to rid myself of sin. I just zip off my affirmations the way I zipped off my prayers."

Nelly returns to the practice of an ancient ritual of her religion of origin. She makes it work in a way that deepens her connection with her Jewish heritage. She integrates a childhood spiritual ritual with prayers that capture her unique life situation and struggle today.

A Story from Nelly

Lately I have been doing the Friday night Sabbath ceremony at home. I choose this particular ritual because women all over the world have always been the ones to light the Sabbath candles. It also makes sense in my life to ritualize Friday at sundown, which is the end of my work week and a transition into another mode, the weekend. My mother went to Israel, and I asked her to bring me back Sabbath candlesticks. I thought it would be helpful to get them from the center of contemporary Judaism. I light the candles every Friday night. I feminize the prayer. First I say the prayers in Hebrew, or my own remembrance of the Hebrew prayer; this connects me to the ancients. Then I re-create the prayer anew each week and say it in English. I make the prayer relevant to my life and to my spiritual questions. This week as I lighted the candles, I prayed, "Blessed art Thou, the Creator and the Destroyer, who summons me to the Process of Life and Death, so that I might expand and stretch to my fullest, and become all of what I am meant to be.

When I light the Sabbath candles I feel I am channeling something very old and very deep. I am honoring my Jewish background. I live by the ocean, so I can watch the sun drop into the ocean and do the ritual precisely at sunset, the time prescribed by the Jewish tradition. This connects me to the patterns and cycles of nature. The candles burn down all evening, and I am comforted by the warm glow.

The ritual of candle lighting, found in many religions and cultural settings, is an example of a common yet powerful ritual that can be reintegrated into our lives in a meaningful way. In a candle lighting ritual we work with the energy of fire, an element familiar to all of us in our everyday lives. The image of the flame easily kindles warmth in our hearts. Mary still practices a Native American candle lighting ceremony she learned from her parents.

> *"When I was a child my father would light a candle each morning and offer a prayer to the Creator. It is a way that my people pay homage to the sun, giver of life to me and to the planet. Now each morning I light a candle at my prayer altar. I connect with the flame of the candle and the flame of life in my heart. I give thanks for this fire and this life."*

As a child Carolyn loved the lights at Christmas; their light helped her to feel warm and comforted. Her family lighted candles on the Christmas tree in accordance with a Western European tradition stemming from rituals honoring the return of the sun in winter. As an adult, she researched the old European Winter Solstice holiday and discovered a whole spiritual tradition that had been lost to her. Carolyn now practices a similar yet different candle lighting ritual at Winter Solstice.

> *"Today when I light the solstice candles I think of my English and Celtic ancestors who endured long, cold winter evenings together. I can sometimes feel all of us huddling together waiting for the sun to return on the longest day of the year. I burn candles often in January and February, not only at the Winter Solstice; this helps me stay warm emotionally and spiritually. It feels like a very supportive thing to do. When I light the candles I feel connected to my ancestors and to the life force that dwells within all creatures on earth."*

Creating New Rituals

> *"A good ritual is an activity that brings us closer to our God. It's a signal that we want to know her, an invitation for her participation in our life. Ritual also provides a safe way for us to get to know each other."*

As we can see, women are reserving bits and pieces gathered in their spiritual journeys for later integration into new collective participatory actions that help them connect with their authentic spirituality. Some call these actions rituals.

There is a vast variety of rituals, ranging from very simple practices performed alone in a matter of minutes to long, involved ceremonies with many participants. However simple or complicated, rituals are made up of a variety of ingredients: words, actions, music, special adornment, and spiritual objects. When participating in ritual we may use all of these ingredients or only one. For example, think about the difference between an elaborate wedding ceremony and the repetition of grace at the dinner table. Most likely the wedding ceremony uses all the elements of ritual available. It is designed to evoke a strong emotional and spiritual bond that will last a lifetime. The spirit of the ritual is designed to touch not only the individuals at the center of the ceremony but everyone in attendance. When we say grace at the dinner table the degree of spiritual involvement is usually less; therefore, fewer words, actions, and spiritual regalia are required.

Personal rituals can add spiritual significance to traditional occasions such as birthdays, graduations, and other family celebrations. Religious ceremonies like weddings, funerals, and memorial services are sometimes enhanced by the addition of personal rituals that hold special significance for the participants. Women use ritual to help them get through the rough spots in a day or the particular difficulties of a given task. Performing a ritual can help change frustration to patience. Simple rituals that take only minutes to perform can lift our spirits. Lighting incense and affirming we are at peace with ourselves, for example, can help us find tranquillity.

Lily uses personal ritual to bring spiritual meaning to a social event and creates a spiritual sharing experience for herself and her close friends. She uses an altar and the importance of the objects placed upon it to deepen her connection to the celebration of her birthday.

"I did a wonderful birthday celebration for myself about three years ago. I wanted to honor my Inner Child. I invited my very favorite friends and told them we were having an afternoon tea. I chose my friends very carefully. It was just my network of women friends, with whom I share a lot.

"The table I set up became incredibly important to me, like an altar. It had a combination of woman things and little girl things on it. The process of setting that up was spiritual for me. I knew each piece of the preparations of that altar/table. The table was incredible; it helped us to do some important sharing. I remember my five-year-old just loved it; she was transformed. It was a very meaningful ritual for me. I really created something special, a healing bridge to my past."

Tina talks about her unique way of creating a spiritual space for herself using jewelry making and ritual adornment. The ritual with her necklaces helps her be present for her work and to detach from her work when it is completed. To make the necklaces, she uses objects very much like those she gathered in the woods as a child: pieces of quartz, bits of wood, feathers, shells, and beads.

"The drive for using this necklace was to have something to help me with the incredible letdown I would feel after finishing a photography session. When I put the necklace on, I acknowledge that I am going into a concentrated, focused state, and when I take it off, I acknowledge that now I am a 'regular person' again. It really works. I used amber for this necklace because it has a calming effect as well.

"Since that time I have made a lot of necklaces. When I was having difficulty getting pregnant, I made necklace after necklace, one for each phase of the ovulation process. My relationship with these necklaces is very ritualistic. When appropriate I hang the necklaces outdoors in the trees to get the energy of nature and be cleansed."

In order to establish or renew your connection to ritual, it is helpful to review your past participation in ritual. You will notice that some of your experiences were very public—rituals taking place in a temple or church, for example, with many participants. Others were more private—family rituals and ceremonies with close friends. Perhaps you will recall totally private rituals that you performed alone at home or outdoors.

My Connection with Ritual

Use this exercise to explore your participation in ritual.

Close your eyes and begin by using whichever grounding meditation most helps you to come into a comfortable relationship with yourself. Now allow your mind to travel back in time. See yourself involved in a ritual that was meaningful to you. You may find yourself in public, or you may find yourself alone. Notice if you feel a spiritual connection. How does the feeling of connection happen? What are you doing at the time?

If it feels comfortable, explore another past ritual experience in the same manner, asking yourself the same questions. When ready, come back to feeling your breath and your body sitting on the earth. Open your eyes.

Here are some questions to help you write about this exercise.

Was I alone or in public? What was I doing that I enjoyed? What felt good about this experience? Was there anything that felt uncomfortable? What benefit did I receive from this practice? Do I still participate in rituals like these?

Now make a list of rituals that were important to you. Put a check mark next to those that you still use.

Creating Private Ritual

Elements of Ritual

For the most part spiritual ceremonies are made of these elements: words, actions, music, adornment, and spiritual objects or images. Think of a familiar religious ritual, and see if you can identify the different elements. Notice how spiritual objects were used, how music added to the experience. As you build your own ritual, however simple or complex, you will want to take note of the elements you are using. Elements of ritual that are familiar and comfortable will bring the best results. Discover where you feel most connected. Which elements hold the most power for you?

Circle the elements of ritual that appeal to you most.

WORDS   ACTIONS   MUSIC   ADORNMENT

SPIRITUAL OBJECTS AND IMAGES

Begin by choosing one central element to place at the center/heart of your ritual.

Establishing a Time Frame

Because the primary purpose of ritual is to deepen your spirituality, you will want to make sure that all activities correspond directly to your own spiritual needs and understanding. Creating ritual is a very personal experience. You will have to decide when and how often you want to perform your ritual. In the morning or in the evening? How many times a week? Some rituals can be performed every day; others maybe only once a year. It doesn't matter what time or date you choose as long as it works for you. By doing this you are creating a form, a ritual calendar that speaks to you, a safe and comfortable structure for your practice.

A Word About Prayer

Basically prayers are words we say out loud or to ourselves that help us to open to our spirituality. Whether we are praising God or asking for healing and protection, prayer can create a verbal pathway to the divine. When using prayer to renew your spirituality you might try reciting a prayer from a religious text. See if you can connect to the words. Discover if they hold meaning for you. You may find that your own words, spoken with feeling, are your most powerful prayers.

Choosing Ritual Objects

You will want to choose objects to which you feel drawn spiritually, objects that interest you, but also with which you feel comfortable. A crystal wand, for example, although very beautiful and mysterious looking, may prove too unfamiliar and difficult to integrate into your personal ritual. To begin, you will want to look for objects that hold personal meaning for you. Start considering things that are already familiar, objects that already hold meaning for you: a branch from the cedar tree out back, a flower from your garden, an image from your bedroom wall. Let these personal objects speak to you. They can tell you of their spiritual qualities and how they might be used.

Working with a Spiritual Object

Choose an object or image to which you are drawn. Place it on your altar or in your spiritual space. With your eyes open, contemplate the object. Relax your eyes, and gaze at it for a while. Notice its form and color. Ask yourself, What feelings do I get from this object? What kind of energy does it project? Ask your inner voice how this object can be helpful to you. How could it be used in your ritual? End your meditation with gratefulness to your inner voice.

It's important to develop ritual practices that work for each of us as individuals.

Applying Ritual Techniques

Here is a list of ritual techniques. Each has a history of use in a spiritual context. Let your eyes drift over the list. Notice if any of these techniques jump out at you or feel friendly to you. If so, try incorporating one into your spiritual practice.

1. Burning incense
2. Lighting candles
3. Listening to inspirational music in the morning
4. Observing a moment of silence before eating
5. Reciting a prayer each evening at sunset
6. Drawing and interpreting a tarot card
7. Drinking water, tea, or another beverage as part of a ceremony
8. Using an herb, plant, or root for a spiritual purpose
9. Bowing or kneeling before an altar, spiritual object, or spiritual image

You might want to research some of these practices. Learning about their traditional use is another way of opening yourself to new possibilities.

Attending a Public Ritual

If you are not familiar with public ritual, you might consider attending one. If you feel uncomfortable going alone, invite a friend to accompany you. If you are familiar with a certain type of public ritual, you may want to branch out and try something new—perhaps by attending a religious observance that holds meaning for a friend.

There are many ways to experience public ritual. You can remain the observer, taking in and evaluating the scene from a distance. There is nothing wrong with this if it is how you feel most comfortable. Public rituals also can be opportunities for strong spiritual connection and deepening, however. Remember, authentic spiritual experience can occur only in a context of trust and mutual respect. Participate in the ritual to the degree you feel comfortable.

Public Ritual

Attend and participate in a ceremony that interests you. Notice the parts of the ritual that particularly appeal to you. Think about the elements of the ritual and how they affect you. Circle the elements that speak to you most:

WORDS   ACTIONS   MUSIC   ADORNMENT

SPIRITUAL OBJECTS AND IMAGES

Is there anything you might like to take from this ceremony and apply to your own use of ritual?

We suggest you use your sense of inner knowing or "at homeness" when deciding whether to incorporate ritual acts into your spiritual practices.

Integration

This exercise may help you clarify the role of ritual in your spiritual life.

Contemplate the questions that follow; you may want to record your responses.

How has ritual played a role in my spiritual journey?

Would I like to create a spiritual connection with a ritual object?

Am I more comfortable with public rituals, or private ones?

What is my general feeling about using spiritual rituals in my life today?

Whatever your vehicle for spiritual connection, it is of paramount importance that you remain connected to yourself. Without this personal connection, extravagant rituals or captivating religious works of art will only serve to divert you from your path. Each spiritual experience should be grounded in a feeling of authenticity and integrity.

Listening to Your Intuition

10

"Intuitive knowing is a spiritual event, It involves seeing things clearly, seeing things as they really are."

We live in a culture that relies on reason and logic to obtain knowledge and understanding. Nonrational ways of knowing tend to be discouraged. How many times have you put forth a vague feeling about something, a tentative hunch about a situation, only to be greeted by a derogatory remark about women's intuition? In spite of, or perhaps because of, this seemingly patriarchal emphasis on logic, women retain an apparent facility with intuitive thought.

The use of intuition for accessing spiritual knowledge has long been the domain of women. Although women appear to feel more comfortable relying on intuition, intuitional thought occurs in both women and men; it is part of our inheritance as human beings, a way of knowing ultimately available to us all. Angela, a Presbyterian minister, discusses what she sees as the gift of intuition and its historical use by women in the Jewish and Christian traditions.

"I think intuition is heightened the more mature one's spirituality becomes. From a Judeo-Christian perspective, when you look at women in the scriptures, intuition is their strongest and most consistent gift. They never question what they encounter. It is the men in the scriptures that are questioning. For example, the woman who is crazy sees Jesus and she says, 'This is the holy one.' The people tell her to be quiet. Jesus touches her, and the woman pours oil over him. She knows who he is. All the women know who he is because they intuitively recognize the power. Women who have a hard time with their spirituality ought to go back and claim the powerful women in the scriptures."

Intuition can be like an apparition, here one minute, gone the next. Its mysterious appearance, however, is not an accident: a few crossed wires in the brain creating a special opening to hidden knowledge. Intuition is cultivated in stillness, by being with oneself in very much the same way one prays or meditates. The magic or mystery of intuition arises from its ability to unlock the door to direct knowledge without the use of rational thought. Its quality of knowingness can be described as a feeling of penetrating a situation with the mind, going under a problem, or seeing within it. Helene describes the use of her intuition as shining sunlight on a foggy situation.

"The fog clears, and I am left with the truth. I can see the real picture."

Because intuition does not provide a logical pathway to knowledge, when asked from where the knowledge comes, or how we know it, we cannot rationally say, for when we use our intuition, we tap into knowledge that is part of our consciousness but normally exists beyond our awareness, information that until a moment before had been unavailable to us.

It is only natural, then, that our inability to explain intuition in rational terms might undermine our trust of it. We may also doubt our intuition because we are inexperienced and therefore unsure of our intuitive impressions. We may have intuitive feelings but not know how or when to act on them. Some of us may doubt that we receive any reliable information at all. Exploring the connection between our intuition and spirituality can also raise questions.

When considering these doubts it may be helpful to remember that although sometimes overlooked, intuition has played a part in traditional religion. Some denominations of Christianity rely on introspective knowing to come into closer contact with God. Maggie remembers an intuitive connection with the Holy Spirit.

"Characteristics of the Holy Spirit were pretty feminine, for example, sensing the spirit speaking in a breeze; this was the intuitive way of knowing."

Christian contemplative prayer, for example, involves applying intuition to spiritual concepts like faith; it is hoped that intuitional investigation will reveal deeper spiritual knowledge. A devoted Christian asking for guidance with a problem may use the Bible as an intuitive tool. In prayer, one may feel a special scripture or verse seemingly appearing from nowhere, providing the comfort and knowledge needed to overcome the difficulty.

Traditional religions teach us that to establish a moral and ethical direction in life, we must rely on our conscience; an inner voice that tells us right from wrong. Consulting our conscience, we ask for inner guidance on how to proceed in a given situation for the good of all concerned. The phrase "Let your conscience be your guide" is one of the cornerstones of Christian morality and can be understood as an intuitional experience.

Women approach intuition from a variety of experiences and beliefs. Some of us have spent years developing a relationship to our intuitive abilities; others will feel as if such an exploration is brand-new. Attitude is formed by experience. Let us take a moment to examine our beliefs and attitudes toward the use of intuition.

Beliefs About Intuition

Write out any messages about your intuition you have internalized from family, friends, or religion. Take time to look them over. Pick one belief that you will examine further, and write it here. You can examine this belief by discussing it with others. Pick three friends or family members and ask each one if they share this belief about intuition. Allow yourself to listen to the resulting opinions without feeling you need to defend a position. You are just exploring.

The Voice Within

Intuition brings us knowledge, and that knowledge can take different forms. Many of us rediscover our intuition by opening to our spiritual selves, by paying attention to messages and feelings of a spiritual nature. Although perhaps hesitant at first, many of the women we interviewed spoke of the benefits of relying on their intuitive voice. Generally, intuition was not seen as a mysterious force rooted in superstition. On the contrary, women felt that intuition involved a "deep inner knowingness" or, as one woman put it, "my natural ability to access truth." In some cases truth was spoken of as an inner voice. Intuition is an inner event; there is a felt need to connect with an inner sense of knowing and to open from that point outward.

While traveling in Europe with her mother, Carol was involved in a serious bus accident that killed many of the people onboard. By paying attention to her intuition, she mysteriously saved both their lives. The experience opened her to the belief in a spiritual power beyond herself. Carol was sixteen years old at the time.

A Story from Carol

We were returning from a day in the Black Forest, late in the afternoon. My mother and I were sitting near the front of the tourist bus, when I suddenly felt a desire to move to the back, where there was more room, so I could sleep the rest of the way. This was very unlike me, because I never was able to sleep in public places and never took naps in the afternoon. However, I insisted we move to the back of the bus. Only minutes after we changed seats, our bus collided with a large transport truck. Everyone in the front of the bus was killed and those seated in the rows in front of us seriously injured. I was not hurt at all. My mother suffered minor cuts and bruises. I remember feeling this strange timeless feeling as I emerged from the bus. This feeling lasted for a couple of days. I felt a sense of awe when I realized what had happened. I had received divine counsel; someone or something spoke to me, telling me to move to the back of the bus, and I followed the directions. This event fostered a curiosity about what I now call intuition. It confirmed for me a belief in the nonrational world that has never left me.

In childhood we rely heavily on our intuition, not having fully developed our capacity for rational thought. Our inner voice speaks to us more clearly and we are perhaps more likely to listen. Unfortunately, as we progress through the educational system our natural intuitiveness is discouraged in favor of scientific investigation and reason. The curiosity and openness of childhood gives way to more measured and logical ways of experiencing life. We can lose our ability for nonrational thought.

Nelly remembers a childhood experience of trusting her intuition. She received intuitive knowledge about potential danger to herself and others. She trusted her sense of knowingness, and it was validated by her mother.

A Story from Nelly

When I was eight years old, something happened in my community that created a lot of fear and anxiety. Some kids had planted bombs around the school that they had made from their chemistry sets. One morning I awoke from a dream and told my mom they had found the bombs in a sewer across the street from the school. But the bombs had not been found yet. A couple of days later, the police discovered the bombs exactly where I had indicated.

My mother was very impressed with this, and I got a lot of praise. This story is often retold. It's become a bit of a family myth. After that I felt good whenever I got an intuitive flash. My experience was put in a positive frame and not associated with anything fearful. Trusting my intuition had literally kept me safe, because I stayed away from the sewer where the bomb was planted. I grew to trust my intuition more. To this day, whenever I have the sense that something is going to happen and then it actually does happen, I feel safe and at peace. I know that I take care of myself in this way.

Nelly tells us of an experience later in life when she again felt protected through paying attention to her intuition.

"One day at work I got the message to go home and meditate during my lunch break. That was the only day I ever did this. During meditation my inner voice directed me to pray to the Great Spirit for protection. I had never prayed to the Great Spirit before. That very evening on my way home from work I was in a serious car accident. My car was torn up except where I was sitting. The police told me, 'You were very lucky; you could have been killed.' I believe my intuition protected me by guiding me to the Great Spirit."

Cultivating Intuition

Here are two exercises that can help as you begin to explore your intuition.

Childhood intuitive experience. Use free-form writing to put yourself in touch with a childhood intuitive experience. Write about how your childhood messages might have protected and instructed you.

Feelings about people. Spend some time daily jotting down feelings you may have about people in your spiritual journal. These feelings will be fleeting impressions, intuitive glimpses. They can happen when you talk to people or when you dream or think about them. Then put the notebook away for a while. When you feel ready, take it out again and reread what you have written. What thread of truth was hidden in what you were feeling at the time you wrote? What do your words tell you in retrospect? Is the information helpful to you?

Sometimes it is hard to trust ourselves. Self-trust is a learned experience. Not all of us have been taught to trust our perceptions, given accurate and consistent feedback and the unconditional love needed to back it up. Even today a woman can often find her opinion, or even the glimmering of an idea, snuffed out before she gets the chance to test it. Consequently, we may feel a lack of confidence in our inner sense of knowing.

Another potential complication is that the intuitive voice takes different forms. It can also convey different things. Consider the stories of Carol and Nelly. Both felt protected and reassured by their intuitive messages, but their intuitive messages came in different ways. Carol gets an unusual idea and follows it; and Nelly receives specific knowledge about an event in a dream. What is important is not how our intuition speaks to us but the quality and intention of its message.

Intuition

Think for a moment about the last time you had a feeling or a hunch about something. What type of message was it? What did it convey? Circle the responses that fit most closely.

ASSURANCE   COMFORT   PROTECTION   KNOWLEDGE   GUIDANCE

In our culture the intuitive experience is seen as unusual and infrequent. However, as women investigate their use of intuition, many report receiving intuitive messages more often than they had originally thought. It can be exciting to realize that we are in touch with our inner voice, but the quandary remains: Which messages should we trust, and should we act on the information received? It may be helpful to know that whatever form your intuitional messages take, each encounter can be handled in a similar manner.

Intuitive messages need to be investigated before they can be put to good use. A questioning attitude is helpful; an overcautious attitude will undermine your spiritual progress; a naive, unquestioning trust could cause undue confusion or harm. (The questions in the exercise "Questioning Doubt" on page 35 will be helpful in striking a balance between mistrust and gullibility.)

Whether you consider yourself a veteran or a newcomer, we suggest that you consider three basic questions when examining your intuition: What is the message? What is its intention? Is the message meant to be shared?

What Is the Message?

As interesting or important as an intuitional message may seem, it is best not to act until you are sure you understand it. You might practice writing down some intuitional messages you receive about everyday events. Sometimes all you will get is a vague feeling about something. That's perfectly OK. Sometimes we have to sit with a feeling awhile before we can see meaning in it. You may want to write the meaning in your spiritual journal for future reference. It can be interesting to consult it later to see if the message actually played itself out in your life in some way.

At times you may feel frustrated when unable to decipher an intuitive message. If this happens, we suggest a gentle and patient attitude. You might want to simply put the issue aside and go on about your day. If you revisit your intuitional feeling later, you may see its meaning in retrospect.

What Is the Intention of the Message?

Take time to contemplate the intention behind your intuitive message. Is the intention comfort, protection, assurance, knowledge, or guidance? You will be better prepared to understand your message and to act on it if you understand its purpose.

Is the Intuitive Message Meant to Be Shared?

Although our intuition may supply us with helpful information or support, often it is not meant to be shared by others. In fact, in some instances, sharing intuitive knowledge will create rather than clear up confusion. As we consider sharing an intuitive feeling, we can sometimes imagine potential negative consequences for ourselves. When you are moved to share an intuitional message, always check out your motivation. When sharing, explain that it is your truth, not necessarily anyone else's. If in doubt, keep it to yourself.

We also suggest you review the exercise "Sources of Support" earlier in the book on page 26. Ask yourself who might be your most appropriate support person as you explore your intuitive voice. It will be helpful to share your doubts and fears with someone else. You may be confident that a spiritual leader or teacher can help you in this matter. Support is essential, but you are the final authority. Decisions about the validity and importance of your intuition rest with you.

A helpful way to check out one's intuitive messages and to develop intuition is to use a tool—like tarot cards, rune stones, and the *I Ching*—specifically designed to deepen our connection with intuition. You might feel more comfortable having objects, images, and writings with which to compare your intuitional flashes. Tools such as these can be purchased in spiritual bookstores with accompanying instructions. You may find classes and support groups available as well.

Divination Tarot

This exercise can be adapted for using other tools of divination. Focus on your intuitive feeling or message; affirm out loud that the card you pick will shed light on your intuitive understanding. Now draw a tarot card from the deck. Sit quietly and contemplate the image on the card. Ask yourself if the card in any way validates or contradicts the feeling you are having. Look for symbols that may enhance the meaning of the intuitive thought you are having. You might note this card in your journal or leave it out on your altar to look at again in a couple of days. Then ask the same question again. In retrospect, was this card a validation of my intuition?

It is interesting to notice that intuitive abilities have often been associated with people in rural, nonindustrialized societies, living closer to the natural rhythms of life. When we are raised close to nature, we come to respect and understand her natural patterns that affect our lives. For example, a farmer living off the land is directly influenced by patterns she perceives in the weather. She learns to read the "signs of nature." One way to think of intuition is as a way of understanding patterns that are beyond our control. When our lives are in harmony with the patterns and cycles of nature, these forces eventually become part of our awareness.

Personified Intuition

Religion and culture can also influence the way in which intuitive knowledge is revealed. Some religions provide examples of the intuitive voice speaking to us in human or near-human form. In the Christian tradition, angels and saints are sometimes messengers of comfort and support. For Randy, personified intuitive experiences began in childhood. Growing up an abused child, she received spiritual sustenance from an inner voice she initially thought of as her guardian angel. From the experience of listening to her guardian angel, she has learned to respect knowledge coming from other spiritual sources today.

"God felt like a scary man who was big and far away. So as a child I connected to angels 'cause they weren't that scary. I had a guardian angel. We had to pray and kneel by the side of the bed. It was then that I would talk to my guardian angel and get an answer that was very comforting for me. That is still true for me today. I can get very quiet and listen inside and get an answer. What has changed is

who I think I am talking to. As a child I talked to my guardian angel, to Jesus, and sometimes to God. Today I feel my answers come from a guide, a being who is pure light, or from the ground of being. When I pray I sometimes think of the Goddess. I experience layers of connection. It reminds me of when I was a child, when it was easy to connect with my guardian angel."

Marie feels that growing up Roman Catholic and hearing about angels and saints at an early young age made the concept of spirit guides more accessible to her.

"The idea that there were beings with messages for me who lived in another reality was already part of my spiritual belief system."

When Catholicism ceased to work for her as a adult, Marie found that she was drawn to her "guides."

"Sometimes they feel like family. I don't attach any particular gender to my guides. I was told that at one point my grandfather was there trying to make up for being so mean to me in life. At one time I had a Native American spirit guide. I sometimes feel my mother with me and my grandmother. I greet them by holding my hands out in front of me. I sometimes feel a lot of heat and energy. I have an intuitive awareness that we are not here by ourselves, that we are here to do work and that they are here to help us. I feel connected to my guides through some karmic adventure. Perhaps they were family to me once or people I have helped in another time."

Marie explains that she receives direction about decisions and choices she must make in her life. She uses her guides to find answers to difficult life question she is facing.

"There are different kinds of help we can get from intuitive knowledge. I ask for guidance and help to be led in the right direction. I am given respite from having to be so responsible, to have all the answers myself."

Inner Teacher/Inner Voice

The inner teacher is a personification of your inner voice, or intuition. If you feel it could be helpful to work with a personification of your inner voice, you may want to try the following exercise.

Begin by using Grounding 3, Become a Tree, on page 12. When you are ready, imagine your inner teacher before you. Get a sense of your relationship to your inner teacher at this time. If you would like a closer connection, ask your teacher what you can do to strengthen communication. State that you would like to hear your inner teacher's voice more frequently and more clearly. Affirm that you will be open to messages from your inner teacher. Affirm that these messages come from a sacred place within you.

Messages of Comfort

Often we receive intuitive messages when we are emotionally vulnerable. These messages provide us with clarity, inspiration, and hope. Three women talk about messages like these; each receives her message in a nonrational manner, from a feeling of intuitive understanding. Each woman internalizes the knowledge and benefits from it.

"There was a time when I was trying to reach into myself. I was starting to write, and I was scared that I wouldn't be able to do it. I turned on the radio just as I was being overcome with feelings of insecurity. The lyrics came in for 'Bridge over Troubled Water.' I intuitively understood this message from my mother. I felt the strong presence of my mother. We always communicated through music. I thanked her out loud. It was real basic encouragement. This felt like a spiritual experience."

COLLEGE STUDENT, 55

"I remember a time when I was lying in bed crying, feeling a sense of loss. I was very upset. I remember the sense of someone lying in bed next to me, and I smelled a familiar scent and recognized it as my great aunt's perfume. Then I had this tremendous sense of solace and peace that everything was going to be all right. I used to smell this perfume as a child when she took care of me. Whenever I was sad, she would take me in her lap and console me. I remembered how she would wrap her big skirts around me. My aunt was a very loving and nurturing woman."

VISUAL ARTIST, 31

"The strangest experience I ever had was with the yellow blanket my grandmother made for my son. A few years after she died, I was going through some stuff trying to decide what to get rid of, and I came upon the yellow blanket. As I held the blanket in my hand I had an experience of my grandmother being right there with me. It happened at a very quiet time when I was going through things calmly and slowly. It happened very quickly. I knew something very serious was happening. I knew I had to keep that blanket. At the time I felt fine, not at all

confused by this. But afterward when my logical mind took over, I became frightened. It was like I got knowledge or a message that I was not prepared for. Today the blanket is not that important to me. I realize it could have been something else that triggered those feelings. The most important thing is that I felt her there with me, and she was all right. After that experience I lost all my fear surrounding Grandma's death. I had been so worried about her death and all the suffering she had gone through. But now I know she is OK. Her essence is OK. I feel a whole lot more peace about her passing."

MOTHER, 36

Leticia tells us about an important spiritual experience in which she felt intuitively comforted. She had been feeling very upset and angry because she had suffered a miscarriage.

"My friend Pat was praying for me, and I felt two hands on my shoulders. When those hands touched me, it really scared me. I tried to see who it was, but there was no one there. I just broke down and started crying and crying. Then the hands became gentle and caressed my shoulders for a while. Finally the feeling left. I believe it was an angel."

Stories of other people's intuitive insights and experiences can also be spiritually comforting. Claudia tells of being comforted by a story told to her of a relative who received a powerful message from an unnamed spiritual source.

"Stories were most important to me as a child. There is a story in our family of a relative, Eliza Snow, who was in a coma and came back to life. She taught primary school and remembered seeing one of her students in heaven while in the coma. There is no way she could have known that this child died. The child had been missing and was later found dead. I was able to touch into something spiritual through this story. Eliza Snow had brought back knowledge from the unknown. She made the spiritual world real for me."

Florence talks about being called to trust the presence of God at her side. She speaks of this experience much the way one might speak of receiving intuitive knowledge. She knows God is beside her.

"I remember after I was separated from my husband, my family was falling apart. I called an Episcopal priest who was my spiritual mentor to come over and bless my house. After the ceremony was over and everyone left, I was in the living room crying and crying. I distinctly felt a comforting arm around me, and I knew it was the arm of God. I felt he was calling me to trust, and I believe that he

was right there with me. It was so powerful and so tangible. It felt like my dad with his arm around me, nurturing me, saying, 'It's OK, sweetie, I'll take care of it.'"

Comfort

If you feel a need for spiritual nurturance and comfort in your life, try the following exercise.

Use one of the grounding exercises to establish a sense of calmness and presence within. Now allow yourself to open to your heart. Feel your heart center in your body. Let it open and expand to the world around you. Take three deep breaths, letting go of any tension you may be holding. Now open yourself to a feeling of comfort and support. Understand that it comes from a spiritual source appropriate to you. Let the feeling in. Now prepare yourself for an intuitive message about comfort and safety. Ask yourself in what ways you can make yourself more comfortable in your life.

Uncomfortable Messages

Generally, intuitive thought is considered helpful to us. Messages give us direction, comfort us, and keep us safe. In some cases intuitive messages can be considered spiritual teachings. Sometimes, however, we may feel uncomfortable receiving intuitive knowledge. Having an intuitive negative feeling about a person or a situation or receiving knowledge of a painful event, although potentially helpful, is naturally difficult to process or integrate. Leticia tells of her struggle to understand and accept her intuitive abilities. She comes from a tradition of spiritism and supernatural belief; her family's spiritual practices involve the use of intuition, psychic connections with the living, and spirits who have passed on. Although frightened by it as a young girl, as an adult Leticia is attempting to embrace her gift, to strengthen her spiritual connection. Leticia's story illustrates that, for some of us, there is a close connection between psychic occurrences and intuitive knowing.

"My mother was Pentecostal, and my father was Catholic, and both were from Puerto Rico. I was raised Catholic, but I really didn't relate to it too well. I remember when I was in church I would feel something pulling my hair or yanking on my clothes. I'd turn around, and there was nothing there. These kinds of psychic things happened to me a lot when I was little. I have a twin sister; she

would see things. I would feel them, especially things that felt wrong. It could happen in small ways. Like once I locked the door because my mother told me to, and then it flew open. My mother accused me of not locking the door, but I know I did. I even put the chain on. I knew the door flying open wasn't good because it didn't feel good.

"I know that my grandfather who lived with us did black magic in his room with an altar. At the time it was real hush-hush. I feel the door flying open was connected to his magic. I think he was doing ceremonies and bringing bad energy into the house. I think this was partly why I had some of those experiences. I had some pretty scary dreams or waking visions. I can remember how they felt. They were very awful. Even talking about it today, I feel upset. My sister was seeing things in those days, and I knew it wasn't right. She shouldn't have been seeing things move, a broom dance, for example. I know how to judge these psychic occurrences by how I feel when they happen. It all depends on the feeling I get. There are good feelings and bad feelings. I just can't imagine anyone going with a bad feeling. I go with something comforting, something soothing.

"Today I can walk into a room and feel negative energy if it's there. My grandmother will call and talk to me about these things, which is nice. My family accepts this part of me now."

Leticia works with her dreams and visions using her intuition to decipher hidden meaning and knowledge.

"In my dream I saw some children of our family. I saw one child with a lot of darkness around him. I saw two sisters singing in the choir; one was very shadowed out, the other very sparkly and bright. I've been trying to put all these pieces together, trying to understand what it all means. In my dream Grandmother told me to pray for them. This was a dream I studied all day long, trying to feel the meaning. It was so real; I knew in my heart that it was real.

"Sometimes I wonder why a person is so much in my heart that I think about them four or five times a day, so then I may pray for them because it feels like they need help. I feel they are in pain of some kind. Sometimes when I pray for people, later on I hear that they really were tired and they really were upset that day. I've just started realizing that I get these spiritual messages."

Grounding and Safety

When receiving messages or feelings that feel unwelcome or uncomfortable, it is helpful to come back to yourself through grounding. This helps you to establish boundaries and separate yourself from any unwelcome thoughts or messages. You can use this tool to comfort yourself. The Mother Earth Meditation is particularly helpful when you feel unsafe.

After a complete grounding, ask yourself any of the following questions. Let your responses come to you from your sacred place within.

1. Is this message something I need to pay attention to?

2. What is the source of these uncomfortable feelings?

3. Do these feelings remind me of other messages I have received before?

4. Is this a message from my inner voice, or am I just worried about something?

Precognition

Another form of intuition is precognition: knowledge from an unknown source about a future event. This kind of intuitive experience allows us a glimpse into the future. Our intuitive thoughts have a predictive quality to them. When this happens it seems as if time stands still or ceases to exist; we may have a sense of the timelessness of existence. Not all intuitive messages include knowledge about the future, but it is not uncommon. Cheryl sometimes receives notice of her relatives' impending passing before it happens. Although she admits it is scary at times, she welcomes these messages. For Cheryl they are confirmation of her belief in other dimensions of existence and her own intuitive abilities.

"I remember the day my daddy died when I was ten years old. He wasn't married to my mom, and he had another family. On Sunday my mother and I were having breakfast, and my mother asked me to pass her something, and I didn't hear her. Instead I just looked at her and said, 'Daddy's dead.' Then the phone rang, and it was his sister telling us he had just fallen off the roof and broken his neck. The same thing happened when my grandfather died. He was real sick with cancer. It was my mom's turn to take care of him. As she was leaving to go bring him home, I told her that he wasn't coming back with her to our house. When she got to the hospital he was dead. I had known ahead of time. When my husband died, I was at an AA meeting, and someone called me to the telephone. When she called me to the phone, I got incredibly sad, and I knew I would never see my husband again. In fact, it was my son on the phone, telling me my husband was dead. My mom has this same kind of ability, but she mostly denies it."

Intuitive messages sometimes come to us in dramatic ways. In the case of her sister, Cheryl managed to hear the message clearly and use it positively.

"I was reading in bed at night, and as I turned over I saw my sister Virginia's image on the wall, and she was bleeding. I blinked my eyes, and I saw it again. The next day my brother called and told me where Virginia was. I went right over there to see her. I felt like God had given me the opportunity to see her and tell her some things I needed to tell her. We'd been having a hard time since I got sober. So when she died I felt complete."

Cheryl goes on to explain her connections to other lifetimes and how messages from the past strengthen her.

"I know that this is not my first lifetime—I've been here before—because I have some experiences where there is no way that I should know what I know. I can be talking to someone, and while we are talking I can think in my mind exactly the thing they are going to say next. The only thing I can attribute this to is that I must have had this conversation sometime before. I remember when I was in the sixth grade I would close my eyes and see myself in Egypt. I was wearing the tunics they wore, and I was playing by the water with a dish. This image has come to me periodically throughout my life, maybe twelve or fifteen times. It feels very real. There is one memory in which I am on a slave ship coming over here, and I am having hot coals poured down my throat. Some mornings when I awake from this dream, my throat is so sore I can't talk. I can still feel the coals cutting into my throat. I feel these dreams are spiritual messages to me to never forget where I came from and the suffering of my people."

How often in retrospect have we regretted not following an inkling, a feeling in the pit of our stomach? Women are now learning to trust uncomfortable feelings, even though they may be disturbed by negative messages or warnings. Illogical negative feelings about a person or a situation can be difficult to understand and accept. We can have an intense emotional reaction to disturbing intuitive messages and become confused, losing ourselves in emotional reaction rather than simply staying with the intuitive feeling and seeing where it leads.

Alice struggles with her negative feelings, searching for the intuitive knowledge behind them.

"All weekend I had the feeling something was going to happen to me personally. I tried to think positively, to tell myself, 'Oh, no,' but the feeling was overwhelming and would not go away. I was not able to pinpoint what was going to happen. During the weekend at theater rehearsal I would tell people that I felt

really bad, and they would ask, 'Are you sick?' and I would say, 'It's not a physical thing; I just don't feel well.' On that Sunday night I was in a very tragic car accident. Afterward I was really aware that my intuition had tried to warn me to stay home. Unfortunately, the message wasn't that clear. At the time it didn't feel like it was something I could prevent. Now I always try to listen to my intuition. I call it wisdom, actually."

Sometimes we may feel our intuition warning us of a potentially difficult or dangerous situation. You may want to protect yourself when this happens.

Protection

Use any of the following suggestions that are compatible with who you are to further your sense of spiritual protection:

1. Do free-form writing in your journal on "my sense of protection."
2. Place familiar sacred objects with which you have a strong spiritual connection in your sleeping space and generally around your environment.
3. Fill yourself with loving intentions toward all beings.
4. See beauty everywhere you go.
5. Consult with a spiritual teacher or mentor.
6. Affirm that you are filled with goodness and light.
7. Perform any type of physical exercise to regain closer connection with yourself and your body.

Some women, like Florence, felt their "call" to religion come in the form of an intuitive message. Florence hears the voice of God in her intuitive message.

"I was dissatisfied because I hadn't been feeling a sense of community at my church, and then in the middle of the night, I heard a voice saying, 'Try St. Michael's.' The first time I attended St. Michael's, the priest preached on community. I knew that was a call. Some might say that was my intuition. My view is that God called me. I think he calls people of all religious denominations."

Coincidence

When a coincidence occurs in one's life, it can be interpreted as spiritual if it is no longer experienced as meaningless or accidental. A connection between events becomes apparent; one feels order and purpose behind apparently coincidental events. Ann spoke of feeling spirituality working through synchronistic occurrences in her life.

"There were a series of 'coincidences' in my life. Some very specific needs of mine were being met in a very blatant and yet anonymous way. It felt like I was experiencing miracles. One example is that I was involved in this college ministry. I was having financial difficulties at the time and would invariably receive anonymous checks from people from the church that met the specific amount of financial need. A friend of mine who was a minister in my church had a child who died of SIDS. I sent them a portrait of their child as a gift. Months later, I was overdrawn in my checkbook by two hundred dollars because I had forgotten to write down a check. I was panicked. That same week I got a letter from that family with a check in it for two hundred dollars. This kind of thing happened many times. I understood that God was the only one who understood the specificity of my needs. I understood that as God providing."

Not all meaningful coincidences are as obvious as the ones Ann describes. Sometimes we need to look a bit deeper to discover them at work in our life.

Meaningful Coincidence

As time passes we may gain insight into apparently meaningless occurrences. One of the most effective and practical ways to learn to discern meaningless coincidence from meaningful coincidence is to keep track of each coincidental event that occurs. In your journal, note any feelings or intuitive messages you have about the coincidence at the time it happens. Later, in retrospect, review each event, looking for meaning that may or may not have been apparent at the time the event occurred.

Take some time now to recall any recent intuitive moments.

Dissecting the Intuitive Moment

Write down one example of an intuitive message you have recently received. Notice what type of intuition it was.

Think about the underlying intention of the message. Was it comforting? Did it provide guidance? Were there predictive qualities to it? Did you feel comforted by the knowledge?

Did you take any action based on this intuition? If so, how did it turn out for you?

Nurturing
Relationship and Community

11

Community is the circle that embraces us, the safety net. Community is the line that connects us, the heart line. We bond in relationship and through these relationships give birth to spiritual community. Our friends and family extend a guiding hand when we hit obstacles on our healing journey. They offer comfort and wise words when we are confused. They remind us of our inherent beauty when we doubt ourselves. Friends and family can be role models as they travel their own spiritual paths with integrity, compassion, and courage.

Although the spiritual journey is actually a landscape of many terrains and dimensions, for a moment let us imagine the path as linear and one-dimensional. Some people are behind you on the path, others beside you, and still others ahead of you. All these people are essential to your spiritual community.

The people behind catch you if you stumble or fall. They soothe you and calm you when you need rest and rejuvenation. These are the members of your community who are there for you. They understand you and are accepting and nurturing of your spiritual journey. They are your spiritual family.

The people ahead of you are beckoning you forward on your healing journey. They know the section of the path ahead, for they have traveled it. They know where the potholes lie, where the sharp cliffs descend. They know the places of utter beauty and remind you to remain alert and delight in the scenery. These people are your guides, your teachers, your mentors. Although they have been down the path, you cannot walk in their footprints; you have to find your own footing. But they are there to lead you on.

There are those who travel beside you. They are walking beside you for this segment of the journey. You look over at them and see yourself reflected. You feel stronger as you see their strength. You feel more beautiful as you see their beauty. These people are spiritual friends and partners.

The spiritual healing journey is even more complex and multidimensional than this description. We travel many paths, sometimes at the same time. The healing journey is a mosaic in constant flux.

Think of your spiritual community in an expansive way, as including all the people in your life with whom you share spirituality. With some of your community you may share spiritual practice; with others you may share spiritual conversation; with others you might simply sense support. You will turn to some members of your community for guidance or teaching; others may turn to you for direction and mentoring.

Community Support

Spend some time now connecting with your spiritual community through this exercise, the one on the next page, or both.

In this exercise you get a clearer picture of your spiritual community by graphically representing them. Draw a line horizontally across the middle of the page. This line represents the lap of your spiritual journey that you are on right now. Near the center of the line make a representation of yourself. Then graphically represent other members of your spiritual community on this line. Place the people or groups of people to whom you feel most connected on your journey on this line. You can represent these people or groups of people however you like. You might write down their names, or draw stick figures, or use photographs or symbols that represent them. You might want to adjust their size to represent the importance of your connection to them right now in your life. Place them ahead of you, beside you, or behind you. Think about why you have placed them where you have placed them. Then find a word or feeling, or perhaps a body movement, that describes your connection to this person.

Because community can be a nurturing spiritual home and a source of spiritual renewal, it is important to take the time to appreciate and acknowledge your community. Remember to acknowledge everyone in your community—yourself, your family, your friends, and your cultural and religious communities.

Appreciating Spiritual Community

In this exercise you use guided imagery to more fully acknowledge and appreciate your community. Imagine yourself at the center of a circle that is your spiritual community. Send yourself your own loving support for your spiritual renewal, speaking the words of acknowledgment aloud. Think about who sits closest to you in this circle, who the most supportive people in your spiritual community are. Express your appreciation to each of them. Speak these words aloud. Think about who is included in your larger spiritual community. Be expansive. Include everyone who supports and validates your spirituality. Acknowledge how this larger community encourages you on your spiritual path. Speak aloud words of acknowledgment and gratitude. Allow your community to grow even larger, to include all people throughout the world and across time who are on the spiritual path. Acknowledge your inherent connectedness.

Self-Love

Imagine community like a net. Each member of the community is a point on the net, and each relationship is a connecting thread. The strength and flexibility of the net really begins with the vitality of the individual points, and the basis of this vitality is self-love. Self-love and self-respect are the foundation of healthy relationships and trustworthy community.

When we are self-loving, we consider our happiness and take care of ourselves. We recognize our needs and express them to others. We remember to nurture our body, mind, and spirit. Self-respect and self-love provide a necessary foundation for spiritual development. Think about how you care for yourself.

Write About Self-Loving

Take time to write the responses to these questions in your spiritual journal. How do you care for yourself? How do you acknowledge and validate yourself? What do you do that gives you renewed energy and hope? Notice if the answers come easily and if you feel satisfied with your responses.

Self-love needs to be cultivated. We must commit ourselves over and over again to taking good care of ourselves. We then become able to know and honor our needs and to balance the different interests and relationships in our life. We discover a natural zest for life.

Creating Self-Love

The following exercises guide you through two ways of cultivating self-love. Work with either or both.

Guided imagery. Sometimes it can be easier to access self-love through our love for another. In the exercise you will use the technique of guided imagery to create self-love out of your love for another. After grounding and relaxing yourself, allow someone you love very much to appear before you. Feel the love you have for this person flowing out toward her or him. Let the love build up in your heart and mind. Then, instead of sending all this love to another, let some of it be for you. Let it flow back to yourself. Feel your love encircling your loved one and yourself. Feel the strength of your love. Feel the appreciation you are giving yourself. Sit in this loving energy for as long as you feel comfortable.

Self-loving activities. Make a list of ways that you might care for yourself better. Brainstorm many possibilities; don't worry right now about whether they are realistic. Just keep adding to the list until it seems as if you have run out of ideas; then think a little longer and come up with a few more. Leave the list for a little while. When you return to it, choose one thing to do for yourself and implement it.

Here are some things others have tried:

1. Each evening before bed I remind myself of one thing I enjoyed that day.
2. I imagine patting myself on my back and telling myself that I am doing really well.
3. I bought a new stuffed animal that I cuddle with when I feel discouraged.
4. I got a massage.

Our society and our religions have taught us, as women, to place the needs of others before our own. We have been taught to give of ourselves, and although this can open spiritual doors, it can also disempower our spiritual essence.

We might believe that caring for ourselves is selfish and so put our needs aside whenever possible. Discounting our needs can lead to resentment, bitterness, and a need to control. We can lose touch with our natural vitality and openheartedness. Then our generosity and love have gone awry. How can we include our own needs in the equation considering all involved?

Loving relationships involve give and take, surrendering and asserting ourselves. Relationships that function from a base of mutual respect can succeed
in attaining a delicate balance of both. Surrender is commonly defined as the
giving up of power and control, yielding to the influence of another. Given the
level of abuse and domination at work in our society, this kind of surrender can
lead us down a dangerous path. Perhaps we need to discover a different kind
of surrender, one that does not imply domination of one over another, but instead is for mutual benefit.

Linda, who was sexually abused in childhood, knows that spiritual surrender must be very different from her experience of personal powerlessness and
resignation as a victim of abuse.

> *"I have to look at surrender in a whole new way—a way that does not have to do
> with giving up power."*

Listen to Nelly as she clarifies her understanding of surrender in relationship through remembering a time in her past when she understood spiritual
surrender in a way that hurt her.

A STORY FROM NELLY

*When I entered college I had lots of questions without many satisfying answers. I
felt real out of place in the world and didn't like myself very well. I started studying comparative religions. I was intrigued by the notion of surrender and egoless-
ness that I read about in Buddhism.*

*At about the same time I became involved in my first long-term sexual relation-
ship. I gave myself up to my partner, thinking that was what was meant by surrender. Denying my own needs and visions, I went along with what my partner
wanted and forgot about myself. It was like I had no backbone, like there was
nobody home inside of me. I was devastated when he broke up with me and told
me that love had turned to pity.*

*I still have lots of questions about surrender, but I do know that for me a loving
relationship must include self-awareness and self-love. Then I can bring myself
more fully into the relationship. Then I stand on firm ground and can make better decisions about when to assert my needs and when to surrender to a higher
need or spiritual value.*

Lauren recently divorced her husband, realizing that she had lost herself
in the marriage. In this way she reclaimed her spirit.

"Before I left my husband I felt numb and empty. When I went to counseling, I said I felt like I was dying. You talk about someone with a 'broken spirit'—that's what it was like. I felt I had to get out of my marriage so that I could be myself again. There was no other lover; I hadn't left for someone else. It was just for me. I'm doing a lot of thinking now, asking myself what my goals are. I am feeling better about myself. I'm stronger, and I have more of a feeling inside again. That feeling inside is the spiritual force!"

At times, it can be spiritually liberating to put our needs aside for a higher benefit. Sharon has carefully considered when surrender is liberating rather than constricting. Using awareness, Sharon skillfully dances between nurturing her own needs and attending to the needs of others.

"When I am very present and aware, I can make clearer choices about when to put my needs aside. For example, I can remember nights when my child cried and I chose to stay awake with her because that was what was needed at the time. That act of placing my needs aside and not choosing sleep was uplifting and strengthening and gave me energy. It was a clear choice made from a place of awareness."

As women, we may find that before we can surrender ourselves, we have to honor ourselves. In order to pursue our spirituality, we must transform inner negativity into inner love and compassion. For many of us, the path to our God or Goddess is through the development of our own inner divinity.

Self-Honoring Ritual

Ritual has great transformative power. Remember the suggestions on ritual in order to create a ritual that is self-affirming. Decide whether you would prefer to have a private ritual or to invite others to share it with you. When do you wish to do this ritual? Choose a time that is realistic and honors your other needs. Choose the elements you wish to include in the ritual, considering which feel comfortable and fit with the meaning and intent of the ritual. Because the purpose of this ritual is self-affirmation, think about elements that feel very nurturing and affirming. Do you wish to include actions? music? adornment? specific objects and images? Most important, enjoy!

Loving Relationships with Others

Love is what bonds us to one another. In the net, threads join together the individual points. Likewise, in community, relationships bring our individual lives together. Relationships are a perfect arena in which to practice some of the most fundamental spiritual values. To treat others with love, respect, compassion, and acceptance is to honor spiritual values that are refined as we deepen our spirituality and are tested in relationship. In relationships, as in community life, we walk our spiritual talk.

Whether due to biological predetermination or social conditioning, women tend to be more relationally oriented than men, with a special skill and ability to connect intimately with others. Psychologists have recently formulated theories of female development that emphasize growth through relationship. They suggest that an emphasis on autonomy and separation may be a male-oriented value. In a more women-oriented model, loving connections with others facilitate personal development.

Similarly, some religious traditions favor an individualistic spiritual journey in which autonomy and separation are emphasized. One sometimes spends time in isolation, where one connects to oneself, one's inner voice or inner vision, and eventually emerges refreshed and spiritually illuminated. Through these practices we strengthen our ability to detach. This ability to step back and detach from difficult and puzzling situations is a skill necessary to the preservation of one's identity and can ensure the authenticity of one's experience. However, to remain consistently apart from others while in spiritual relationship to oneself and one's God ultimately may not prove satisfying. Responding to the needs of others can be a spiritual path and a sign of our spiritual evolution.

Angela, a Presbyterian minister, understands compassionate, just, and loving relationships to be fundamental to spirituality.

> *"The Talmud and the Bible both start with relationship. God created out of a desire to be in relationship. In the Garden narratives, the relationship was broken (the fall); hence, all human relationships suffer brokenness. I do not think we can have a deep spirituality when we have broken or abusive relationships. In my tradition Jesus models how to relate in human form. Jesus embodies what it means to be in a relationship in a way that shows compassion, love, and justice. To be Christ-like is to be in this kind of relationship with yourself and those around you."*

Relationships can beckon us forward on the spiritual journey. As a young adult, Ann was searching for close relationships. After some painful experimentation, she discovered a Christian community in which she was able to relate with authenticity and integrity.

"I grew up in a small town and had a very narrow view of life; basically everything was safe. When I went to college I was exposed to all these new values and found that I had to pick and choose among them. I began experimenting in relationships with men and tried to adopt their values. There were some things going on that didn't feel right to me, that conflicted with my values. I felt a lot of psychic pain because I had given up my inner sense of right and wrong to be accepted by this crowd.

"After a while, I ran into some people who had a love that was not conditional. For the first time there was something real in my relationships. It was no longer about how well you could go through the motions. Those people were religiously affiliated. There was something different about their lives that really impacted me. I was ready to give up the old way of relating that wasn't working. This was when I made a commitment to 'God's way of things.' I was looking for a way to do relationships in which I didn't have to sacrifice integrity. These relationships brought me back to the church. I felt a sense of love that goes beyond what we normally experience because we shared the common belief that people are more important than things and that God is a part of our relationships."

Both Angela and Ann have searched for their relational values and have integrated them into their daily lives. What relational values were you taught in your religion and in your family? Are these values useful in your life now? The exercises that follow use two different methods to clarify the values you were taught and the values that you now honor.

Relational Values

A checklist. Get out two different colored pens, pencils, or crayons. Use one color to check off the qualities in relationships you were taught in your religion and your family. Use the other to check off the qualities you currently value. Add to the list other qualities of relationship.

> Fidelity
> Forgiveness
> Truthfulness

Tolerance

Loyalty

Equality

Obedience

Respect

Caring

Appreciation

Sacrifice

Sharing

_____

_____

Recording your values. Tape-record yourself talking about values that are important to you in relationship. Begin by imagining yourself still living within your family of childhood. Thinking about what you learned about relationship in your family, in your community, and in your religion, Complete these sentences:

I was taught _____.

I believed _____.

It was important to me that _____.

Now repeat the exercise, expressing what you value in relationship now.

I believe _____.

I need _____.

It's important to me that _____.

Relationships take many forms as our love is expressed in different ways. Love can arise out of the special affection felt between a parent and a child. Love between adults can be based on sexual attraction and desire, the tenderness felt by lovers. Relationships are formed through the bonds of commitment and affection between friends. A different kind of love expresses itself as a universal concern for the good of humanity, an unselfish loyalty expressed toward a neighbor or even a stranger. However we form the relationship, in relationship we have the opportunity to reach beyond our particular strand on the net and to feel connected with the whole, to touch into a basic unity and interconnectedness with all of life.

Relationships with Family

A spiritual perspective can help us build and nurture a healthy family, and family life can be a wonderful arena for spiritual growth. But just what is it we mean by family? Some define a family legalistically, as relationships of blood and marriage. Others consider a family to be those who are bonded by love and commitment. Our differing beliefs about family touch a very deep and sensitive vein. Perhaps our commonality lies in a longing for enduring and sustaining relationships. It can be helpful to clarify how you define family and who constitutes your own family.

Defining Family

For this exercise you will need a recent dictionary and your spiritual journal. Look up the definition of *family*. Read each of the definitions, and consider if each is relevant in your life. When a definition is relevant, list any family member that you include under this definition. When you have read all the definitions, check and make sure that all of your own definitions of family have been addressed. If not, write down other definitions, and be sure and list family members who are included under them. Then go through your list of family, and put a star next to the family members who play an important role in your life.

As our society rapidly changes, we see the structure and nature of families changing. As we move through this discussion of family relationships, we will make generalizations about family, some of which may not apply to your family. Please adapt these ideas to fit your own experience.

In childhood our first impressions about love and trust are learned in our family relationships. These relationships set the stage and act as models for other relationships, including our relationship with our God or Goddess. If we are fortunate we are nurtured by the deep and unconditional love of our parents. Adeline explains how she experienced her mother's unconditional love.

"I was always very close to my mother. I can still remember the softness of her touch. I always felt that she loved me regardless of what I did, not because of what I did. I didn't think she loved me because I got good grades in school or because I was clean or the other things I did or didn't do. I never felt I had to earn her love."

Spiritual connection can be greatly influenced by your mother. For many of us, she is the first spiritual guide, and her influence sets the course for our spiritual journey. Our mothers can model both spiritual opportunities and spiritual limitations for us as we grow into womanhood.

As a child Maureen shared an active spiritual life with her mother; Maureen's mother modeled her own understanding of the teachings and practices of Catholicism. These early experiences continue to guide and inspire Maureen.

"I was a nontraditional Catholic, and that was 100 percent my mother's doing. I got the formal training of the Catholic church, but more important, I got her interpretation of Catholicism. My mom was a mystic. She had a very personal relationship with God and Jesus. When my mom and I went to mass together, we experienced the transubstantiation at Communion. We actually felt the infusion of spirit.

"I realize my mother opened a lot of doors for me. I ended up believing we are all connected to our spirituality, and there really isn't too much in between unless you choose to see it that way. Mother seemed to have a direct pipeline; she saw spirituality in everything. She saw a sunset as one of the most exciting things in the world to celebrate. She honored the earth; she worshiped it. It was natural with her to have conversations with saints. She has a special relationship with Saint Anthony, for example, and used his services in order to locate missing things that were important to her. Then she would find these things and know it was the intervention of Saint Anthony. As a child, I found it very natural to talk to saints, like calling up your next-door neighbor and having a conversation. My mother's spiritual influence set the stage for spiritual experiences I now have as an adult."

Like Maureen, Marie was inspired by her mother's spirituality. However, Marie found that she could not embrace all of her mother's spiritual teachings.

"My mother was a very spiritual person, and we went to church together regularly. I loved being with her in these moments and felt very close to God. However, she was not at all comfortable in her sexuality. She dressed very plainly and wore almost no makeup. Somehow I was given subtle guidance from her that sex and men were dangerous, and I should beware of any sexual feelings. For instance, I learned to masturbate when I was very young and knew I couldn't talk about this with my mother. I loved her very deeply and wanted to please her, yet

I also felt very confused about denying these powerful feelings I was having. My mother inspired me to love God and to have a spiritual practice, but her religious beliefs turned me against myself for several years. It wasn't till I was in my twenties that I figured out how to love my body and how to be sexual without fear."

Darlene had a childhood spiritual experience of deep devotional love for her mother during an altar call at a Pentecostal church service. Darlene felt a deep connection to her mother, and this love inspired an important spiritual opening. Darlene now understands this experience was her first encounter with the Sacred Feminine.

"At the age of five I had the conversion experience they call getting saved. It was Mother's Day, and the preacher said that if you wanted to have your sins forgiven and have Jesus in your heart you should come forward. I did, and I remember crying and feeling really moved and having my heart open. But this opening wasn't about God; it was about realizing how much I loved my mother. I never told anyone this. Everyone said, 'Isn't it wonderful she got saved!' Getting saved was a big deal in my church, but that wasn't what the experience was about at all for me. It was about my love and devotion to my mother. So I puzzled over that. Now I think this was one of my first encounters with the Goddess."

Nelly talked about her father's emotional connection to her and to his religion.

"It felt the same, the way he loved me and loved Judaism; it was right from his heart. It was without words. I feel teary as I remember this strong connection."

Sylvia's father was an important person at their temple, and religious involvement supported family life.

"I liked hanging out with my father at temple. We were an important family, and I felt very identified with the group. It felt good to have an identity and a cohesive family."

Our siblings can have a deep impact upon our developing spirituality. The close, nurturing relationship Elaine had with her older sister set the stage for a spiritual awakening.

"She was older, mature, and nurturing. She tells me she was delighted when I was born. When I was twenty-five years old, I was visiting with my sister, and we were in the bedroom we shared as children. She started talking about truths of the universe, a conversation about transcendence. Although I had never had a conversation like this before, I remember thinking, 'I remember all this.' What she said wasn't new. It was like she was reminding me of something I already knew. I remember writing down a list of my truths and running out and telling my father. After this I began practicing yoga and meditation and connecting with the transcendent."

Bridget had a very meaningful spiritual connection with her grandmother in which she felt calmed and opened to the Spirit.

"My grandmother's storytelling was very important to me. She came from a very beautiful region in Ecuador that is the seat of one of the most ancient and important cultures in Latin America, a pre-Columbian matriarchal culture. She told me an incredible number of stories about spirits. At a very young age, I accepted these ghosts, apparitions, devils, and self-protective charms. When I was upset, I would calm myself down by asking her to get into bed with me and tell me these stories. The stories were a basis for accepting some other way of relating to Spirit and to other realms of existence."

Looking at your family tree can stimulate your thoughts about the influence of your family upon your developing spirituality.

Family Tree

Refer to your family tree and think about the primary relationships in terms of spiritual influence.

Ask yourself these questions: What did each family member transmit about spirituality? In what way was my mother the guardian of the spirituality of my family? my father? my grandmother? my grandfather? Were there other family members who influenced my spirituality?

Sometimes the most direct way to get information about family influences is to ask. In this next exercise we suggest a conversation with your parents. If you are unable to speak to your parents, you can have the discussion with another family member or friend who knew your parents well. Very often some important insights come out of these conversations, so you might want to tape-record the conversation or jot down some notes afterward.

A Conversation with Your Parents

Have a conversation about their spirituality with your mother and/or father. See if you can determine what ethical values you have adopted from them. Ask them about the spiritual influences in their lives. See where your spirituality resonates with theirs and where it differs.

When we become adults, we create our own families. For most of us, the nucleus of the family is an intimate sexual relationship. Most of us bring tremendous hope and expectation into these relationships. When we infuse these relationships with spiritual awareness, we can find more balance and satisfaction.

Our spirituality can guide us toward relationship decisions. Cheryl understands that strong emotions are also part of God's gift and uses her connection to her emotions and to her God to guide her to clarity.

"I find that when I have conflict with someone it causes me to have conflict with my Higher Power, so I need to clean up the conflict as soon as possible. When I am pissed off at someone and then I start to pray I can't talk to my God as clearly. When I am meditating I can't listen as well 'cause I am distracted by the conflict.

"There was a lot of conflict in my relationship. I decided it wasn't working, and I wasn't going to see him anymore. I came home today and was sitting on the floor kind of chilling out and thinking about how I was feeling. It occurred to me that rather than hold off on what I was feeling, why not go ahead and feel what I was feeling 'cause I was real fortunate that God had allowed me to feel. Once I accepted the feelings, it was easier to figure out what I wanted to do and not do. The majority of the pain was because I was in conflict with myself. Once I sit still and relate whatever is going on to me and to the God in my life, then I usually get it figured out. It is just when I have my stuff all twisted up inside that it gets so messy."

Intimate relationship can be an incredible spiritual teacher as you bare your soul to another. Diane uses her lovemaking to deepen her spiritual connection with her partner and with the universe. She surrenders to a higher spiritual reality through an ecstatic union with her lover.

"Lovemaking can be an act of worship. I have had experiences in lovemaking in which I lose all sense of a personal self. My lover becomes a Goddess or the Buddha Tara, and I am her devotee. My love reaches out to the world. It is the ultimate act of surrender, of opening into the universe. In our union we are united not with ourselves alone but with the body of the universe. I keep focused on my breathing during lovemaking, keeping it slow and steady, resisting my body's urge to quicken the breath. In the space created by the even breath coupled with intense and pleasurable sensations, there is tremendous expansion. The transformation of energy is tangible. It is sacred space."

In our intimate relationship we can find wonderful opportunities to share spiritual moments together. For Diane, lovemaking led her into deep spiritual connection. The possibilities for sharing and connection are infinite when we open to ourselves, to each other, and to the life we share together. Consider how spirituality may affect your current relationship. You may like to explore this with a partner.

To My Beloved

A conversation. Set aside some special time to spend with your beloved. Begin with a conversation, each of you expressing how it is that you feel spiritually connected to each other. Does it just seem to happen by chance? Is it related to what you are doing? Is it about how you are feeling? Is it about remembering your spiritual beliefs and living them out in your love? See if there are any ways the two of you can create more opportunities for spiritual connection.

A letter. Write a letter to your beloved. Express any wishes you have about how you might share your lives together in deeper spiritual connection. Are there any hidden dreams you have about your spiritual life together? Write them down now. After you complete this letter, see if there is any part of it you would like to share with your beloved.

The love of a mother for her child is perhaps one of the deepest kinds of love. This love demands an incredible sensitivity and surrender to another.

Parenting requires an agile combining of deep attachment with the ability and willingness to let go and allow the child to develop into her or his own person. This ability to connect and let go as needed is an important spiritual skill.

Connecting and Letting Go

Think of one way you have been closely connected to your child(ren) and this connection has guided and supported her or him. Then think of one way that you have let go of your child(ren) when that was the best thing. Affirm your ability to connect and let go. If you are not a mother, you might try this exercise thinking about another relationship.

As a mother, Sharon found a treasure, the ability to be present in everyday life. Sharon discovered her authentic spiritual path, one that was filled with love and ease.

"I came home to my spiritual path through birthing and mothering my first child. For many years before this I had gone to meditation retreats and practiced mindfulness, being present and aware in each moment. But this practice was torture for me. After five years of meditation practice, I felt my mind was as easily distracted as when I began.

"Then I remembered a story I had heard at retreat about a young woman who lived in India who was a slave in someone's household. She wanted to have a spiritual path, but she didn't have any time for formal spiritual practice, so she choose as her path to be mindful in her everyday life. She used washing clothes and cleaning the house and scrubbing dishes as her mindfulness practice. She became very enlightened. I decided that this was all I could do and what I was going to do in this lifetime. Before that I had the fantasy that I was going to go into a monastery or something like that.

"This all came about at the same time that I gave birth to my daughter. I was very inspired to be mindful because I loved her so much, and it was such an obvious route to being a good parent—to be there in the moment and to do what had to be done. So I started caring for my daughter as my practice in mindfulness, and it wasn't torture! It was real reinforcing, because I was working with this baby who loved mindfulness attention and was very responsive. For example, when I was rubbing her back, my mind might wander off, but I would bring my attention back to what I was doing. I still continue to practice mindfulness with

her, but it is much more complex now that she is six years old and there is more complex interaction. It was a wonderful gift that she gave me, this opportunity to find my spiritual path, because basically it has been an easy path for me. As much as I have thought and believed that the holiest of paths is to be mindful, doing it with her is more satisfying because it includes love."

Through mothering Sharon was able to practice mindfulness, a spiritual perspective she deeply values. If you are a mother, contemplate how mothering aids you on your spiritual journey.

A Contemplation for Mothers

Think of one spiritual value that is important to you. Now contemplate these questions: How do I express this spiritual value in my mothering? How can I more deeply practice this value in my parenting? Am I teaching this value to my children?

Spiritual Friendships

The precious gems in our spiritual life are spiritual friendships, the foundation of support groups and the glue of religious community. With our spiritual friends, we can share our deepest spiritual insights as well as awkward moments of spiritual confusion. Our spiritual friends can support us as we venture into spiritual exploration, as we test out new ideas and new practices.

As a child, Linda had a special bonding ceremony with her closest friends.

"We made up the ritual ourselves and took vows and made pacts that connected us to something bigger. We knew that no matter what happened in the material world, no matter where our parents moved the family, no matter what conditions changed, we had a pact that superseded these changes."

As an adult Linda turns to her friends as her spiritual advisers.

"Being open to my friends and talking about my moral dilemmas and the huge questions in life is a really important part of my spirituality. My friends remind

me to turn to my Higher Power when I am too confused to see clearly. I need to
be humble and ask others how they deal with things."

Sharon forges community with the people around her as she lives her spiritual ideals in her daily life.

"My close friends are my spiritual sounding board. I talk about my spiritual issues, dilemmas, or thoughts with my friends. I talk to my friends when I feel judgmental about how to find more compassion. At work my boss is like a friend, and she helps me resolve the ethical dilemmas of working in a huge bureaucracy. My friends are important companions as my spirituality evolves."

Cheryl found a spiritual friend and spiritual adviser through Alcoholics Anonymous.

"He's not like any concept of a spiritual adviser you might have. He's a street hustler from New York City and a real neat human being. He loves me unconditionally."

Nelly realizes how essential her spiritual friendships have always been and how, through interviewing women, her friendship circle has expanded.

A Story from Nelly

I remember the day that I met Barbara just like it was yesterday, even though I was only three years old. I suppose I somehow knew what an important person she was to become in my life. For many years she was my closest friend and confidant. Together we explored every path in the forest. Together we played every fantasy we could imagine. Adolescence seemed to pull us apart as our paths diverged. Now, forty-one years later, our spiritual beliefs have brought us back together. I know that I can always pick up the phone and Barbara will bridge the differences in our lives and the miles between us with her spiritual wisdom.

Throughout my life my community has been woven of many spiritual friendships. Carol has been my most consistent spiritual buddy as an adult; we have shared our spiritual journeys for twenty years now. Over the years I have traveled with many spiritual buddies, women with whom I ponder my deepest questions and bare my innermost thoughts, women to whom I come when I feel confused, scared, uncertain, with no sense of spiritual path beneath my feet, women who have known me over time and distance and who can remind me of my journey, where I have come from and where I seem to be heading.

I just came from the interview with Marilyn. I feel charged in every cell of my body. My heart is pumping. I feel so alive and connected. Her story is magnificent. A woman's spirituality is a pearl—so precious, usually so hidden and protected. A pearl develops in the hidden environment of a shell and comes from a mere grain of sand. A woman's spirituality, often hidden from view, develops from the very basic stuff of life and transforms into a very precious jewel.

Marilyn's spiritual story is so different from my own. Raised in a small town in Louisiana, she tells her story with a slight Southern drawl, giving each word the time and focus it deserves. My speech is fast, rushing in that New York way. Yet her story resonates with mine on a level much deeper than the words we choose or the history we tell. This is my spiritual community, a web of spiritual friends supporting and cushioning my spiritual journey.

Acknowledging Spiritual Friendship

Think about a spiritual friend who has been important to you. Write a letter telling that person what it has been like to share spiritual friendship with her or him. Mail the letter if it feels like the right thing to do.

The basis of spiritual friendship is deep listening and honest sharing. Take an opportunity to open your heart and share with a friend.

Telling Your Story, Listening to a Friend's Story

Get together with a friend who shares your interest in spirituality. Plan to spend an hour or two together. Interview each other, choosing from among these questions, the questions that were asked of the women who were interviewed for this book.

How would you describe your religious background? What about your religious background worked for you? What about your religious background was difficult or did not work for you?

Describe spiritual/psychic experiences of childhood. Have you ever had such an experience that seemed particularly important to you? How did you feel about these experiences; what were they like for you? Have you ever had experiences in nature that seemed particularly important to you? How did you feel about them; what were they like for you? What relationships support your spirituality—as child and adult? How do you satisfy your spiritual needs now? Do you currently use prayer or ritual? Do you believe in God, Goddess, Supreme Being, Spirit? How do you get support for your spirituality? Do you have a spiritual community? Are there other issues that come to mind when you think about your spirituality?

Spiritual and Religious Community

Our spiritual and religious communities are where we go for spiritual nurturance and support. Angela said it very well:

"I think community is essential to really nurturing our spiritual self. I understand the church to literally be the people, not the building."

We find community in many ways. Some of us remain affiliated with the religion of our childhood. Others leave traditional religions and discover new spiritual groups and communities. Some find fulfilling community through family and friends. However we make the connection, community can be a wonderful source of spiritual renewal and inspiration.

Community and connection are particularly critical to women; however, difficulties can arise as we search for community. We may not know where or how to look. We may not trust our inner sense of what kind of community is right for us. We may be drawn to a different community than our husband, partner, or other family members. As we validate our own truths and find our own spiritual practices, we may grow away from our community. When we think for ourselves and act out of our own spiritual convictions we may risk censorship from our community. Some communities seem to be unable to tolerate differences in belief, needing rigid models to feel safe and connected. When communities function in this way, they become traps rather than forces for liberation, healing, and growth.

How can we weave a community in which there is enough freedom to evolve and enough of a container to feel safe and grounded? How can we find the courage within ourselves to question and, when appropriate, to disagree with our community? These are questions that we must continually answer for ourselves. There is no one answer; there is no simple answer; there is no enduring answer. Listen to three women answer these question for themselves. Listen to the kinds of issues that come up for women who stay within their religion of origin and the issues of those who choose to leave.

Claudia has chosen to stay within the religious community of her childhood and of her family. She cherishes the caring network of the Mormon church and uses it to her advantage both personally and professionally. The community was there for her in her time of greatest need. She has reframed her lower status as a woman as an opportunity to refine her own beliefs. Claudia has found her own way within a church that does not encourage individual paths.

"I am a Christian, a Mormon, who needs to be in the structure of religion. I was raised in a structure of religion. I like the conservative values of organized religion, such as the caring network that reaches out to everybody. I have taken my religion, which I have had a lot of problems with and which is a patriarchal religion, and have found a way to work within that structure.

"I enjoy the community. Mormonism is a service-oriented religion, a lay religion. Every member of the church works for no pay; it is a lay clergy. I have the opportunity to be a 'visiting teacher.' This means I am responsible for three women and go see them once a month. I go with a companion.

"Today I went and visited a woman with a serious neuromuscular condition. I felt she might be suicidal. I asked her if she was suicidal, and she was. So now I switched hats, I put on my therapist's hat. The church will pay for her therapy for a year. I asked her if she wanted therapy, and she cried and said she did and that this was an answer to her prayers. Although she says she doesn't believe in the Mormon church anymore, I am sure the church will pay me to be her therapist. That is the kind of network my religion offers me. As her therapist I can call in the community to meet her needs. I can call on somebody to bring food to that woman tomorrow and to pay her rent. With just a phone call, I can get someone to go tonight and change her sheets and sit with her all night. Being a therapist and working with the Mormon church, I can call up these kinds of resources.

"You have to understand that I am a cultural Mormon. I don't consider myself a true believer. I don't buy everything. My family has been in the church for six generations, and it is easier for me to be a Mormon than not. Show me a church that would give me more and I would join, but I have never found a church that would.

"Seven years ago my son and my nephew were killed in an auto accident, and that was the hardest look at death I ever took. Actually at that time I was work-

ing on a surgical unit with people whose kids had been killed. I think the Lord had put me in this job. I had just written an article on grief and loss for the American Journal of Nursing. I knew all the literature. When my son and nephew were killed, I called the bishop to get a blessing. One of the blessings was that I would guide my family and my cousin's family through this. Because of my guidance, I think my family did very well with this tragedy. We did some very unusual things: They were both totally burned, but we had the remains of their bodies wrapped in gauze and had a body part available to see.

"Theology is not useful when you have a great loss like that. What is helpful is people being there with their arms around you. The church came through for me when my son died. They were there to answer the phone. Even a belief in God didn't matter at that point, because all that is relevant is getting through it and living, because you think you are going to die.

"The Mormon church has an incredible belief that when you die you go to heaven forever, and you are going to be with your family for time and eternity. If you have a temple marriage, you are married for time and eternity. Personally, I am not sure what happens when you die, though I really believe that my son is part of me now, that there is some human string of consciousness that we are all in together. I had a dream in which I asked my son, 'How are you?' and he replied, 'I am.' I never could have made that up. I never could have thought to say that.

"My message is, if you like your church, think about staying. Try to figure out a way you can live in the culture. Realize that religion is a cultural thing. Don't cut off emotionally if you have been hurt. Try and go back and take what is good about it. Reorganize yourself in such a way that you can take what is good for you; even if you don't take it in a building, take it in your heart. Don't leave all the things that comforted you as a child. If you can somehow resolve the bitterness, there are all kinds of things you can go back to that will strengthen you and give you the power to touch other people's lives."

In contrast to Claudia, Maggie, a nun for eighteen years, chose to leave her convent and finally the Catholic church. She reached a point at which she was unable to be a representative of a church in which men held the power and leadership, "to play second fiddle." She has a difficult time finding community outside the structures of traditional religion.

"I was a nun for eighteen years. I think part of the essence of Catholicism is community, the sense that we are all in this life together and we need to support each other, the importance of being of service in the world, not just going after what you want.

"I think that within Catholicism and within religious life there was a lot of potential for community, but there weren't very many years in communities where it really worked. For me, it worked once or twice. There was a lot of time when people in religious community were unable to live peaceably together and live out their values.

"I felt it really worked once when I was in a community of four nuns living together on the reservation. We went through a lot of hard times and decisions about how to be among the Native People. But we would sit down together and talk about our values and figure out how we would live them as a group and how to create a structure for that. We had real open communications and meetings. We had regular times to meet and evaluate how things were going. When things got conflictual, we would go to our quiet space together and process it. It worked really well. The irony was when we created the kind of community we really wanted, it got squelched by the order because it was too free, because there wasn't a leader in the group.

"Although the religious community was women, we were really bound by the church canons and the men who were in charge. The order would propose changes, and the men in charge would not allow them. As I got more and more feminized, it got to the point where I had a hard time being a representative of the church the way the leadership of the church was. I had a hard time playing second fiddle to men. I realized that I was getting my support from outside the order. I realized I could better live my spiritual values outside the church.

"I have been out of the convent for eight years now. There is quite a hole left in my life, and I haven't figured out how to find community. I am a member of a social justice group that is faith-based that has filled a little of my need for community. My spirituality is very much about helping the world move forward in its evolutionary process. I choose work that I consider important, like my job at the AIDS project. I work with the underdog, the abused, the throwaways, the poor, the downtrodden."

Sandy Boucher, writer and practitioner of Buddhism, found a spiritual community of women.

"One of the most powerful aspects of my involvement in women's liberation in the 1970s was my coming together with other women in deep, life-changing association. We shared our experience, our anguish, our hope, our transformative energies; we believed in each other and passionately valued our femaleness.

"So it made sense that when I began to engage in Buddhist practice I would be drawn to the 'sangha' or community aspect of Buddhism. I would never have

been able to pursue Buddhist meditation had not my lover at the time found a woman teacher. The ancient teachings, as they were given by this very woman-affirming, innovative Western teacher, challenged and inspired me. They were free of the male bias of the male-led Buddhist centers. The community of women who gathered around this teacher stretched from Portland to Los Angeles, up and down the West Coast. At the retreats held in the Mojave Desert, I would see the same women. We began to know one another and support one another in doing our sitting practice regularly, in discussing the Buddhist precepts and tenets, and seeing how those applied to our lives as late-twentieth-century North American women. Many of us were lesbians, and we felt utterly comfortable in this community, in which the teacher was respectful of our sexual preference and relationships.

"In between retreats in the desert, we gathered together in the Oakland-Berkeley area to create a Women's Sangha. We held weekly meditation sittings on Sunday nights, celebrated the Buddhist holidays with ceremonies, and became a network of women involved in spiritual practice and questioning. Our events provided a safe place for all women to get a taste of Buddhism, to sit regularly if they wished to, to present inspiring materials on Buddhism and women. The group was a great support for my meditation practice and for the questioning of male-supremacist institutions in Buddhism that led to the writing of my book Turning the Wheel. It provided a place to explore our spiritual experience as women, to share that exploration with other women. Though the focus was different from that in the women's liberation groups I had been part of, the Women's Sangha offered the same opportunity for deep and life-changing associations and investigation.

"When I recall the women who attended, I see us sitting on pillows in a circle, eyes closed in meditation, or open as we chanted, our energies merging and strengthening each of us."

The experiences of Claudia, Maggie, and Sandy may have stimulated your thoughts about your own experiences in spiritual and religious groups and communities.

Issues in Spiritual Community

Think about the issues you are dealing with right now regarding spiritual community. Choose one of the following seven questions to contemplate for each day of the week. If you repeat the cycle of questions for a second week, most likely you will find deeper answers.

Does your spiritual community feel adequate? Do you feel supported within your spiritual community? Do you have a voice in your community? Is there room to disagree within your community? Does your community support your individual spiritual growth? Are you able to integrate your spiritual community adequately with the other significant relationships within your life? Do you believe that you deserve a supportive community?

As with all relationships, spiritual and religious communities are strengthened when we give them our loving attention.

Strengthening Community

If you identify as a member of a religious or spiritual community, consider doing something that will create a stronger bond within your community. Here are some examples:

1. Form a women's group to address your needs as women in the community.
2. Do a project together, one that reflects your common values.
3. Go on a retreat together.
4. Network to other communities like your own, sharing your common challenges and opportunities.

Cultural Roots

Culture is about who we are at our very core, about our basic and primordial identity. It is about such things as how we look, what we eat, how we move, and who we love. Through culture we form basic assumptions about life. We discover what is right and what is wrong, what is important and what is not. We find meaning in life. Through culture we connect to our roots, to our ancestors, and bond in community.

There is a very close connection between spirituality, religion, and culture. Each address the basic issues and fundamental values of life. Often they intersect one another. For example, our connection to religion may be primarily a cultural rather than a theological connection. Or our culture may be so central to our life that it serves functions similar to that of a religion.

Like many of us today, Teresa is influenced by many different cultures and has identified strongly with each at different times in her life. As a child she identified as Mexicana and Catholic, and as an adult she identifies as Indian. Teresa has also been very influenced by the recovery and women's communities. She believes her work is to bridge differences and bring women together in community and prayer.

"My grandma was Indian, but she had been pulled away from her tradition at an early age. When she married my grandfather, she moved from her tribal village to the city, never to return to her people. She was very assimilated in the Catholic ways. My grandma took all the holidays from the Catholic church to heart. We went to church even on Saturdays. The days before Easter felt like a punishment because there was so much strictness. There were all these things that had to be done and all these things that we could not do. As a child I was very Catholic. I remember kissing the hands of the priest and wanting to be a nun.

"The outer rooms in the house all looked very Catholic, the living room, the kitchen. But in the back room of our house was a whole other world. It was my grandma's world, and in this room she intermingled things that were Catholic with things from her Indian culture. In the back room was the holy water and the herbs. She healed people through chanting. I quietly stood at the side of my grandma while she was doing healing. Her healing songs were in my head; so were the mysteries of her healing.

"When I was young person I was called some powerful names. I was called Negra, India, and Fea. The lighter-skinned kids were always appreciated more, so Negra was not used in a loving way. And even though my grandma was Indian, the name India was not used in a good way. Fea meant ugly, and I went around half my life thinking I was ugly.

"When I was in my teen years, I let go of both the Indian side of me and the Catholic side of me. When I had my first child I wanted to have her baptized, but my grandma said I couldn't 'cause I wasn't married. So I said, 'OK, I will not practice the way Catholics practice.' None of my kids were brought up Catholic.

"When I was in my twenties I found a new community that was very special for me. I met a family from the Acoma pueblo at a powwow. I don't even know how I ended up at the powwow. Then this woman who was in her eighties got up and put her shawl around my shoulders. She said to me in broken English, 'Get up and dance.' Another woman told me this was a great honor, that Grandma asked me to get up and dance. This elder was a very special woman in the community.

When she was very young she survived a lighting strike. She was considered to have a special wisdom. Even though I did not want to dance in public, I got up and danced.

"I was adopted right on the spot. No legal thing, just the Indian way. I was brought into their family. As time went on, these people did many prayers and healings for me. People were telling me I looked Indian and I do have Indian blood, but I had always thought of myself first as Mexicana. I felt the specialness of being taken in by this family. But also I had to guard it; what did they want? I knew there was good medicine and bad medicine and that people work both ways. But from the first prayer this grandma did, things started changing in my life. There was an opening in me to my prayer life and to an understanding and respect for things.

"Later I moved to California, and at first I was doing a lot of healing and prayers for people on my own, independent from a community. I kept thinking there were no Indian people in California, not knowing then that there are Indian people all over California. It took a couple of years, but I met people who shared this spiritual life and way of things. I took an art class about indigenous people and met some people, and then I met some Indian people at a Narcotics Anonymous conference. Over the years I met more and more Indian people. Now I go to the Point Reyes Roundhouse, and people come from all around. There are several things going on. There's women's gatherings that happen and other gatherings with all the family. At these gatherings whatever needs to happen will happen—like somebody needs a prayer or to connect with a community. We go up there on Friday night, and it starts with a potluck and ends up with dancing.

"We have a women's circle in Santa Rosa, and everybody in that circle is Indian along with something else. It feels like community to me. We call it an inter-tribal women's circle. We acknowledge what we share, spirituality first and, second, what we share 'cause we are female. We've felt the confusion of sometimes not feeling Indian. I don't belong completely in any world. Sometimes if you're part and not full Indian, the Indian communities will not accept you.

"There was a lot of denial of the Indian side of us in our home when I grew up. When I wear bright colors, my aunts want to correct this. The colors are my joy and the brightness of each day. I wear ornaments from the earth like feathers and earrings for my daily walk with my Creator. In the women's circle, color is one of the main topics we talk about. Each one of us has been drawn to colors and clothes without really understanding why we are drawn to them. It's been through humor and pain that we discussed this subject because it is not always understood.

"I feel like it is my responsibility to bridge the differences. I have some friends that are not Indian but have a strong spirituality. I feel my responsibility is bringing all these women together. Only through prayer and tolerance and patience will we get clarity.

"You ask me how I got a stronger spirituality. More and more I know myself and trust myself. I got the self-confidence that my word counts for something. My prayer walks with me. As the years have gone by, I have done a lot of work to find the beauty in me as a dark Indian. I walked around half my life thinking how ugly I was, never recognizing or seeing my own beauty. The beauty was in my heart and spirit and had always been there."

Carol left the culture and religion of her childhood and explored other cultures. Like Teresa, Carol found an authentic spiritual path when she reembraced the culture and spiritual ways of her ancestors.

A STORY FROM CAROL

I have moved a lot in my life, living half my adult years outside the continental United States: two years in Paris, seven years in Montreal, and almost four years in Puerto Rico. I traveled in Europe, Mexico, and China. Each time I moved, my communities drastically changed. I chose this willingly. Each community that I became part of deepened my sense of who I was and who I was not. I used these experiences to discover myself and my spirituality. From the French I learned about my relationship to beauty and its influence on spirit, the importance of knowing one's history and taking pride in it. The Puerto Rican culture taught me about genuine openheartedness and exposed me to spiritual mysteries.

Although I learned the language, customs, and values everywhere I lived, ultimately I remained a cultural outsider. A few years ago I realized that I had been filling the void I felt inside with bits and pieces of other people's ways. My experiences had given me a spiritual feeling of unity with all peoples and taught me that the world was my community. But where was my individuality? What was my history and culture?

These questions took me back to my religion of origin and my Western European culture. I have found that there are parts of my background that I must reject like male dominance, puritanism, and class and racial prejudice. I have also come to realize a spiritual connection to my past and my ancestors. Most of my family were poor folk who lived close to the land in England, France, and Germany. They were farmers and clergy. My mother's people came from Westbury, a town in England near Stonehenge. A simple life close to nature, spiritual teaching, rituals honoring the seasons and the elements—these are the things that are close to my heart. I came to understand that the spirituality of my ancestors was not so different from my own. Sometimes it seems as though I have gone on a long spiritual journey only to come home to myself.

As we have heard from Carol and Teresa, there can be an essential spiritual passage when we connect to our cultural roots. How does your culture influence your spiritual journey?

Cultural Values

Write down the name of the culture or cultures with which you identify. Be inclusive. Then using free-form writing, write for five minutes about what values you learned from your culture. Think about how those values affect your spiritual journey.

Though finding our spiritual roots can provide a strong spiritual link, it is also true that when we reach across cultural differences we find a wonderful opportunity for spiritual connection. When we knock down the fences that divide us, we can delight in the richness of diversity. As we reach beyond our known culture, we can expand into the mysteries of the unknown.

Tina is Unitarian, and in her church social equality and improved race relations are important religious values. Tina's political work has focused on healing the rift between races. Tina understands this drive as basic to her spirituality.

"When I am able to connect across the race barrier, there is this incredible release of heat and light. I think of this like a law of physics. It feels like a spiritual moment. It is my experience that human beings have an incredible drive to connect across the race, class, and gender barriers that divide us."

For Leila, her culture and religion were the same. As a child she learned a great deal about her culture as a Jew, but very little about the religion of Judaism. As an adult, Leila has returned to her culture and in the process discovered deep spiritual roots in the religion of her childhood. Leila values multicultural experiences and reaches out to heal the wounds of intercultural hostility. She investigates just how far she can question the traditions of her religion without losing the essence of the culture.

> *"Two years ago our seder was co-led by a Palestinian, and we had Arabs and Palestinians as guests. We read from the Koran at the seder. I think of myself as very politically progressive, and even I had to think about how I felt about such a nontraditional seder. It takes a certain amount of order to live a life. The order of the seder carries a symbolic meaning and power. You get to ask a lot of questions about the order; it is a very dialectical process. You question, but if you question it out of existence, you do not have an order or a culture."*

Cross-Cultural Experiences

Think about an experience with a person from another culture that did not feel successful. Think about what made that experience difficult. What spiritual lessons did you learn in this interaction? Then think about an experience with a person from another culture that was successful and about what made that experience successful. What spiritual lessons did you learn in this interaction?

Reaching Out to a Larger Community

We are all part of the same web. We share this planet and all her resources. We depend upon one another to survive and to thrive. At the same time that we are separate individuals, we are intricately bound to one another. At birth we arise out of the body of another woman, and at death our bodies return to the earth to create new life forms. In the years between, we birth and nurture many forms of new life. In our early years and in old age, our interdependence is undeniable. In the years between, this reality is more subtle, yet in truth we are always dependent on one another for basic survival, as well as for spiritual sustenance.

It is this awareness that ultimately guides us to understand that we are part of a much larger community. Some of us think of this as the human community. Others understand this community to include all life forms. As we expand our understanding, we naturally increase our compassion.

There are many ways to reach out and create more expansive and inclusive communities. Through her family's example, Diane Mariechild learned the value of reaching out with kindness.

"I consider my mother my first spiritual teacher. She taught me that God was love and that we were all children of God. I learned through her example that God's love was expressed through kindness and caring to others. My mother was always present with a comforting hug and a huge pot of spaghetti sauce, whether it was for a new mother, a bedridden neighbor, or a grieving family. No matter how little money there was, my mother shared whatever she had. 'There's always enough food to put an extra plate on the table,' she'd say. My friends were always welcome. She told me how her family struggled to get food, especially when my grandfather broke his legs. They lived in a poor, mostly black neighborhood. It was the black people who shared food with them. When my grandfather didn't have work, it was a black man who gave some of his gardening clients to my grandfather. She never forgot such kindness, and those experiences have made her accepting of people's racial and cultural differences. She remembers being treated badly because she was Italian. She didn't grow bitter; she grew in compassion. She remembered that pain and didn't want us children to ever treat anyone unkindly because they were different. One of her close friends through school was a boy who had cerebral palsy.

"My mother would help the neighbor's kids sew their Halloween costumes. She'd tell me stories of her childhood—like the time one of her neighbors helped her design and sew her graduation dress. That was one of the many stories she would tell of the generosity of their Jewish neighbors. Although my mother was a devout Christian, she didn't believe some of the dogma. For example, she didn't believe that only Christians would 'go to heaven' or find peace after death. Although she felt a deep and personal connection with Christ, she didn't believe he was the only teacher or the only way.

"My maternal grandmother, who died several months before I was born, was an uneducated Italian immigrant—Catholic, without the dogma. My mother described her as gentle, patient, and kind, without the fiery temperament my mother struggled with. When my mother left the Catholic church to marry my Baptist father, which was quite radical in their time, her mother told her this: 'All paths lead to the center; the different religions are like spokes of a wheel all coming into the hub.'"

Carter Heyward speaks of some of the ways she has reached out beyond her church home. She reminds us to acknowledge the small movements toward connection.

"To build other kinds of spiritual networks can be difficult, but as a feminist I think it is possible because we share values about spiritual community regardless

of whether we are Jewish or Christian or Wiccan. It is an expanded sense of community, a network of women who somehow know we are all important to one another even if we don't know each other's names.

"Building community is so critical, and it can be so hard. Part of the issue is where you are geographically located as well as your financial resources. The literature that is being written is so important to the women who read. The spiritual resources are there now in written word. Women who pick up a book on feminist spirituality often will then follow up with a call or contact and then perhaps choose to come to seminary, or leave an abusive marriage, or see a feminist therapist who encourages them to do what they really have wanted to do with their life. Women contacting other women even if not explicitly spiritual— talking about our lives, thinking about options, what hurts and what empowers. The small things count."

Expanding Spiritual Community

Take a moment to think about whether you would like to feel more sense of spiritual community. Listed below are some ways you might expand your community. Check off any ideas you might like to pursue. Then think more specifically how you might do that. Add to the list to suit your needs and preferences.

———— Read new spiritual books.

———— Go to a meeting of a spiritual group.

———— Start a new spiritual group.

———— Attend a spiritual workshop or retreat.

———— Set aside time to spend with a friend pursuing common spiritual interests.

———— Worship with a religious group.

When we are open to it, we can find spiritual connection in unlikely places as our sense of spiritual community expands. Hallie Iglehart Austin relates an experience of opening her heart to a total stranger. It was a very cold night just a few days before Christmas.

"I was walking around the city with a friend of mine. I was totally bundled up in my warmest coat. We passed by a homeless person sitting on the sidewalk. He

had a piece of cardboard in front of him and on it was written 'Merry Christmas.' The juxtaposition of his situation and the extreme cold and this little sign he had out just went straight to my heart. I caught myself having walked a few steps past. We went back, and I gave him some money, what little cash I had left. It wasn't very much. He looked up at me. He had this incredible light in his eyes, and his eyes connected right with mine. He said 'Thank you, may you have a wonderful Christmas.' I have never felt so much contact from a stranger. This man was so truly grateful that I walked away sobbing. Even though he was in the condition he was in, he opened himself up to me and gave me a lot back."

Leila speaks of her spiritual journey as one of learning to be of service in her community, a value that is essential to Judaism.

"The value of service is everywhere in Judaism. You have to wrestle with how you bring God into the world through your divine acts. I am referring to everyday acts, like taking a friend to the airport or reaching out to your sister when she is in pain. Central to Judaism is the act of avoda, or service. This is how you realize your own divinity and create divinity in the world. It is not just that God exists, but our actions of service create God."

As Leila suggests, all our acts are essentially spiritual acts—the miraculous experiences, like Hallie's, in which we connect deeply to someone so very different from ourselves, along with the everyday acts, like taking a friend to the airport. Each moment provides the possibility to live in greater connection and community with others. Each moment holds the opportunity for our hearts to open, to touch greater acceptance and compassion.

Interconnectedness

In this exercise we will be using contemplation to investigate the experience of the interconnectedness in our lives. Spend a few minutes to become quiet and centered.

Try contemplating the following ideas. Read through each paragraph. Take time to contemplate each idea. Discover if the concept presented is true for you. If it does hold true, then investigate how that truth affects your life and the way you perceive the world around you. After you have spent time in contemplation, then write down some of the thoughts that came into your mind.

We are connected to all other breathing beings through the air that we breathe. We are connected to other people, to animals, and to plants through the air we share. We breath in; air enters our bodies and is changed inside our bodies. We breathe out, sharing the air with others nearby, in the same room, the same car, the same bus, the same auditorium. The plants breathe air too, imbuing it with the oxygen that is essential to our life. We exhale carbon dioxide, essential in the life of plants.

Air circulates. The winds carry air around the earth. We share the air with people, animals, and plants around the world. We share the air with people on all the continents, of all colors, of all nationalities, and in all life situations.

When people pollute the air, we share the polluted air as well. When Mt. Saint Helens erupted, the ash of the volcano circulated around the world. How else does sharing air affect your life?

We are connected to one another through the food we eat. Most of us are dependent on many others to provide the food that nourishes us. We are connected to the people who prepare the soil, sow the seed, plow the field. We are connected to the people who tend the young plants, water the plants, pick the food from the plants. We are dependent on the people who truck the food, who process the food in the factories. We are connected to the storekeepers who purchase the food, display the food, sell the food, bag the food. We are connected to the people who prepare the food, cook the food, serve the food, wash the dishes. We are connected to all these people; they all help sustain our lives.

Choose another area of your life. Contemplate and acknowledge the various ways in which you are connected in this area as well. Think about all the different people involved. Be as expansive and thorough as you can be.

Endings and New Beginnings

12

It is time now to acknowledge your journey and to plot new directions. Your healing and renewal are not complete. Healing is never finished; there is always new territory to explore. And renewal is an ongoing process; there is always opportunity to come more into touch with your authentic spiritual path. You have, however, reached the conclusion of this book; this lap of your journey is nearly complete. Take a moment now to review and acknowledge your travels.

Checking In with Yourself

As you conclude this journey, different kinds of change and transition may present themselves. You may sense a completion, that your spiritual healing work is complete for now. Or you may know that this healing cycle is not yet complete, but you need to take a break. Taking time for rest is honoring your care and commitment to yourself, acknowledging the natural cycle of ebb and flow. Perhaps it is time to put more time and focus into other interests in your life. Then again, maybe you feel motivated to deepen the healing work you have begun and to continue journeying with this book. You might return to an earlier chapter in the book, reread portions of it, and try some exercises that you chose to skip initially. You might start spending time with spiritual friends and community. Allow choices that resonate with your inner needs.

The Next Step

Become grounded and quiet inside. Then use whatever method is most useful to answer the question below. You might, for example, use free-form writing or contemplation or use a divination tool like the tarot to tap into your intuition. Trust your own sense of what approach is best for you right now.

Question. What is the next step on my spiritual journey?

Take some time to contemplate whether a period of rest might be helpful now.

Rest and Rejuvenation

Allow yourself to become grounded and quiet inside. Focus on the center of your body, in the area of your belly or chest. As you focus, ask for a body sensation or an image that represents the energy of your spiritual renewal process right now. Gently focus your attention on the sensation or image you receive. Does it guide you toward rest? You may feel this kind of guidance as a sense of heaviness, fullness, or overload. Check in with the energy level of your spirit. Does your spirit feel pulled to more stillness? Honor whatever you discover. If you feel drawn toward rest and rejuvenation, respect these inner needs.

Reviewing and Planning Ahead

Traveling your authentic spiritual path is a courageous choice that can open your eyes and your heart. Healing can lead you through difficult passages, and renewal can guide you to joyous and beautiful vistas. Take some time to review your journey of renewal, the journey you traveled while reading this book and working through the exercises. As you review the terrain you have traveled, it might be helpful to open your spiritual journal or refer to your spiritual time line.

Throughout this book we offered many different ways to access greater awareness and spiritual renewal: mental imagery, writing, focus questions, or new activities. Some approaches were most likely more helpful than others.

Healing Tools

Make a list of the healing tools that have been helpful to you. You might refresh your memory by looking over the exercises you completed and rereading entries in your spiritual journal. Under what circumstances might you use a particular healing tool? Refer back to this list if you become discouraged, confused, or disconnected.

In "Developing a Firm Footing" you acquired some basic perspectives and practices that can continue to serve you on your journey forward. Think about those that have become spiritual habits, ways of being in the world that are natural to you and no longer demand a great deal of effort. Also remind yourself of those that you want to reinforce with more practice. Remember obstacles that can block your journey, and note helpful hints to guide you forward. Impatience, self-doubt, and frustration may block your way; patience, generosity, and openness to change can be welcome companions on the path.

Traveling On with a Firm Footing

Take some time to contemplate what each of these words means to you now and how you wish to integrate them into your spiritual life in the days to come.

> Self-trust
> Spiritual space
> Support
> Structure
> Intention
> Gratitude

Add other words to this list, reminders of how you can travel on with a firm footing.

In the section on spiritual alienation, you looked at the ways you encountered spiritual alienation and discovered healing practices. You investigated obstacles blocking your relationship with God and issues arising out of your involvement with religion. You investigated other obstacles that hinder you. Remember the issues that touched you most deeply. Remember the healing you invoked. Make note of any unfinished business.

The Healing Journey

Begin with a grounding exercise. Now spend some time reviewing the healing work you have done. Imagine yourself standing on your time line, standing at the point that represents right now, this very moment in time. Then imagine yourself looking back into the past, back into the healing work you have done about spiritual alienation. Think about whether your vision of God has come into clearer focus. Has your relationship to religion changed? What else have you examined with healing awareness? Express gratitude to yourself and your spiritual source for the healing you have experienced. Now imagine yourself looking ahead into your future. What is the healing work that lies ahead? What is your direction for healing? Take out your spiritual journal and write down what you discover.

In the section on spiritual connection you explored many possible paths of connection. Most likely you traveled through some familiar terrain; maybe you also discovered new passages. How do you most naturally connect to your spiritual center, to your God? Which connections bring you the greatest joy and peacefulness? How might you revisit these connections? Very often we know what brings us spiritual connection, but we forget to pursue these connections. Many of us find that making lists organizes our lives. A "to do" list can help you make time and place for what is important to you.

Reminders

Make a list of the activities that bring you spiritual connection. At first, brainstorm, listing anything that guides you toward greater connection; censor nothing. Be wild and free in your ideas. Next review the list, circling any ideas that seem both valuable to you and possible in your life. Make a second list of the circled activities, possibly assigning dates and times for attending to these activities. If this list or your assigned dates seem overwhelming, think about simpler ways to accomplish your goals. Remember to give yourself enough time to enjoy and feel nurtured by these activities.

The spiritual journey is a journey toward inner freedom and sustaining connection. It is a miraculous journey through the mundane matters of life. After we clear the briars and brambles that block our path, we find direction. Our direction is guided by our spiritual values.

Spiritual Values

Spend a few minutes allowing your mind to drift over the work that you have done. Remember the exercises or ideas that were the most important to you.

Let your mind be free and go where it chooses. Then take out a pen or pencil and write down three spiritual values that are essential on your journey. Think about how you express those values in your life. How might you realize each value a little more fully? Where might you find support for these values?

Ending and Beginning Again

It can be helpful to think about how you deal with endings, because change can sometimes be difficult. Change also brings excitement about new adventures to come. Ending this book can serve as a model for the other changes in your life.

When there are endings and change, the ground shifts beneath us. We may feel as if we are at the edge of a cliff overlooking the unknown, leaving the old ways of being and not yet knowing the new ways. It takes foresight and courage to trust in the new ground that lies ahead. When we lose touch with the old familiar ground, we can become vulnerable and feel fearful and contract inside. A common response is to run from endings by, for example, becoming too numb or too busy to notice. But then we are less able to make good choices in plotting new directions. Conscious endings, when we move on with full presence and awareness, can be quite liberating. The death of the old gives birth to the new.

Each of us has our own ways of dealing with endings. Probably we have negotiated some endings in our lives more gracefully than others. Spend some time understanding how you most skillfully move through endings.

Ending with Grace

Think about an ending in your life that felt successful; it might be the ending of a relationship, or a project, or a spiritual affiliation. Ask yourself these questions:

What kind of feelings accompanied this ending?
What kind of support did I have for this ending?
How did I take care of myself during this ending?
What did I learn from this ending?

Think about whether there are lessons you want to remember as you navigate through endings in the days to come.

Celebrate and commemorate this ending. Rejoice or pay tribute. Create a regal ritual or spend a moment in solemn appreciation. Enjoy your solitude or invite your friends and family. Adorn yourself with the colors and forms that delight you or invoke the aesthetics of simplicity. Practice abandonment to your creator or practice the discipline of reverence.

An Ending Ritual

Create an ending ritual that marks an ending and completion of this book. Create whatever kind of ritual reflects your needs and experience. Look back to the chapter on ritual to remind yourself of the elements of ritual. In your ritual consider including gratitude toward yourself for your efforts, to others who have supported you, and to your God. Consider affirming your intention to continue your journey of renewal.

As you move forward on your spiritual journey, you may discover many modes of travel. Sometimes you will float downstream; other times you will scale the mountainsides with ropes and crampons. You may fly on the back of a hawk or dance with your ancestors. At times the journey may seem like a leisurely stroll and at other times like a triathlon.

Do it your own way, respecting the world you share with others and knowing that you are guided by a larger wisdom and compassion. Remain grounded as you soar to freedom. Do it your own way, while you consider the possibility that we may all be traveling home to the same source.